History of Intellectual Culture

History of Intellectual Culture

―

International Yearbook of Knowledge and Society

Edited by
Charlotte A. Lerg, Johan Östling, and Jana Weiß

Current Advisory Board:
Peter Burke, University of Cambridge
Heather Ellis, University of Sheffield
Tiffany N. Florvil, University of New Mexico
Adam Kola, Nicolaus Copernicus University, Torun
Suzanne Marchand, Louisiana State University
Pierre-Héli Monot, Ludwig Maximilian University, Munich
Herman Paul, Leiden University
João Ohara, Federal University of Rio de Janeiro
Swen Steinberg, Queen's University, Kingston, and German Historical Institute, Washington, DC
Emily Steinhauer, Royal Holloway, University of London
Eugenia Roldán Vera, Center for Research and Advanced Studies (CINVESTAV), Mexico
Christa Wirth, University of Agder

History of Intellectual Culture

Volume 2
2023

Modes of Publication

Edited by
Charlotte A. Lerg, Johan Östling, and Jana Weiß

DE GRUYTER
OLDENBOURG

This publication has been kindly supported by Lund University Library.

ISBN 978-3-11-107783-3
e-ISBN (PDF) 978-3-11-107803-8
e-ISBN (EPUB) 978-3-11-107808-3
ISSN 2747-6766
DOI https://doi.org/10.1515/9783111078038

This work is licensed under the Creative Commons Attribution-NonCommercial-NoDerivatives 4.0 International License. For details go to http://creativecommons.org/licenses/by-nc-nd/4.0/.

Creative Commons license terms for re-use do not apply to any content (such as graphs, figures, photos, excerpts, etc.) that is not part of the Open Access publication. These may require obtaining further permission from the rights holder. The obligation to research and clear permission lies solely with the party re-using the material.

Library of Congress Control Number: 2023940913

Bibliographic information published by the Deutsche Nationalbibliothek
The Deutsche Nationalbibliothek lists this publication in the Deutsche Nationalbibliografie; detailed bibliographic data are available on the internet at http://dnb.dnb.de.

© 2023 with the author(s), editing © 2023 Charlotte A. Lerg, Johan Östling, and Jana Weiß, published by Walter de Gruyter GmbH, Berlin/Boston. This book is published with open access at www.degruyter.com.

Cover image: Word Cloud generated with WordArt.com.
Printing and binding: CPI books GmbH, Leck

www.degruyter.com

Table of Contents

Preface —— VII

Section I: **Individual Articles**

Anastassiya Schacht
Soviet Public Health and Its Pattern of Involved Non-Attachment in International Organizations —— 3

Carlos Fernando Teixeira Alves
Knowledge and Society: The Role of Two Universities in Southern Europe in the Early Nineteenth Century – the Case of Coimbra and Salamanca —— 29

Carl-Filip Smedberg
Ordering the Social: The History of Knowledge and the Usefulness of (Studying) Social Taxonomies —— 51

Section II: **Modes of Publication**

Charlotte A. Lerg, Johan Östling, and Jana Weiß
Modes of Publication: Introduction —— 71

Chelsea A. Rodriguez
Digital Newspapers, Material Knowledge: Grappling with the TimesMachine Digital Archive as a Repository of Knowledge —— 77

Elena Falco
How to Read Wikipedia: Design Choices and the Knowing Subject —— 99

Elisavet Papalexopoulou
Women of the Word: Translation and Political Activism in the Age of Revolutions —— 111

Jean-Pierre V. M. Hérubel
Higher Education Institutional Histories: Observations, Discussion, and Definitional Glossary of the Publication Genre in Canada and the United States —— 123

Section III: **Engaging the Field**

Bennet Rosswag and Christoph Schmitt
The Objectification of Meaning: A Systems-Theoretical Approach to (the History of) Knowledge —— 147

Anton Jansson
Review Essay: The History of Atheism, Secularism, and Humanism: Recent Works and Future Directions —— 163

HIC Conversation with Marnie Hughes-Warrington, Chiel van den Akker, and Moira Pérez, edited and introduced by João Ohara
Pasts and Futures for the Theory and Philosophy of History —— 189

Contributors —— 203

Preface

We are excited to publish our second volume. While *History of Intellectual Culture* (*HIC*) is still comparatively young (as is, arguably, the field of the history of knowledge in general), our aim is to establish an international, interdisciplinary, and open-access yearbook for a wide audience.

First and foremost, we would like to express our collective thanks to our devoted authors, dedicated reviewers, and editorial board who helped make the first two volumes a success. In selecting contributions, we seek to represent not only various disciplines dealing with the broad range of the field (as laid out in our introduction to the first volume). We also see our yearbook as an outlet for both established and emerging scholars.

In addition, we will continue to encourage non-native English speakers to submit articles. While this has and will continue to pose (linguistic) challenges, we hope to provide as much support as needed for non-native English voices to be heard in the wider academic community, which to this day is dominated by anglophone histories (of knowledge).

Unintentionally, albeit very fittingly, the thematic sections of our first two volumes on "Participatory Knowledge" and "Modes of Publication" relate to our mission and build on each other. We hope that this year's articles will be useful and thought-provoking to a wide audience. We are very much looking forward to input from guest editors regarding future themes.

May 2023

Charlotte A. Lerg, Ludwig Maximilian University, Munich
Johan Östling, Lund Centre for the History of Knowledge (LUCK), Lund University
Jana Weiß, The University of Texas at Austin

Section I: **Individual Articles**

Anastassiya Schacht
Soviet Public Health and Its Pattern of Involved Non-Attachment in International Organizations

Abstract: This contribution analyzes the pattern of how the Soviet drive to participate in international public health expert organizations was permanently entangled with the state's agencies of academic policing – and political agendas proper. Using the League of Nations' Health Organization, the World Health Organization, and the World Psychiatric Association as case studies, I reconstruct how Soviet politics intervened with scholarly endeavors and forced scholars to take on political roles and decisions. Through a three-step longitudinal comparison, my article provides an insight into the restrained pattern of Soviet expert engagement. The contribution argues that, although the state's surveillance and domination over scholars were sustained throughout the entire studied period, each new iteration of detachment and withdrawal was less total in scope and more difficult to legitimize for the domestic expert community itself.

Keywords: expert organizations, international organizations, authoritarianism, knowledge circulation, public health

1 Conflicted Soviet Internationalism

An international, cross-cultural, and transnational exchange of ideas has been one of the central, formative events of intellectual life for centuries – and most prominently so in the timespan since World War I. Throughout this century of political turbulence and excessive violence, intellectual cooperation – and especially in public health – frequently remained one of the few unwavering domains where internationalist thinking survived regardless of autarky- or confrontation-driven national politics. With the scope of research ever-growing concerning processes of connection and interchange in expert communities and intellectual coopera-

---

Acknowledgment: The author most warmly thanks the people, who contributed greatly to the creation and quality of this text, be it in form of editorial consideration, intellectual wit, organizational support, proof-reading patience, and human warmth: Peter Becker, Sophie Brocks, Charlotte A. Lerg, Johan Östling, Jannis Panagiotidis, Katharina Seibert, Martina Steer, and Jana Weiß.

ə Open Access. © 2023 the author(s), published by De Gruyter. [cc) BY-NC-ND] This work is licensed under the Creative Commons Attribution-NonCommercial-NoDerivatives 4.0 International License.
https://doi.org/10.1515/9783111078038-002

tion,[1] it is ever more crucial to systematically study cases of detachment and disentanglement that may reveal patterns behind conflicts and contestations of otherwise converging international engagement.

A particularly interesting example of this conflicted (involved, but often deliberately non-attached) engagement may be traced regarding the case of Russia. Over the last one and a half centuries, Russia went through several political regimes and ideologies. Each new regime sought to adopt the ways how it allowed its decision-makers, but also experts and citizens to interact with their international communities. Over and over, experts entitled to reach out beyond state borders had to adopt a very distinctive behavior, balancing between a genuine interest in international exchanges and the necessity to perform visible acts of political loyalty to their regime.[2]

This contribution surveys this peculiar pattern of politically pre-defined international disengagement on behalf of Soviet public health experts as seen in three cases throughout the century. It starts with the early Soviet and largely one-way collaboration with the League of Nations' Health Organization (LNHO) – an example that is somewhat longer in temporal terms but the most coherently disengaged in its structural logic.[3] From the interwar period into the late 1940s, the text moves on to the next example of non-attachment as it discusses the Soviet withdrawal from the newly-established WHO in 1949. With the WHO caesura overcome in the mid-1950s and international cooperation in public health productively including the USSR from then on, my third example highlights the narrower institution and yet another episode of the Soviet All-Union Society of Neuropathologists and

---

[1] For the sake of brevity and given the specificity of the focus group under study, I use these terms interchangeably throughout the text, referring to medical experts in their dual role as both research-conducting, academia-policing scholars and intellectuals and their more practical activities in the professional maintenance of public health systems.

[2] For this dual loyalty, as the author aptly labels it, see Nikolai Krementsov, *International Science Between the World Wars: The Case of Genetics* (London: Routledge, 2005), 6–10.

[3] There has in the last twenty years been a rich scholarship on Soviet entanglement with international public health efforts in the interwar period. For Soviet-German cooperation, see works by Susan Gross Solomon such as *Doing Medicine Together: Germany and Russia between the Wars* (Toronto: University of Toronto Press, 2006) or "Thinking Internationally, Acting Locally: Soviet Public Health as Cultural Diplomacy in the 1920s," in *Russian and Soviet Health Care from an International Perspective*, ed. Susan Grant (Liverpool: Palgrave Macmillan, 2017), 193–216. From more recent research on the Soviet-German bond in the interwar period, see Yulia Ratmanov and Pavel Ratmanov, "Transfer of the 'social hygiene' idea from Germany to Soviet Russia in the compilation of the curriculum on social hygiene in 1922," *Vestnik obŝestvennogo zdorov'â i zdravoohraneniâ Dal'nego Vostoka Rossii* 1, no. 1 (2020): 3.

Psychiatrists (AUSNP) withdrawing from the World Psychiatric Association at the very end of the Brezhnev era in 1983.

Based on these three cases, I argue for a distinctive pattern of conflicted internationalism traceable to Soviet authoritarianism interfering with expert communication across state and ideological borders. On the one hand, there is an apparent and continuous interest among the medical experts themselves to engage with the international community, whether for knowledge and technology exchange on behalf of the Soviet population, or for the globally defined good.[4] On the other hand, this genuine interest in cooperation has continuously been obstructed by the Communist regime. Government actors would, if not entirely prohibit expert communication with actors abroad, at least continuously narrow down the room for maneuver in which professionals could cooperate without fearing repression at home. The fact that the state invaded and sustainably transformed the scholarly and medical landscape meant that international cooperation primarily served as political representation. Cooperation would thus immediately be severed as soon as the Communist entanglement of medicine and politics was seen as contested. In the case of the WHO, this challenge was the result of presumed unfair treatment as a newly recognized superpower.[5] In the case of the World Psychiatric Association, this was the result of the psychiatrists involved finding it practically impossible to resolve a conflictual deadlock, in which they would be contested on politically motivated misdiagnoses and the mistreatment of dissidents. The anxiously ambivalent scenario of international cooperation available for Soviet public health experts might be labeled involved non-attachment: not entirely withdrawn and

---

[4] The former would be applicable to the interwar phase of early Soviet medicine, largely rebuilding the public health system; for instance, through the adoption of the social medicine model, which would be adopted from the broader non-Communist European debate and LNHO engagement, additionally reaching the USSR via its German cooperations and reappropriated for use and further export as the Semashko model (cf. contributions in György Peteri, ed., *Imagining the West in Eastern Europe and the Soviet Union* (Pittsburgh: University of Pittsburgh Press, 2010); Milena Angelova, "Visionarity and Health: The Semashko Model and the Sovietization of Public Health in Bulgaria (1944–1951)," *Balkanistic Forum* 3 (2021): 74–103. For the latter (i.e., the global good apart from the export of public health models to the postwar Warsaw Pact states), consider the massive Soviet engagement with the WHO's large-scale eradication programs within and despite the Cold War context. For a coherent overview, see Marcos Cueto, Theodore M. Brown, and Elizabeth Fee, *The World Health Organization: A History* (Cambridge: Cambridge University Press, 2019).

[5] Document Notification by the Union of Soviet Republics concerning participation in the World Health Organization, Executive Board, Seventeenth Session, Provisional Agenda Item 7.2. EB17/32 from 15 December 1955.

isolated but ready to threaten and perform accordingly in case of political – not epistemic – necessity.

This long observational focus may seem unusual, given the salience of dynamic changes in Soviet public health practices, which, in turn, may be further dissected within each of the periods under study. This contribution acknowledges the abundance of research undertaken with regard to each of the mentioned periods (which I discuss further below), such as research growing increasingly important with the new iteration of Russian political and military violence, in turn translating into a disruption of scholarly and medical cooperation yet again. Precisely this disruption of politically forced non-attachment is what forms the primary focus of this contribution. To reveal this pattern, we need to carry out a longitudinal observation of this trend.

2 The Pattern Emerges: Early Soviet Cooperation with the League's Health Organization

I start my analysis of the Soviet pattern of "involved non-attachment" in public health efforts at the onset of both the Soviet regime and the League of Nations. Both topics have in recent years enjoyed good coverage in research and a certain change in historiographic paradigms. East European Studies in the last two decades, mostly referenced in the previous section, have offered a complex picture of Soviet internationalism, not limited to exclusively highlighting its isolationist tendencies. For research on the League of Nations, it has seen a continuous revaluation. It is no longer seen as merely a failed predecessor to the UN, but the first attempt to create a truly global form of internationalism with a far more nuanced approach to its agencies, structures, and its short- and long-term impacts.[6]

Clearly, international and in particular medical cooperation with Russian involvement thrived before the 1920s. The Tsarist Empire was deeply involved in the internationalization of public health efforts throughout the nineteenth century,

---

[6] The literature here is vast and ever-growing, starting perhaps with Susan Pedersen's "Back to the League of Nations," *The American Historical Review* 112, no. 4 (Oct. 2007): 1091–1117; Glenda Sluga, *Internationalism in the Age of Nationalism* (Philadelphia: University of Pennsylvania Press, 2013), or Glenda Sluge and Patricia Clavin, *Internationalisms: A Twentieth-Century History* (Cambridge: Cambridge University Press: 2017). On the sustainable impact of the League of Nations on the UN, see M. Patrick Cottrell, *The League of Nations: Enduring Legacies of the First Experiment at World Organization* (Milton Park: Routledge, 2018). Regarding public health internationalism in the interwar period, see Josef L. Baron, *Health Policies in Interwar Europe: A Transnational Perspective* (Milton Park: Routledge, 2019).

whether in the form of gradually emerging sanitary controls,[7] exchanges of experts, practices, and legal frameworks,[8] the early work of the Red Cross,[9] or early cooperation on cross-nationally comparable lists over causes of death – out of which the present-day International Classification of Diseases originated.[10] My choice of topic, however, is based on the unprecedented consolidation of many public health bodies and initiatives under the umbrella of the League of Nations – simultaneously with the political seizure of power by the Bolsheviks in the collapsing Russian Empire.

In the early years, the newly formed Bolshevik state found itself in almost complete isolation. Former political and economic networks had been seriously disrupted during World War I and were now further contested due to the mutual antagonism of ideologies. On one side of this dichotomy, the early Bolsheviks sought to stir and propel any tension abroad that might trigger a world revolution.[11] Their animosity toward the non-communist West was met with an equally strong sentiment of rejection and suspicion.[12]

---

[7] On the emerging international regime of sanitary controls in Russia, see Charlotte E. Henze, *Disease, Health Care, and Government in Late Imperial Russia: Life and Death on the Volga, 1823–1914* (Milton Park: Routledge, 2011). For a quite rare scholarly touch on nineteenth-century colonial medicine in Central Asia under imperial rule, see Anna Afanasyeva, "Quarantines and Copper Amulets: The Struggle against Cholera in the Kazakh Steppe in the Nineteenth Century," *Jahrbücher für Geschichte Osteuropas* 61, no. 4 (2013): 489–512. For the interwar period of early Soviet transformation, see Paula Michaels, *Curative Powers: Medicine and Empire in Stalin's Central Asia* (Pittsburgh: University of Pittsburgh Press, 2003).

[8] Nancy Mandelker Frieden, *Russian Physicians in an Era of Reform and Revolution, 1856–1905* (Princeton: Princeton University Press, 2014). Based on Frieden's analysis of how the medical profession in late imperial Russia evolved through the standardization of both curricula and administrative structures and their coevolution, also see Angelika Strobel, *Die "Gesundung Russlands". Hygiene und imperial Verwaltungspraxis um 1900* (Bielefeld: Transcript, 2022).

[9] For the imperial period, see Inge Hendriks et al., "Women in Healthcare in Imperial Russia: The contribution of the surgeon Nikolay I Pirogov," *Journal of Medical Biography* 29, no. 1 (2021): 9–18. For the early Soviet transformation of the nursing profession, see Susan Grant, *Soviet Nightingales: Care under Communism* (Ithaca: Cornell University Press, 2022).

[10] See File *Nomenclature of Causes of Death. Russia*, in the League of Nations Archive, R843/12B/60650/22685.

[11] Zara Steiner, *The Lights that Failed: European International History 1919–1933* (Oxford: Oxford University Press, 2005), 131 ff.

[12] Diaries by officers of the Rockefeller Foundation's International Health Division reveal a general policy of this foundation to sever any cooperation with Russian scholars around the turn of the 1920s. Regardless of whether a medical expert was a political refugee, a scholar stranded in the newly-formed Bolshevik state, a devoted red cadre, present in the US or abroad doing fieldwork in the post-revolutionary empire, the Rockefeller Foundation did not finance anything until the middle of the 1920s. This does not, however, mean that the USSR did not profit from Rockefeller fund-

However, despite its resentment against the collective West, and the League of Nations representing it, the Soviet government was clearly interested in establishing international cooperation with them. In the early 1920s, amidst and during the aftermath of the Russian Civil War and largely lacking diplomatic recognition, the Bolshevik regime acquired medical assistance for epidemic relief and control offered by the League's Health Committee.[13] Within its national borders, Bolsheviks continuously sought to subdue the country's intellectuals, be it by a coordinated reorganization of academia – and healthcare – under the full control of the state, by repressing those opposing this transformation,[14] or by purposefully investing in those being more cooperative. On the one hand, intellectuals were swiftly ascribed as a class hostile to the new state of workers and peasants. The entire educational and training system was uprooted and then gradually subdued to the needs and political desires of the new government. Former academic qualifications were withdrawn, curricula redrafted, and any protests against imbalances in this process were suppressed.[15]

---

ing at all. A considerable part of the LNHO budget was until 1934 covered by the Rockefeller Foundation – and the LNHO pioneered cooperation with the Soviet public health system. For the Rockefeller Foundation's engagement with international public health, see Josep L. Barona, *The Rockefeller Foundation, Public Health and International Diplomacy, 1920–1945* (Milton Park: Routledge, 2015); and Paul Wendling, "American Foundations and the Internationalizing of Public Health," in *Shifting Boundaries of Public Health*, eds. Patrick Zylberman, Lion Murard, and Susan Gross Solomon (Paris: Boydell & Brewer, 2008), 63–86. For the Rockefeller Foundation's hesitance to cooperate with the Soviet regime, see Susan Gross Solomon, "'Through a Glass Darkly': The Rockefeller Foundation's International Health Board and Soviet Public Health," in *Studies in history and philosophy of science. Part C, Studies in history and philosophy of biological and biomedical sciences* 31, no. 3 (2000): 409–418.

13 For the Health Committee's Director Ludwik Rajchman negotiating donations of essential drugs with the Soviet Narkom (minister) for Foreign Affairs Maxim Litvinov, see, for instance, Letter by Rajchman to Litvinov date 02.11.1921, R824/12B/15255/17135.

14 For Bolshevik advances against the universities' autonomy, subsequent protest by professors, and state suppression of this protest, see Kontantin V. Ivanov, "New politics of education in 1917–1922: Reform of High School," in *Timetable of Changes: Review of Educational and Academic Policies in the Russian Empire – USSR (late 1880s–1930s)*, ed. Alexander N. Dmitriev (in Russian, Moscow: Novoe Literaturnoe Obozrenie, 2012), 360–379. For the politics of the cooptation of scholars, see Evgenia Dolgova, *Birth of Soviet Science: Scholars in the 1920s–1930s*, (in Russian, Moscow: Rossiyskiy Gosudarstvenniy Universitet, 2020), 152–176.

15 For the Health Committee's Director Ludwik Rajchman negotiating donations of essential drugs with the Soviet Narkom (minister) for Foreign Affairs Maxim Litvinov, see, for instance, Letter by Rajchman to Litvinov date 02.11.1921, R824/12B/15255/17135. For academic qualifications under the new regime, see Dolgova, *Birth of Soviet Science*, 88–90. For the reinstalment of curricula, see Dmitry A. Andreev, "Proletarisation of High School: 'New Student' as an instrument of educational politics," in *Timetable of Changes. Review of Educational and Academic Policies in the Russian Empire –*

However, even though medical professionals suffered the same amount of deprivation as their peers in other fields of knowledge, they were at least in dire demand by the new regime. It was on their shoulders that the fight against the consequences of famines and epidemics of typhus and postwar syphilis was carried out. Thus, the pragmatic need to retain power was coupled with the demand that the population be covered by public health systems, thereby permitting medical professionals to be recognized by the Bolsheviks in terms of their expertise.

With public health as such in a dire crisis after World War I, and following four years of civil war and famines, as much assistance as possible was absolutely crucial. From international expertise, Soviet medical experts might obtain aid in stocking up their depleted facilities and libraries[16] but also getting reattached to networks of knowledge and technical assistance for addressing the epidemiological challenges they were facing. With little to no investment, their government could harvest the benefits of medical internationalism, which it dearly needed at the time.

Zooming out to the international level, the LNHO pioneered cooperation with the Bolsheviks. Arguably, this was less for the sheer sake of cooperation, as dealing with the Bolsheviks was in the early 1920s seen as a negative political liability. Yet, at the pragmatic level, it was once again the exceptional role and importance of maintaining public health that allowed the buildup of early cooperation. The director of LNHO, Ludwik Rajchman, lobbied to donate pharmaceuticals and vaccines and to initiate campaigns for the prevention of typhus epidemics, or at least containing them within the Soviet borders.[17] Throughout the first half of the 1920s, several courses aimed at public health staff and nurses were carried out within and outside the USSR – in Kharkiv, Moscow, and Warsaw in 1923,[18] and again in Moscow in 1925 – with the LNHO covering the costs of such courses as well.[19] Starting in 1922, a program of interstate exchange and training for medical experts was

---

USSR (late 1880s–1930s), ed. Alexander N. Dmitriev (in Russian, Moscow: Novoe Literaturnoe Obozrenie, 2012), 494–523.
16 File *Supply of books and scientific documents to universities impoverished by the war. Dossier concerning Russia* (1922) in the League of Nations Archive, Geneva, R1049/13C/24805/23815 (Jackets 1 to 4).
17 File *Epidemics in Russia – Dr. Rajchmann (to Mr. Litvinoff) – Announces the intention of the Epidemic Commission of the League to make a gift of essential drugs to the Russian Health Commissariat. Advises negotiations between Russia and Poland for the purpose of establishing a Sanitary Convention* in the League of Nations Archive, R824/12B/17135/15255.
18 File *2nd series of courses of instruction at Kharkiv, Moscow, and Warsaw 1923. Services of professors* in the League of Nations Archive, R846/12B/28475/23967.
19 File *Training Courses for Public Health Personnel (Russia, etc.) 1925. Courses finances* in the League of Nations Archive, R846/12B/39721/23967.

launched,[20] in which the Soviets were also welcome. One of the first participants to profit from this program was none other than the Soviet People's Commissar (i. e., minister) for Health Nikolai Semashko.[21]

Semashko is a seminal figure for what turned out to be a complete relaunch of the public health system both under a brand new political regime and based on a highly novel organizational framework. Throughout the 1920s and well into the 1930s (i. e., as long as it was politically possible to pursue such an aim), Semashko vigorously managed the grand enterprise of internationalizing the Soviet public health system, or as Gross Solomon aptly puts it, "re-claiming place" for it.[22] As shown in the recent monograph by Pavel Ratmanov, Semashko stood at the apex of a broad campaign propagating the successes of the early Soviet public health system in the US and Western Europe.[23] Nevertheless, no expertise or talent for propaganda can withstand the pressure of totalitarianism. Given his well-documented track record with the LNHO, it may come as a surprise that Semashko would argue for the full autarky of accomplishments in public health when publishing his *Outline on the Theory of Soviet Organisation* in 1947. The League's cooperation programs are entirely missing in this text, and no state but the USSR features positively in the book. What is heavily highlighted is rather the dichotomy between the all-is-well Soviet Union and the decaying imperialist rest of the world. The book, even though published in 1947, largely fits into the interwar trend traced for the public health sectors of other nations that first seriously profited from the international system, be it via the LNHO or its independent but close funding partner the Rockefeller Foundation. For Semashko, this was only included in the text to deny any positive impact of such a cooperation while profiling the presumed national spirit of the positive changes that occurred.[24]

Collective effort for the USSR's own benefit – which was then sold to domestic audiences with as few strings of responsibility attached as possible – was how Semashko characterized early Soviet involvement with international public health efforts, which may come across as harsh only at first sight. Reappropriating gains

---

20 File *First Interchange of Sanitary Personnel: Sept-Dec 1922* in the League of Nations Archive, R837/12B/20109/25371. For the League's cooperation with the Rockefeller Foundation in organizing and funding these courses, see Barona, *Rockefeller Foundation*.
21 See *Miscellaneous correspondence respecting First Exchange of Sanitary Personnel: September-December 1922* (LON Archive, R837–12B-20109–25371).
22 Gross Solomon, "Thinking Internationally," 193–216, here especially p. 196.
23 Pavel Ratmanov, *Soviet Healthcare at the International Stage in the 1920–1940s: Between "Soft Power" and Propaganda (Western Europe and the USA)* (Vladivostok: DVGMU, 2021).
24 Erik Ingebrigtsen, "Privileged Origins: 'National Models' and Reforms of Public Health in interwar Hungary," in Gyorgy Peteri, *Imagining the West in Eastern Europe and the Soviet Union* (Pittsburgh: University of Pittsburgh Press, 2010), 36–59.

from international public health efforts in this way, largely via the League, was described as if this was an outcome of national efforts alone, a trope that several states in Eastern and Central Europe used in the interwar period.[25] From their very first years in power, the new political regime adopted a strategy of least possible alignment for the maximum possible benefit for itself. The early 1920s saw extensive correspondence between the LNHO (in the person of Director Rajchman or Deputy Director White) and the Soviet officials, typically represented by Narkom (minister) for Foreign Affairs Maxim Litvinov.[26] Negotiations concerned how the LNHO's activities in Soviet Russia should be framed. The Soviet side allowed access to all medical and sanitary facilities across the country, yet vehemently blocked any idea of recognizing the diplomatic immunity of international officers while in the country, or the League as an actor in general.[27] As the Bolshevik regime consolidated over the course of the 1920s and was subsequently recognized by the League, this stance started to soften ever so slowly. It is remarkable that the very same Litvinov who negotiated the LNHO's aid with no strings attached in the early 1920s would be hailed in the Soviet press of the mid-1930s as the one who brought the USSR into the League as a full member.[28]

The case study of interwar involvement with international public health efforts reveals an emerging pattern that we also encounter in parts 2 and 3, in the postwar Soviet engagement with the WHO and the World Psychiatric Association (WPA). One aspect of this pattern has already been mentioned above: the omnipresence of state interests behind scholarly and public health-related internationalism. Political reasoning allowed, restricted, or prohibited international exchanges in the public healthcare domain and decided on the way that international cooperation might take. Political reasoning also had the prerogative to interpret the impact and reassign credentials for it, if it chose to do so. This process of reappropriating international inputs as nothing but national accomplishments was

---

25 Consider contributions in György Peteri, *Imagining the West in Eastern Europe and the Soviet Union* (Pittsburgh: University of Pittsburgh: 2010) and in particular Erik Ingebrigtsen's conceptual paper suggesting that the Hungarian example of these politics constitutes one instance of the series: Erik Ingebrigtsen, "'National models' and reforms of Public Health in Interwar Hungary."
26 Cf. Rajchman-Litvinov correspondence in the League of Nations Archive (R838–12B-20398–20398); White-Litvinov correspondence in ibid. (R838–12B-20492–20492).
27 File *Relation between the Health Committee of the League and the Russian Government – Communicated by Dr. Rajchman – Records interview between himself and Litvinoff at Genoa regarding this question* in the League of Nations Archive, R838/12B/20398/20398.
28 So, for example, in the country's popular journal *Ogoniok* from 9 October 1934, no. 19 (505), which, apart from a detailed report on the events of Soviet admittance to the League of Nations, featured Litvinov's photo on its front page.

introduced and is thus especially easy to trace for the interwar period.[29] In the USSR too, a large part of the improvements to the Soviet public health system, even if achieved with considerable support from international actors like the League of Nations, would become reinterpreted for the domestic population as Bolshevik-created accomplishments. This must have been profitable for Soviet interests, since it was not attached to any long-term responsibilities implicitly included in a committed membership or recognition.

A few decades later, during the early years of the World Health Organization, Soviet participation appears from new angles of involved non-involvement.

3 Ambivalent Superpower: The USSR's Early Engagement with the World Health Organization

The reinstatement of peace and order after the end of World War II brought to life a new global umbrella organization – the UN – as well as several specific agencies, less universal in their focus though not in scale. Unlike in the interwar period, these agencies were structurally autonomous from the UN and its ruling mechanisms, albeit clearly maintaining their close bond with the mother organization, both in public and inherently integrated into the inner architectures of these agencies.[30]

Another difference from the interwar creation of the League consisted of more of the world's recognized powers now explicitly binding themselves as nations sponsoring and carrying the largely upscaled and complex organizational body of practical internationalism. The League had the Big Three (Britain, France, the US) to bring it into existence, while many global and regional powers of the day were more or less deliberately omitted from membership, and the US never fully joined.[31] Both the political landscape and the desire to embrace international

---

29 I can only but warmly recommend a wonderful conceptual text on this pattern of interwar reappropriation by Erik Ingebrigtsen – in this case, done on a Hungarian case study (Ingebrigtsen, "Privileged Origins"). Hopefully, research on this niche for interwar USSR will eventually be carried out.

30 For the comprehensive history of the World Health Organization, see Cueto, Brown, and Fee, *World Health Organization*.

31 On the limited internationality and the ultimate overpowering by the Big Three (and then Big Two), see Klaas Dykmann, "How International was the Secretariat of the League of Nations?" *The International History Review* 37, no. 4 (2015): 721–744.

cooperation changed dramatically after World War II.[32] The UN and its many agencies were drafted as "all-inclusive" by design (we return to this later) and were now supported by the newly established superpower quintet: the United States, the United Kingdom, France, China, and the Soviet Union.

No longer an outcast, but rather a war-winning power, the USSR entered the era of postwar internationalism under radically different premises compared to two decades prior. In discussions preceding the establishment of the WHO, special consideration was regularly paid to what the Soviet position might be on a given issue and how Soviet interests might be accommodated in advance.[33] The Soviets were reserved slots for representatives to meetings of the Technical Preparatory Committee in 1946, and the inability of the Soviet delegate to make a prepared statement on the birth of the WHO at one of many preparatory meetings was, though bitterly commented upon in a private diary, still duly and readily accepted.[34] While negotiating, the Soviet side managed to get not only one, but three representatives. While also federal member states of the USSR, the Byelorussian and Ukrainian Soviet Republics ended up becoming two additional individual member states of the organization. Thus, the USSR acquired freedom of action, where two additional votes could be automatically counted on toward any motion it suggested or blocked – and any motion could be shifted or proposed by one of these two proxies when convenient to the Soviet Union. The USSR was thus one of the founding powers and an exceptionally well-positioned player in the WHO both at the declaratory stage in 1946 and when the organization was finally and de facto launched during the First World Health Assembly in 1948.[35]

This helped little. A year in and several months before the Second World Health Assembly of 1949, the Soviet Union sent a telegram proclaiming its decision to withdraw from the WHO.[36] The reasons listed in support of the walkout concerned the allegedly unfair preferential treatment given to the US-American mem-

---

32 On the origins of the UN in the wartime agreements of the Allies, see Dan Plesch, *America, Hitler and the UN: How the Allies Won World War II and Forged a Peace* (London: I.B. Tauris, 2011); Mark Mazower, *Governing the World: The History of an Idea* (London: Penguin Press, 2012).
33 For the exasperation expressed by a Chinese official regarding such treatment, see "Item 4. The Origins of the World Health Organization: A Personal Memoir, 1945–1948," in *Szeming Sze Papers, 1945–1988*, UA.90. F14.1, University of Pittsburg Archives, B.1, F.16, 1982.
34 Ibid.
35 See, for example, the editorial "The First World Health Assembly," *American Journal of Public Health* 38 (October 1948): 1448–1450.
36 Here and later in the passage, I quote from the WHO's document *Notification by the Union of Soviet Republics concerning participation in the World Health Organization, Executive Board, Seventeenth Session, Provisional Agenda Item 7.2.*, EB17/32 from 15 December 1955.

bership.³⁷ Accusations went into more detail and included, for example, a somewhat quicker executable right for the US to leave the WHO. Should they ever want to, this withdrawal was possible with only one year's notice, not two as in the case of other states.³⁸ Unfair as it may have sounded, the US carried the largest financial burden of all nations, sponsoring over one-third of the WHO's annual budget in these early years.³⁹ The Soviet contribution, on the contrary, was far more modest in monetary terms, less so in representative power. In addition, it also enjoyed its boosted presence via two additional memberships for the Byelorussian SSR and Ukrainian SSR. Closing the monetary argument, the USSR was found to be in arrears on its fee payment for more than half a year in 1949 as it left the organization.

Clearly, there was a positive bias towards the US in the early WHO, just as in, arguably, all agencies of the newly created UNO – or rather the recreated, remodeled, and upscaled LON – much so with the help of US-American monetary investments too.⁴⁰ The US indeed enjoyed certain preferential treatment, even though the same might have been said about the USSR with its additional representing republics. The argument regarding preferential treatment might thus be considered plausible for the delegations of many nations – however, it must be approached with a good measure of critical thinking for the Soviet side.

Instead, it is logical to interpret the withdrawal in 1949 through macropolitical considerations that had little to do with the World Health Organization as an agency or its mission to promote global public health.⁴¹ The postwar wave of Soviet isolationism from the WHO aligns neatly with both the beginning of the Cold War and its often competing attempts at internationalism,⁴² but also with the last wave of

---

37 Also debated by Charles Easton Rothwell in his "International Organization and World Politics," *International Organization* 3, no. 4 (1949): 605–619.
38 Cueto, Brown, and Fee, *World Health Organization*, 52–53.
39 Ibid.
40 On the World War II origins of the UN and the strong US-American commitment to this project, see, for instance, Plesch, *America, Hitler and the UN*. On the structural continuity and change between the League and the UN, see Amy L. Sayward, *The United Nations in International History*, (London, New York: Bloomsbury Academic, 2017): 7.
41 Cueto, Brown, and Fee, *World Health Organization*, 66.
42 The context of the Cold War triggered an explosive growth in the number of international organizations – a process that, on closer inspection, revealed less of the broader acceptance of internationalist thinking but rather a reduplication of organizations and unions on two sides of the Iron Curtain and the political dichotomy this symbolized (cf. Thomas Davies, *NGOs: A New History of Transnational Civil Society* (London: Hurst & Company, 2013)), 133–135. For the competition between the superpowers, although rather applicable for a somewhat later timeframe, see Peter Ridder, *Konkurrenz um Menschenrechte: Der Kalte Krieg und die Entstehung des UN-Menschenrechtsschutzes von 1965–1993* (Göttingen: Vandenhoeck & Ruprecht, 2021).

Stalinist terror unravelling in the USSR. With regard to the former, the logic of Stalinist terror and accompanying isolationism had already been tested during the interwar period, stylized as self-protection against the constructed enemy of the whole world outside the Soviet borders, with the vicious powers of imperialism just waiting for a chance to infiltrate and sabotage the USSR. Anything that did not play by Soviet-only rules was very easily labeled as hostile and dangerous to its Communist ideology and was to be rejected.

There was definitely a basis for this hostile sentiment in the US-led liberal political landscape of the early Cold War. With Soviet Communism serving as the only ideological alternative to Western liberalism, now greatly strengthened and on equal footing, the anxiety concerning the potential takeover by this ideological adversary was only too palpable. Jamie Cohen-Cole's study of the new interest in the US in psychology scholars reveals how this authoritarian thinking gradually came to be firmly associated with the ideological adversary in Communism – and in Communist expertise too.[43]

This confrontation of worldviews proved unavoidable also when it came to postwar reconstruction and public health. Where the US was set on investing in relief and reconstruction under the Marshall Plan, it clearly sought to oust what Communists might have suggested.[44] James Gillespie mentions the difficulties faced by the UNRRA when Soviet authorities in Czechoslovakia took over the materials of the organization, yet relabeled them as Soviet prior to distribution.[45] In countering the Marshall Plan, the USSR came up with the Warsaw Pact as the most effective alternative it could find under the given circumstances. Aimed at its newly gained satellites in the new Eastern Bloc, it was to make sure that the new Communist countries rejected the offer of Marshall Plan reconstruction assistance.

There was even more momentum with regard to gradually diverging views on public health and how it should be approached globally. Similar to many other spheres covered by the activities of international organizations, this early postwar period saw unprecedented ideological clashes in the field of public health. While both sides of the Iron Curtain agreed that the best way to ameliorate global public health would be through gradually improved standards of living and the eradication of diseases, the envisioned paths toward these goals varied globally. The USSR highlighted the importance of economic growth, whereas the US rather pledged po-

---
[43] Jamie Cohen-Cole, *The Open Mind: Cold War Politics & the Sciences of Human Nature* (Chicago and London: The University of Chicago Press, 2016).
[44] See, for instance, David Ellwood, "The Propaganda of the Marshall Plan in Italy in a Cold War Context," *Intelligence and National Security* 18, no. 2 (2003): 225–236.
[45] James A. Gillespie in Gross Solomon, Murard, and Zylberman, *Shifting Boundaries*, 120.

litical self-determination and individual autonomy. The Communist bloc invested its energy into supporting decolonization – a fair and reasonable intent, which in addition to its thoroughly positive intention simultaneously contested and undermined the authority of Western liberal powers, all of whom had a rather poor record from the colonial era. This is not to say the Soviet Union was not colonial, because it was. Yet, the issue of Soviet colonialism was hardly an issue in the era under discussion and has only slowly emerged as a historiographic topic in later years.[46] Similarly, the walkout from the WHO was partially justified with reference to US-led negligence with regard to economic underdevelopment and poor working conditions endangering health globally.[47]

To what extent the USSR's withdrawal was a matter of divergent approaches to public health practices – or rather a matter of great geopolitical games played well outside of the realm of intellectuals and medical experts – is visible from the rapid shift in stance after Stalin's death in 1953. Among the medical experts themselves, their level of interest in international cooperation on behalf of global public health efforts might have been unchanged as compared to the moment of the USSR withdrawing from the WHO. Yet, it took political and not scholarly interest and will to allow Soviet public health professionals to rejoin the international terrain.[48]

In 1955, a revived interest in being a part of the global public health scheme was manifested at a session of the UN's Economic and Social Council, and the Soviet wish to be readmitted into the WHO was received, processed, and agreed upon quickly.[49] Given that the Soviet return automatically brought back other members from Warsaw Pact states, which had withdrawn out of expected solidarity, the WHO managed to regain its global aspirations and avert the risk of fragmentation and a subsequent erosion of legitimacy induced by the rejection of the universality of the agency.

A closer look reveals that the USSR and its allies found themselves not reentering the WHO anew, but rather reactivating memberships that, based on the in-

---

[46] This has become a contemporary issue too, following Putinist aggression against former Soviet colonies and its constituent republics. For the Soviet vs. US-led rivalry in the sphere of competing world visions, see Ridder, *Menschenrechte*.
[47] Cueto, Brown, and Fee, *World Health Organization*, 63.
[48] On the impact of political destalinization in public health in general, see Paula Michaels, "Soviet Medical Internationalism amid Destalinization, 1953–1958," *The Soviet and Post-Soviet Review* (published online ahead of print 2022). doi: https://doi-org.uaccess.univie.ac.at/10.30965/18763324-bja10070): 1–24. Though impossible to discuss in detail here, for an intriguing account of how the concurrent rise of psychopharmacology actually prevented the destalinization of Soviet psychiatry, see Benjamin Zajicek, "The Psychopharmacological Revolution in the USSR: Schizophrenia Treatment and the Thaw in Soviet Psychiatry, 1954–64," *Medical History* 63, no. 3 (2019): 249–269.
[49] File EB17/32 of December 15, 1955 by the Executive Board of the World Health Organization: 2.

ternal logic of the WHO, were not regarded as terminated but postponed.[50] As briefly mentioned above, the claim of the UN system in terms of universality deliberately avoided introducing a mechanism for states to cancel their memberships. The difference here lies in the fact that complete withdrawal eliminated all mutual responsibilities and duties, while an inactive membership was still implicitly included in the general mission and vision of the agency, while still also requiring that prescribed fees are paid. Throughout its five years of inactivity, arrears on Soviet payments were calculated and presented in the WHO's fiscal reports, and the same applied to the USSR's other proxies: the Byelorussian and Ukrainian SSRs and all other returning Eastern Bloc members. Though the latter group was expected to pay its arrears sovereignly, the collected debt for the USSR and its two proxies by mid-1955 exceeded a truly astronomical sum of $3.5 million, plus over $600,000 for the fiscal year of 1955 (in current value, each of these sums would be roughly ten times greater).[51] Even though subsequent reports show that not the entire debt but a sum of roughly more than $1 million was internally accounted for and settled as partial payment for the arrears, the financial issue was considered finished by 1957.[52]

It took more than a year for Soviet medical experts to be able to rejoin activities run by the WHO. Documentation is available for over two decades, well into the mid-1970s, on individual new members being nominated to the agency's diverse expert advisory panels and committees, each of these working groups addressing individual prominent diseases (e. g., in various years, brucellosis, lepra, malaria, or the plague), a spectrum of diseases (e. g., the Mental Health Panel or the panel on zoonoses), particular scholarly problems (e. g., the standardization of pharmacopoeia or biological standardization), or challenges regarding the management of public health systems (e. g., health education or international quarantine). Soviet medical experts joined their first panels and committees by the middle of 1958 with two professionals, V. Ershov and V. Soloviev, listed as experts on the Health

---

50 The head of the WHO, Brock Chisholm, insisted on this inactive status rather than accepting the withdrawal in 1949 (Cueto, Brown, and Fee, *The World Health Organization*, 64). In fact, the WHO was deliberately devised with no exit option, as apparent from the expert discussions preceding the establishment of the WHO. Minutes of the Technical Preparatory Committee for the International Health Conference. Held in Paris from 18 March to 5 April 1946. Thirteenth Meeting (held on Wednesday, 27 March 1946, at 2.30 p.m., Palais d'Orsay, Paris). United Nations, World Health Organization, Interim Commission: 26.
51 Statement showing the Status of Collections of annual Contributions and of Advances to the Working Capital Fund as of 30 April 1955 in the File A8/AFL/11 of 13 May 1955: 3.
52 Statement showing the Status of Collections of annual Contributions and of Advances to the Working Capital Fund as of 30 April 1957 in the File A10/AFL/12 of 8 May 1957: 3.

Education of the Public Panel and the Virus Diseases Panel, respectively.[53] No longer prevented from doing so by their government's isolationist and boycotting drive, medical experts joined in and contributed avidly. Only including expert panels and committees (i. e., not counting the permanent staff at WHO headquarters), the numbers still speak for themselves.

Within a year, the number of experts convening to consult with their international colleagues on various aspects of global public health management reached 60 scholars, and within half a decade, by the mid-1960s, this figure had doubled. From this time on, roughly more than 150 medical professionals from the USSR would, on various occasions, be travelling abroad, obviously entitled to responsibilities of representation, but more importantly the imperative to discuss, exchange knowledge, and scout technology and potential cooperation. In terms of intellectual creativity, Soviet medical science indeed had much to offer. In the years to come, cutting-edge specialists joined the global exchange of medical ideas, including Zinaida Ermolieva, a medical doctor who independently, and parallel to Fleming, synthesized penicillin during World War II, or virologist Viktor Zhdanov, who played a crucial role in the WHO's global Smallpox Eradication Program.[54] Andrey Snezhnevsky, who served as an expert on the WHO's Mental Health Panel in the 1960s, was a seminal figure in his discipline at home, even more so as his nosological model of schizophrenia, which quickly became the mainstream model in the USSR, in later years of his international fame became closely associated with the politics of psychiatrically (mis)diagnosing dissidents.

Accusations of politically rather than medically motivated diagnoses had mounted ever since the mid-1960s. This was especially true after five medical histories could be smuggled out of the USSR and presented publicly to be scrutinized by international psychiatrists in 1971.[55] In response to this conflict, the World Psy-

---

[53] Report on Appointment to Expert Advisory Panels and Committees by the WHO's Executive Board of 2.1.1958 (EB21/46): 21, 79.

[54] Cueto, Brown, and Fee, *World Health Organization*, 119.

[55] The issue of the political abuse of psychiatry has evolved into a broad epistemic debate on psychiatric ethics, responsibilities, and the limitations of the profession, as well as on the effective means to counter large-scale ethical rule-breaking in medicine. From key authors at the time, the best account of the logic behind Soviet psychiatric abuse is presented in numerous publications by Sidney Bloch and Peter Reddaway. See their *Russia's Political Hospitals: The Abuse of Psychiatry in the Soviet Union* (London: Victor Gollancz Ltd, 1977); Sidney Bloch and Peter Reddaway, *Psychiatric Terror: How Soviet Psychiatry Is Used to Suppress Dissent* (New York: Basic Books, 1977). See also Reddaway's personal recount of the events in *The Dissidents: A Memoir of Working with the Resistance in Russia, 1960–1990* (Washington, D.C.: Brookings Institution Press, 2020). An important piece of present-day scholarship on the political abuse of psychiatry is Robert van Voren, *Cold War in Psychiatry: Human Factors, Secret Actors* (Amsterdam: Rodopi, 2010).

chiatric Association – our third case tracing the pattern of Soviet entanglement in global public health management – came to play an active role. Snezhnevsky and his colleagues, many of whom were trained and supervised by him and thus formed an entire school within the field, were abundantly represented in many international organizations with a public health focus. At the WHO, Eduard Babaian, a recognized narcologist, sat on the expert panel for the Organization of Medical Care,[56] followed by, closer to his expertise, on the one for drug dependency.[57] As a popular expert campaigning against the Soviet representatives adamantly rejecting any productive discussion on the accusations mounted against them, Babaian gave interviews to the Western press while staying in Geneva in his capacity as a WHO officer. Equally so, the Soviet representative and deputy minister for health at home, Dmitry Venediktov, used all his diplomatic skills to contain the psychiatric scandal from spreading and entering discussions at the WHO.[58]

Venediktov's engagement is traceable on many occasions and as such, it exemplifies the variation and complexity of the agency and the impact of a high-profile international expert. While Venediktov's actions helped conceal a systematic breach of medical ethics in the story of the political abuse of psychiatry in the USSR, on other occasions his interventions clearly had a positive impact. While the WHO had moved through a major reform of its structure, administrative politics, and mission, Soviet experts and Venediktov in particular supported initiatives granting more voting power, voice, and space for action to representatives of newly decolonized nations from the Global South.[59] The gradual change in the WHO's administrative culture toward cultural and geographic diversification in the 1970s would not have been possible without a superpower like the USSR, which held onto the agency of those outside the industrial countries of the First World.

The reason for this strong engagement on behalf of weakly represented countries was, once again, primarily political. Such self-imposed advocacy aligned perfectly with the strategy pursued by other Soviet experts representing their country

---

56 WHO, *Report on Appointments to Expert Advisory Panels and Committees* of 20 December 1961, EB29/32: 72.
57 WHO, *Report on Appointments to Expert Advisory Panels and Committees* of 3 January 1974, EB53/2: 62.
58 See the File Twenty-Seventh Session of the Regional Committee for Europe. Report by the Regional Director. 10 November 1977. World Health Organization, EB61/11: 1. Here, Venediktov was asked to comment on the ongoing conflict at the WPA and the condemnation of psychiatric malpractice by the congress in Honolulu. Venediktov argued that the issue could not be discussed due to a lack of time and available reliable documentation. The issue was then dropped.
59 WHO, Document EB67/Conf. Paper No. 11 from 30 January 1981.

in other UN bodies. Peter Ridder has coined a wonderfully suitable term – "concurrence for human rights" – when talking about the US and Soviet representatives fighting each other for the recognition of newly independent, upwardly striving countries since the 1960s.[60] In a similar stance, the WHO representatives adhered to their national interest and national loyalty above their social roles as international officers – and even well above their professional identities.

A legitimate objection here would be that this would hold true for most international scholars. The Soviets, indeed, had much to offer, whether it involved their highly valuable medical knowledge in the context of the WHO or their role as an omnipresent adversary against the collective West. It is also true that just as in the case of better representation for Third World countries, the impact of international experts with a very firmly set political vision must not have been altogether negative. At times, it resulted in the reappropriation of mainstream popular discourses, as if reinvented by Western actors.[61] However, on less felicitous occasions, the primary position of politics would force Soviet medical experts to step down from their professional identities and support practices quite incompatible with their professional ethics as medical practitioners, scholars, or simply intellectuals. In the worst cases, should the political system go into a sudden ideological nosedive, scholarly interest was the least important. In this regard, the complete withdrawal of Soviet experts from the WHO in 1948 serves as a clear example.

4 The World Psychiatric Association: Pre-emptive Self-Expulsion

So far, we have traced two cases of Soviet non-attachment in the international public health system in general. Whereas the interwar period showed an avid Soviet interest in incoming aid and cooperation, while maintaining an obstinate resentment toward their legal affiliation with the League's Health Organization, the postwar period saw a more varied, though equally peculiar, participation pattern with the WHO.

Our third example leads us to a more discipline-specific yet equally international case where political reasoning yet again dominated over decision-making. In this example, a conflict was triggered when it was proven that Soviet psychiatry

---

60 See Ridder, *Menschenrechte*, particularly chapters 2–4.
61 On the competition for gender equality as played out across the Iron Curtain, see Kristen Ghodsee, *Second World, Second Sex: Socialist Women's Activism and Global Solidarity during the Cold War* (Durham: Duke University Press, 2019).

had transgressed medical ethics in the name of political expediency. Arguably, the continuous and institutionalized pressure by Soviet government actors on Soviet psychiatry spread the practice of the late Brezhnev era to victimize and sanction political opposition via false diagnoses of mental illness, confinement, and unnecessary, harmful treatment, which ruined the health and reputation of dissidents. The conflict played out on the international stage, where, for over a decade, Soviet psychiatrists would be regularly confronted with charges of politically motivated diagnoses. The politics of the Brezhnev era – making psychiatrists accomplices in the state suppression of dissent and restricting their action space within international organizations – prevailed in 1983. This time, Soviet medical experts walked out of the World Psychiatric Association in order to preempt being expelled.

The Soviet practice of attesting mental disorders to sane but politically active citizens did not begin in the 1960s but earlier, during the Stalinist period. By then, the first accounts of intellectuals being confined to psychiatric asylums first reached international audiences and were only gradually recognized as an issue of interest for human rights groups by the 1960s.[62] Alexander Podrabinek, whose *Punitive Medicine* was the first systematic domestic account of the political abuse of dissidents in the 1970s, traced the roots of unmedical diagnoses to smaller-scale and unsystematic instances of Soviet psychiatrists misdiagnosing and then confining otherwise sane political dissidents. Initially, however, they did so to save these dissidents from capital punishment or the gulag system during the period of Stalinist terror.[63] What had worked as a means to save lives under Stalinism[64] turned into a well-established machine built to systematically persecute political, cultural, and religious non-conformists in the politically milder late Khrushchev and Brezhnev eras. The systematization and institutionalization of psychiatric persecution occurred in the 1960s. One of the "signals" of this turn

---

62 On Western (in this particular case British) expert and lay audiences only gradually developing an interest in the Soviet human rights movement, and its suppression by means of psychiatry, see the recent book by Mark Hurst, *British Human Rights Organizations and Soviet Dissent, 1965–1985* (London: Bloomsbury Academics, 2017).
63 Alexander Podrabinek, *Punitive Medicine* (New York: Chronika, 1979), 24–25.
64 For a comprehensive overview of Soviet psychiatry in its state as a "normal science" throughout the twentieth century (i.e., focused on daily structures and practices, as well as on the limiting impact of state control upon the epistemic landscape within the discipline), see the recently published monograph by Gregory Dufaud, *Une histoire de la psychiatrie soviétique* (Paris: Éditions EHESS, 2021). On the Stalinist intervention in the epistemic action space of psychiatry, see Benjamin Zajicek, "Soviet Psychiatry and the Origins of the Sluggish Schizophrenia Concept, 1912–1936," *History of Human Sciences* 31, no. 2 (2018): 88–105.

came from a public statement by Nikita Khrushchev himself, who claimed that only mentally ill individuals would oppose the Soviet government.[65]

With international awareness concerning this abuse growing outside the USSR, a complex network of advocacy groups developed over the following decades. This network connected otherwise isolated dissidents in the USSR to a series of working groups – such as those around Peter Reddaway in the UK or representative expert societies like the American Psychiatric Association and the Royal College of Psychiatrists – and reached out further to approach politicians, public personalities, and larger international organizations all the way up to the UN. In the end, the result was a multi-level exercise of pressure on the Soviet All-Union Society of Neuropathologists and Psychiatrists.[66] Beginning in 1971, the issue of psychiatric abuse became a prominent topic for popular, lay audiences and medical experts alike.

The entire 1970s passed in an endless search for mutual understanding and dialogue in an increasingly tense atmosphere of ever-new actors joining this widening debate on ethics and responsibility. The World Psychiatric Association sought to retreat to the position of a "science-only" platform, where this science sought to exist beyond any political tension and agency altogether. The WPA thus favored offering diplomacy and continuously sought to avoid even hypothetical risks of acting according to the political biases of the Cold War. (Accusations of bias were leveled from both the Soviet side and the largely US-American and British sides of the epistemic conflict.) The WPA came under public scrutiny and critique for not responding to the continued abuse in the USSR and for being hesitant in its condemnation. The organization's internal documents reveal that there were fears of a split and subsequent decay should they proceed against their Soviet colleagues by condemning, suspending, or expelling them. The experience of other Eastern Bloc satellites leaving the WHO out of solidarity with the Soviet withdrawal in 1949 must have weighed hard on the decision-making process at the WPA. Additionally, no superpower had ever been excluded from larger international bodies involving medical – that is, supposedly scientific, universal, apolitical – cooperation.

Tensions mounted, however, when several national member societies from the UK, US, Canada, and others pressured the WPA Executive Committee to take clear action. At the Sixth World Psychiatric Congress held in Honolulu in 1977, there was

---

[65] Quoted in various sources. See, for instance, Koriagin in *Posev*, No. 12 (1987): 45–49.
[66] For the track record of extremely productive British human rights groups, see Hurst, *British Human Rights*, as well as the classics on the matter published by actors themselves involved in the campaign against the political abuse of psychiatry: Reddaway and Bloch as well as van Voren (see footnote 55).

an explicit condemnation of the misuse of psychiatric expert knowledge and authority for political means. With the Soviet side continuously withdrawing from dialogue on this issue, the next step would almost unavoidably include the expulsion of the All-Union Society from the World Psychiatric Association by the next congress, which would convene in Vienna in 1983. While the WHO maintained considerable neutrality in this case (we may only guess regarding the extent to which this was the result of the smart strategizing of Soviet officers at various levels), the conflict spilled over into the Human Rights Commission of the United Nations, where a detailed inquiry on the issue was also under preparation.[67]

It is in light of this multilateral and heavy pressure, as well as the inevitability of expulsion following the Honolulu Congress, that the Soviet side withdrew from the World Psychiatric Association in mid-February 1983.[68] Much of how this withdrawal played out will unavoidably remind one of the USSR withdrawing from the WHO in 1949. In both cases, the Soviet side argued that it had been provoked into action by unscientific, politicized activities and thus the unfair treatment it presumably experienced while a member of the organization. In both cases, genuine cooperation at the level of expert projects operated well up until the last moment: Marat Vartanian served as a Soviet representative to the Executive Committee, and an unexpected visit by two high-profile psychiatrists from the USSR was paid to WPA Secretary General Peter Berner only a few weeks before the letter of withdrawal. The visit left the WPA official hopeful for further cooperation and a solution to the conflict.[69] Similar to the WHO case, the formal withdrawal was communicated in writing a few months prior to a major professional convention organized by the organization in question: by telegram four months before the World Health Assembly in 1949 and by letter five months before the World Psychiatric Congress in 1983. Curiously, even the timespan of (temporary) withdrawal – that is, until changes in the domestic Soviet political landscape allowed Soviet experts to appeal for readmittance – was surprisingly the same: six years (1949–1955 and 1983–1989, respectively).

---

67 United Nations, Economic and Social Council. Commission on Human Rights. Document "Report of the Sub-Commission on Prevention of Discrimination and Protection of Minorities on its Thirty-Fourth Session. Geneva, 11 August–11 September 1981", E/CN.4/1515 of 28 September 1981: 93.
68 Letter by the Board of Chairs, All-Union Scientific Society of Neuropathologists and Psychiatrists, to President of WPA, Prof. P. Pichot, General Secretary WPA, Prof. P. Berner, Members of the Executive Committee WPA, of 31 January 1983. Sakharov Centre of Democratic Development, Kaunas.
69 World Psychiatric Association, *The Issue of Abuse 1977–1983*, a report from November 1982 stored at the Sakharov Centre for Democratic Development in Kaunas.

There were also obvious differences. While the Soviet walkout from the WHO in 1949 must be interpreted as an unprovoked test of strength and cultural capital as a new superpower, the WPA withdrawal in 1983 was a clear instance of a forced flight to save face, both politically and scholarly. Accordingly, the case of the WPA walkout was followed by an unprecedented amount of backstage diplomacy, wherein high-profile Soviet and Soviet-friendly psychiatrists attempted to build bridges that would allow for the Soviet Union being readmitted.

The USSR's standing as a superpower also played out differently in these two cases. The WHO walkout in 1949 was followed by the withdrawal of six newly Communist states: Bulgaria, Romania, Albania, Poland, Czechoslovakia, and Hungary. Only Yugoslavia did not follow.[70] The situation in 1983 was different. While the GDR communicated a note of protest, it did not withdraw. Similarly, Poland, Romania, Hungary, and Yugoslavia remained members of the WPA, and only three national psychiatric societies from Communist countries joined the USSR in 1983: those of Cuba, Bulgaria, and Czechoslovakia – albeit the latter two only after several months' delay.

We may attribute such a difference to several reasons. In part, this difference must be explained by the fact that for Communist states in the mid-1980s, unlike in the late 1940s, the ratio between expected governmental repression as a result of not following the USSR and the importance of taking part in cross-border intellectual networks had radically changed. All across the Warsaw Pact, even with the still viable danger of repression, the option to self-isolate from international cooperation in Soviet company was not at all a desirable outcome. The degree of international entanglement in the early 1980s was far too high to endanger by means of a largely unnecessary walkout on behalf of other national psychiatric societies in the Eastern Bloc. Arguably, Soviet experts themselves would most likely not have withdrawn had they not felt forced to choose between political and professional loyalties. The choice they made, however, once again proved which of the two aspects prevailed.[71]

---

[70] For the Yugoslav-Soviet split and its impact on the state socialist attempt at internationalism see, on an example of a feminist antifascist movement, Chiara Bonfiglioli, "Cold War internationalisms, nationalisms and the Yugoslav–Soviet split: The Union of Italian Women and the Antifascist Women's Front of Yugoslavia," in *Women's activism*, ed. Francisca de Haan et al. (London: Routledge, 2013), 59–76.

[71] The predominance of political considerations behind the Soviet withdrawal from the WPA is an argument strongly supported in van Voren, *Cold War in Psychiatry*, 203–204.

5 Discussion: Learning from Failure?

Analyzing the similarities and differences in Soviet engagement and disengagement offers a deeper understanding of ideological continuities still shaping Russia's current self-positioning in the international sphere, which – especially noticeable since the Russian invasion of Ukraine and the outbreak of the current war – mostly occurs *on behalf of* rather than *by* scholars proper. It gives us a good clue of how authoritarianism impacts the action space of medical experts, shapes their lobbying or vetoing decisions, and affects a broader world with such decisions. To that end, this analysis provides us with a better way of responding to the interpenetration of political ideologies with international public health efforts.

The traceable differences between the walkouts in 1949 and 1983 demonstrate the impact and progress of an internationalism gradually gaining a foothold against Soviet isolationism. From an even broader view, we might also compare them with our first case study of the USSR's non-aligned public health attachment with the interwar LNHO. Table 1 compares and summarizes three distinctive ways in which Soviet public health management was attached to an international community of experts throughout the twentieth century.

Table 1: Modes of attachment and participation in international public health organizations by Soviet experts throughout the twentieth century.

	LNHO	WHO	WPA
POLITICAL BACKGROUND	Consolidation of Communism, Stalinism	Stalinism to de-Stalinization (the Thaw)	Brezhnevism to Perestroika
ESTABLISHED MEMBER OF THE ORGANIZATION	no	yes	yes
REPRESENTATIVE MEMBERSHIP THROUGH	Individual experts (state denies recognition)	State representatives (via nomination by the Ministry for Health and Academy of Medical Sciences)	Scientific society (with representatives reporting to the KGB upon their travels and actions)
CONFLICT GROUNDS	General non-recognition between the USSR and the LON with cooperation effort by the LNHO.	USSR claims preferred treatment of the USA, lack of support for the reconstruction in Eastern Europe, fundamental difference in the understanding of Public Health	Psychiatric abuse and lack of Soviet cooperation to stop it.

Table 1: Modes of attachment and participation in international public health organizations by Soviet experts throughout the twentieth century. *(Continued)*

	LNHO	WHO	WPA
STATES FOLLOWED	No satellite states	Bulgaria, Romania, Albania, Poland, Czechoslovakia, and Hungary	Cuba, Czechoslovakia
STATES THAT DID NOT FOLLOW	Not applicable	Yugoslavia	GDR, Poland, Yugoslavia, Romania, Bulgaria, Hungary
IO'S REACTION	LNHO shows much interest in ameliorating Public Health conditions in the USSR	Regret expressed by many and at many occasions	Regret with stern reservation
DURATION OF WITHDRAWAL	Not applicable	6 years	6 years

Table 1 hints at an interesting tendency regarding the rather restricted, non-involved Soviet attachment to international organizations toward deeper international cooperation on the part of Soviet experts despite all political obstacles and forced isolationism. From a flat-out rejection of cooperation with the League's Health Organization during the interwar period – at least at the level of political decision-making – Soviet public health management could move a step forward, assuming the role of superpower testing its strength with its early withdrawal from the WHO in 1949. Not benefitting from the walkout and the fact that destalinization was taking over domestic politics meant that Soviet medical experts were able to rejoin the WHO quite soon, where they cooperated prolifically and engaged with partners for the good of global public health systems. Their political agencies, never completely removed, softened and became more refined, as Soviet officers in the WHO combined their own interest as a big player at the WHO with actions that at times resulted in thoroughly positive changes in the long run, such as a greater voice for the countries of the Global South within the organization.

By the 1970s and 1980s, Soviet medical experts were well-integrated international players. To that end, their loud and impactful withdrawal from the WPA showed just how severe the epistemic conflict had been over the misuse of psychiatric expertise for political means. Their preemptive withdrawal from the WPA was, in its functional logic, nothing more than a state-led attempt to mitigate the reputational damage to its psychiatric professionals and the Soviet use of its healthcare model as a tool of soft power worldwide. As long as an open and critical discussion of the political background to the conflict remained out of reach, withdrawal was the only available option. It also took domestic political changes to partially overcome the deadlock of self-isolationism, in turn allowing Soviet psychiatrists to aspire to being readmitted to the WPA, which, under the condition of eliminating documented abuse as soon as possible, was granted in 1989.

The three surveyed case studies in this contribution show a certain pattern in Soviet medical internationalism during the twentieth century. Although never entirely isolated, and most probably genuinely interested in transnational circulations of knowledge and cross-border networking, Soviet medical experts were continuously pressured to adjust their degree of involvement to the political reasoning of their government. This predominance of a political rationale over a professional one might have passed unnoticed in times free of immediate political pressures but could rather quickly escalate to a complete withdrawal if state actors decided accordingly. At the same time, observing the three case studies in sequence, a certain hope may arise regarding the scope of political shutdowns related to medical cooperation: from flat-out resentment toward the LNHO in the early 1920s to the short-term, unprovoked absence from the WHO from 1949 to 1955, to the only hesitantly executed withdrawal from the WPA between 1983 and 1989. Does this hopeful trend allow us to make prognoses about the future character of international medical cooperation in the context of Russia's ongoing war in Ukraine? So far, Russian political actors have only randomly and rather speculatively called for withdrawing from international public health organizations. Experts have not yet followed these calls – though it remains to be seen whether they do should domestic political pressure demand it, just as in the three previous occasions discussed in this study.

About the contributor

Anastassiya Schacht works at the Department of History at the University of Vienna, where her project received a grant from the Vienna Doctoral School of Historical and Cultural Studies. Her PhD research explored how the conflict concerning the political abuse of psychiatry in the 1970s and 1980s evolved, intertwined with tensions of the Cold War, and shaped governmental strategies and professional agendas. This project analyzed the strategies of self-construction and legitimation in international psychiatric networks, action spaces for scholarly autonomy and responsibility, as well as state involvement in the field of science in authoritarian regimes.

Carlos Fernando Teixeira Alves

Knowledge and Society: The Role of Two Universities in Southern Europe in the Early Nineteenth Century – the Case of Coimbra and Salamanca

Abstract: Based on the methodological approaches in the history of knowledge, this article carries out a comparative analysis of the creation of university curricula while taking into account the objectives of the central government favouring a certain type of practical knowledge, for reasons of public health and economic development. In this sense, the Portuguese and Spanish reformers chose to value the various disciplines that encapsulate natural philosophy. This decision, which sought to meet the interests of the objectives of the central governments, ended up causing a complete change in the hierarchy of knowledge at Salamanca and Coimbra. Starting in the early 1770s, we begin to see the introduction of disciplines such as natural history, experimental physics, and chemistry. In turn, these disciplines were accompanied by an obligation to attend practical classes in the various laboratories created as a result of this process.

Keywords: knowledge, curriculum, university, Coimbra, Salamanca

Introduction

In the wake of the Enlightenment, the third wave of university reforms in Europe (c. 1750–1780) left its mark on curricula[1] and led to the emergence and valorisation of new forms of knowledge.[2] This paper follows the periodisation of these three

---

Funding note: This research was funded by the Foundation for Science and Technology (FCT), with the reference FCTPD/BD/128127/2016.

1 Laurence Brockliss, "Os Curricula", in *Uma História da Universidade na Europa As Universidades na Europa Moderna (1500–1800)*, vol. 2 (Conselho de Reitores das Universidades Portuguesas; Fundação Eng. António de Almeida: Imprensa Nacional-Casa da Moeda, 2001), 541–594.
2 Willem Frijhoff, "Modelos", in *Uma História da Universidade na Europa. As Universidades na Europa Moderna (1500–1800)*, vol. 2 (Lisbon: Imprensa Nacional-Casa da Moeda, 2002), 70; Robert D. Anderson, *European Universities from the Enlightenment to 1914* (Oxford: Oxford University Press, 2004), 23–24.

∂ Open Access. © 2023 the author(s), published by De Gruyter. This work is licensed under the Creative Commons Attribution-NonCommercial-NoDerivatives 4.0 International License.
https://doi.org/10.1515/9783111078038-003

waves, acknowledging that further analysis may be necessary. Whereas the first wave took place in the period 1612–1625, the other two occurred in the eighteenth century,[3] during the reforms in Piedmont and Catalonia (1714–1729), and the period 1759–1780, following the expulsion of the Jesuits. The last wave differed from the others in terms of scope, reaching countries such as Portugal,[4] Spain,[5] Italy, and France.

Among the different areas of knowledge that changed during the third wave, the teaching of philosophy (in all its branches) varied significantly. The philosophy and arts faculties (where philosophy courses were often taught) had to significantly update their teaching.

However, this paper only concerns natural philosophy, one of the branches of philosophy associated with the study of nature and its resources, which was taught at universities for a considerable amount of time[6] and encompassed several additional forms of knowledge. After the third wave of university reforms, the evolution of natural philosophy was more rapid and diverse, giving rise to several other disciplines and coming to play a central role at many universities, as in the case of Coimbra and Salamanca.

Nevertheless, the pace of the reform regarding the philosophy curriculum looked different at Coimbra compared to Salamanca.[7] At the Portuguese university, the teaching of philosophy, and the faculty itself, gained autonomy as early as 1772, whereas this process took longer at Salamanca. This was due to the fact that only the arts course (where philosophy was taught together with mathematics) was reformed in 1771, while no new philosophy course was created. At the Spanish university, moreover, philosophy was for a long time considered purely propaedeutic teaching, which provided the basis for training professions such as physicians.

---

[3] For the state of European universities in the old regime, see François Cadilhon, Jean Mondot, and Jacques Verger, *Universités et Institutions Universitaires Européenes au XVIIIe Siècle. Entre Modernisation et Tradition* (Bordeaux: Presses Universitaires de Bordeaux, 1999); Jaqcques Verger, "Les universités à l'époque moderne", *Histoire mondiale de l'éducation* II (1981).

[4] Ana Cristina Araújo, ed., *O Marquês de Pombal e a Universidade*, 2a ed. (Coimbra: Imprensa da Universidade de Coimbra, 2014).

[5] George M. Addy, *The Enlightenment in the University of Salamanca* (California: Duke University Press, 1966).

[6] The discipline of natural philosophy already existed. At the University of Salamanca, for example, it had been taught since the fifteenth century. See Cirilo Flórez Miguel, "Ciencias, Siglos XV-XVII", in *Historia de la Universidad de Salamanca*, vol. III. 1: *Saberes y confluencias* (Salamanca: Ediciones Universidad de Salamanca, 2006), 409–432.

[7] Carlos Fernando Teixeira Alves, "A Ordem Natural nas reformas universitárias de Salamanca e Coimbra (1769–1820)" (PhD diss., Universidade de Lisboa, 2021), 153–159.

These two reasons would define the difference in pace regarding the reform of the philosophy course at Coimbra and Salamanca, respectively.

Albeit to varying extents, the valorisation of the disciplines making up natural philosophy eventually resulted in a new hierarchy of knowledge in the university curriculum.[8] At Coimbra and Salamanca, this process was long and troubled, and it was the result of the governments preferring certain types of knowledge over others.[9] However, this decision was an attempt to further modern science and improve the lives of the respective populations through various scientific advances. Hence, these reforms redefined the university as an institution, placing it at the service of the state and conceptualising knowledge as politically, culturally, socially, and economically relevant.

In analysing this appreciation of natural philosophy, this paper argues that it was part of a strategy adopted by Portuguese and Spanish reformers aiming to improve the national productive sector and to favour the economy, commerce, and industry. At the same time, this valorisation of natural philosophy also reflects a new belief in the mission of the university, as represented by two of the main figures involved in these educational reforms. The marquis of Pombal, the Portuguese reformer, was a diplomat and later secretary of state (1756–1777) and might be considered King José I's right-hand man. He is known today not only for his reforms in education, but also for his work on the state apparatus and the economic and religious sectors.[10] His counterpart in Spain was Pedro Rodríguez de Campomanes y Pérez,[11] the first count of Campomanes and minister of the treasury (1760–1762), who enjoyed the support of the Spanish King Carlos III, another promoter of these reforms. He played a key role in the expulsion of the Jesuits, was appointed inspector in charge of reforming the University of Salamanca, and drew up and

---

[8] Notker Hammerstein, "As relações com as autoridades", in *Uma História da Universidade na Europa. As Universidades na Europa Moderna (1500–1800)*, vol. 2 (Lisboa: Imprensa Nacional-Casa da Moeda, 2002), 105–46; Notker Hammerstein, "O Iluminiso", in *Uma História da Universidade na Europa: As Universidades na Europa Moderna (1500–1800)*, vol. 2 (Lisboa: Imprensa Nacional-Casa da Moeda, 2002), 595–614; Robert Anderson, "Before and after Humboldt: European Universities between the Eighteenth and the Nineteenth Centuries", in *History of Higher Education Annual*, vol. twenty (Pennsylvania: PennState, 2000), 5–14; Frijhoff, "Modelos".

[9] On the relationship between universities and governments and local authorities, see Hammerstein, As relações com as autoridades".

[10] On Sebastião José de Carvalho e Melo or the Marquis of Pombal (from 1769), see Kenneth Maxwell, *Pombal, Paradox of the Enlightenment* (Cambridge: Cambridge University Press, 1995).

[11] Antonio Álvarez de Morales, "La crisis del reformismo en Campomanes", *Revista de Historia Moderna. Anales de la Universidad de Alicante* (1990), 185–195.

oversaw the implementation of the new syllabus in collaboration with the Council of Castile.[12]

The teaching administered at the universities complied with predefined parameters set by the supervisory bodies, namely the Council of Castile for Salamanca and the Ministry of the Kingdom in the case of Coimbra. From the eighteenth century and onwards, efforts were made in both countries to coordinate the various levels of education, although this took a long time to establish. It would thus be premature to talk about the existence of a structured education system at the beginning of the nineteenth century, as this only began to take shape decades later.

For these reformers, the new mission consisted of training specialists in new areas of knowledge, which would allow for mapping, studying, and efficiently exploiting natural resources, especially in colonial territories.

This analysis begins by evaluating the statutes and study plans as sources for identifying changes in the understanding of new forms of knowledge. At the same time, they must also be read as the result of a clash of ideas, motivated by strategies to achieve concrete aims. Second, it focuses on the new perception of philosophy courses created during this wave of reforms at many universities. The creation of philosophy courses followed a logic of specialisation and modernisation designed to respond to the aims outlined by the interests of governments. Finally, a detailed and specific analysis of the different disciplines comprising natural philosophy from the eighteenth century and onwards illustrates how these reforms played out in practice. Subjects such as natural history, chemistry, and experimental physics were introduced at Coimbra and Salamanca during this period, and the contents of these disciplines reveal the motivations of the Portuguese and Spanish reformers and show how the creation of knowledge was governed by particular political and social circumstances.[13]

At the beginning of the nineteenth century, the aims of the reformers had not changed, and the curricular changes we see only represent essential updates following the rapid evolution of subjects such as botany or chemistry. In this sense, the period from 1800 to 1820 preserves the firm notion that knowledge seeks to transcend the university environment and have a concrete impact by re-

---

[12] Later, other figures stood out, such as Gaspar Melchor de Jovellanos, José Moñino y Redondo, the Count of Floridablanca, Pedro Pablo Abarca de Bolea, the Count of Aranda and Manuel Godoy y Álvarez de Faria.

[13] Simone Lässig, "The History of Knowledge and the Expansion of the Historical Research Agenda", *Bulletin of the German Historical Institute* 59 (2016): 29–58.

sponding to social problems,[14] thus leading to the chronological framework for this study. Although the focus is on the first two decades of the nineteenth century, our analysis starts in the 1770s with the beginning of the university reforms at Coimbra and Salamanca. Curricular changes that were initially introduced during this period continued throughout the following decades and would be significantly updated at the beginning of the nineteenth century.

The two case studies, involving the University of Coimbra and the University of Salamanca, are closely related and there are many similarities in their reforms.[15] This study aims to identify and explain the similarities and differences between the two cases being compared[16] while also examining the causes, the level of analysis, and the issue of interconnections, both in an Iberian and a European context. Despite national differences, which resulted in certain specificities, both reforms took place during the Enlightenment and share some of its ideas. Moreover, the reforms began in the 1760s with an exchange of ideas between Portuguese and Spanish reformers.[17] The choice of only two case studies also allows for a more in-depth comparative analysis, working with several primary sources (from both countries).[18] At the same time, the Catholic background influenced the introduction

---

[14] Johan Östling et al., "The history of knowledge and the circulation of knowledge: An introduction", in *Circulation of Knowledge Explorations in the History of Knowledge* (Lund: Nordic Academic Press, 2018), 7–24.

[15] On issues related to the comparative method, widely utilised in this work, see the volume edited by Deborah Cohen and Maura O'Connor, *Comparison and History: Europe in Cross-National Perspective* (New York: Routledge, 2004).

[16] Deborah Cohen and Maura O'Connor, "Introduction: Comparative History, Cross-National History, Transnational History – Definitions", in *Comparison and History: Europe in Cross-National Perspective* (New York: Routledge, 2004), ix–xxiv; Charles Tilly, *Big Structures, Large Processes, Huge Comparisons*, 75th anniversary series (New York: Russell Sage Foundation, 1984).

[17] Carlos Fernando Teixeira Alves, "A Ordem Natural".

[18] The main primary sources used here are: *Estatutos da Universidade de Coimbra (1772)*, vol. Livro I: Do curso theologico (Coimbra: Por Ordem da Universidade, 1972); *Estatutos da Universidade de Coimbra (1772)*, vol. Livro II: Cursos juridicos das Faculdades de canones e de leis (Coimbra: Por Ordem da Universidade, 1972); *Estatutos da Universidade de Coimbra (1772)*, vol. Livro III: Cursos das sciencias naturaes e filosoficas (Coimbra: Por Ordem da Universidade, 1972); *Plan general de estudios dirigido a la Universidad de Salamanca por el Real y Supremo Consejo de Castilla y mandado imprimir de su orden.* (Salamanca: Antonio Villagordo y Alcaraz, y Thomás de García de Honorato, 1771). In the case of Salamanca, I also focus on Juan Antonio Caballero's Plan of Studies from 1807 (transcribed in full by Addy and used here) and the 1820 plan, Addy, *The Enlightenment*; *Informe de la Universidad de Salamanca. Sobre Plan de Estudios, ó sobre su fundacion, altura y decadencia, y sobre las mejoras de que es susceptible: con cuyo motivo presenta un proyecto de Ley sobre la Instruccion Publica* (Salamanca: En la Imprenta de Don Vicente Blanco, 1820). For this work, several primary sources were consulted at the General Historical Library of the University

of many of the innovative ideas in both locations, while the use of censorship reoccurred at both universities. Both Portugal and Spain found themselves in what they perceived to be a state of significant economic, cultural, and scientific stagnation, which led them to become increasingly committed to more practical education.

1 Statutes and Study Plans

The idea defended by the Iberian reformers (the valorisation of natural philosophy and its component disciplines as a growth-enhancing strategy) is properly understood through a detailed analysis of the various statutes and syllabuses from the universities of Coimbra and Salamanca from 1771 to 1820 (see note 19). These sources were crucial not only for the universities, but also for the Portuguese and Spanish governments. Throughout this period, the statutes and study plans (also understood as a regulatory component) reflect these governments increasingly intervening in educational affairs.[19] In the various facets of their statutes and study plans, the universities saw a broad set of rules and provisions that had to be scrupulously respected. In practice, however, this was not always the case.[20] Many of the statutory revisions known today may have simply served as a response to changes already underway, and even when they were intended to stimulate innovation, they may have become obsolete before further statutory revision. Thus, while there are limitations with regard to this type of primary source, their research value should be highlighted when it comes to exploring the intentions and aims of the Portuguese and Spanish governments, especially by cross-referencing the data being analysed with other sources, such as legislation, minutes, correspondence, or reports. To a certain extent, the sources analysed here show us the university as a central agent in the history of knowledge.[21]

---

of Salamanca (BGHUS), the Coimbra University Archive (AUC), the University of Salamanca Archive (AUSA), and the National Archive of the Torre do Tombo (Lisbon, Portugal (ANTT)).

19 Juan Luis Polo Rodriguez and Jacinto de Veja Domínguez, "Fuentes para el estúdio de las Universidades Hispánicas de Antiguo Régimen", in *Historia de la Universidad de Salamanca*, vol. IV: *Vestigios y Entramados* (Salamanca: Ediciones Universidad de Salamanca, 2009), 131.

20 Laurence Brockliss, "Os Curricula", in *Uma História da Universidade na Europa. As Universidades na Europa Moderna (1500–1800)*, vol. II (Lisbon: Imprensa Nacional-Casa da Moeda, 2002), 543–594.

21 Östling et al., "History of Knowledge", 10; Lorraine Daston, "The History of Science and the History of Knowledge", *KNOW: A Journal on the Formation of Knowledge* 1, no. 1 (2017): 143.

Moreover, the way in which knowledge is understood is influenced by several factors.[22] The key factor in the cases under study concerned how governments understood economic and scientific backwardness, assuming that the main goal of scientific knowledge was to provide concrete improvements for society. As argued by Anderson, the university reforms in Spain aimed for total modernisation, considering "educational reform as part of a wider effort to regenerate Spain, to promote economic development, and to catch up with Europe."[23] The lengthy university reforms at Coimbra and Salamanca that began in the eighteenth century and continued into the next one were not understood as a goal in themselves but as part of a broader project aimed at transforming/modernising the Portuguese and Spanish societies. In both Spain and Portugal, educational reforms were accompanied by administrative, economic, and political reforms. In the case of universities, governments viewed these institutions, together with their agents (professors), as part of the preparation to respond to the needs of the Portuguese and Spanish societies in the transition from the eighteenth to the nineteenth century.

With regard to the various forms of knowledge[24] addressed in this study on the basis of study plans, it is important to share Philippe Sarasin's definition of *rational knowledge*.[25] Although this type of knowledge is not confined to educational institutions, it is strongly linked to universities, academies, or other types of educational institutions. This rational knowledge is derived from the educational functions of universities identified by Willem Frijhoff,[26] who defines five essential functions of the university: 1) setting up teaching, 2) providing a form of education, 3) promoting professional training and the study of scientific knowledge, 4) the formation of an elite, and 5) the provision of (a) certain type(s) of discipline. The academic disciplines may also be identified within the context of educational institutions as the result of a rational creation of knowledge taught in a structured way[27] and linked to formal education.[28]

---

22 Lässig, "History of Knowledge", 33.
23 Anderson, *European Universities*, 31–32.
24 Peter Burke, *A Social History of Knowledge*, vol. I: *From Gutenberg to Diderot* (Cambridge: Polity, 2000).
25 Philippe Sarasin, "Was ist Wissensgeschichte?", *Internationales Archiv für Sozialgeschichte der deutschen Literatur* 36, no. 1 (2011): 159–165.
26 Frijhoff, "Modelos".
27 Pierre Bourdieu, *Homo Academicus* (Stanford: Stanford University Press, 1990).
28 Ludwig Fleck, *Entstehung und Entwicklung einer wissenschaftlichen Tatsache: Einführung in die Lehre vom Denkstil und Denkkollektiv* (Basel: Schwabe, 1935); Robert K. Merton, "Science, Technology and Society in Seventeenth Century England", *Osiris* 4 (1938); Edmund Husserl, *Die Krisis der europäischen Wissenschaft und die transzendentale Phänomenologie* (The Hague: M. Nijhoff, 1954);

Through an analysis of these disciplines, in line with the work of Foucault,[29] it is possible to see the relationship between power (in this case, the Portuguese and Spanish governments through their ministers, inspectors, and other representatives) and knowledge (in natural philosophy, conceived of in its broadest sense). Greater bureaucratic demands, combined with the need to reform the business, commercial, and financial fabric of these countries, converged in the creation of the study plans, which were designed – in collaboration with professors from these institutions – to achieve improvements and advances in the respective societies. Thus, the education offered at these universities may serve as an illustration of variations in the understanding of knowledge in different social circumstances.

For instance, the evidence provided by Francisco de Lemos, rector of the University of Coimbra between 1770–1779 and 1799–1821, in his analysis of the importance of the natural sciences, including natural philosophy and many of its associated disciplines, sheds light on the true nature of this reform while also reflecting a general trend present in all university reforms carried out in this period. Amorim da Costa, a Portuguese expert in the history of science, summarises the rector's thinking as follows:[30]

> the establishment of the natural sciences at the university would enable a better knowledge of the natural riches existing in the country, bringing new material resources for industry, with the subsequent development of trade ... The teaching of natural sciences reflects the development of new arts, new manufactures, new factories, and the improvement of existing ones

Iberian reformers, who shared similar ideas due to regular contacts,[31] favoured the introduction of more practical knowledge to promote the rational exploitation of natural resources. In this sense, the (more modern and updated) philosophy

---

Alexandre Koyré, *From the Closed World to the Infinite Universe* (Baltimore: Johns Hopkins, 1957); S. Kuhn, *The Structure of Scientific Revolutions* (Chicago: University of Chicago Press, 1962); Michel Foucault, *The Archeology of Knowledge* (New York, 1972); Jan Golinski, *Making Natural Knowledge: Constructivism and the History of Science* (Chicago: University of Chicago Press, 2005); Kostas Gavroglou and Jürgen Renn, eds., *Positioning the History of Science* (Dordrecht: Springer, 2007); Lorraine Daston, "Science, History of", in *International Encyclopedia of the Social and Behavioral Sciences* (Oxford: Elsevier, 2015), 241–247; Daston, "History of Science".

29 *Foucault, Archeology of Knowledge.*

30 A. M. Amorim da Costa, "As Ciências Naturais na Reforma Pombalina da Universidade – 'Estudo de Rapazes, não ostentaçã de Príncipes'", in *O Marquês de Pombal e a Universidade* (Coimbra: Imprensa da Universidade de Coimbra, 2014), 188, 207–208. Translated from the original by the author.

31 Archivo Historico Nacional de Madrid (AHN), Conde de Campomanes, Caixa 34/Documento 5.

courses were designed with the aim of preparing specialists able to exploit such resources.

Turning to the decision-making process involved in designing curricula, in line with the questions raised by Simone Lässig,[32] we see that, except for isolated instances, decisions were often the result of collaborations between different actors. A large portion of this dialogue and decision-making took place outside the official bodies. For example, Pedro Luis Blanco, the rector at Salamanca, often addressed government representatives in a personal capacity, as did several of the professors. Moreover, the faculty congregations would defend their own interests, communicating directly with the governmental supervisory bodies. The Council of Castile not only went directly to the University of Salamanca congregations when it wanted to propose a change, but also consulted them on a regular basis on issues related to the university.[33]

Hence, during the second half of the eighteenth century and the first decades of the nineteenth century, many decisions were made jointly, with different factions often sharing similar goals. Sources suggest that the final decisions were mainly made by the governments and the Ministry of the Kingdom – which was also the supervisory body for the University of Coimbra – or the Council of Castile, in the case of the Spanish university. However, the administrative and educational boards also influenced many of these decisions, interacting directly with their supervisory bodies.[34]

One notable difference concerns the degree of government intervention. The rescinding of professorships at the University of Coimbra may here serve as a useful example. In order to remove teaching staff who were less supportive of the reforms, 13 professors were forced to retire in 1772, while 33 new professors whose ideas were closer to those of the reformers were appointed, together with 20 additional replacements.[35]

---

[32] Lässig, "History of Knowledge", 40.
[33] Alves, "A Ordem Natural", 18–22.
[34] See, for example, the draft of the 1766 medical plan, Archivo de la Universidad de Salamanca (AUSA), Informes y correspondencia de assuntos universitarios. Lecciones inaugurales, XVII-XIX, AUSA 2031.
[35] Teófilo Braga, *Historia da Universidade de Coimbra. Nas suas relações com a Instrucção Publica Portugueza*, vol. III: *1700 a 1800* (Lisbon: Por ordem e na Typographia da Academia Real das Sciencias, 1898), 420–425.

2 The Philosophy Course: A Comparative Approach

The university reforms at Coimbra and Salamanca began in the eighteenth century and extended throughout the following century, accompanied by profound changes in the curriculum. The University of Coimbra had a total of six faculties from as early as 1772 – when the faculties of philosophy and mathematics were added – whereas no new faculties were created in Salamanca until the 1790s, when the new faculty of philosophy was founded. This only occurred after a thorough reform of the curriculum for the arts, as well as theology and canonical and civil law.

Natural philosophy, one of the disciplines retaining a close connection with the study of nature and natural products,[36] remained on university curricula in Europe until well into the nineteenth century. Its great advantage was its constant adaptability, which enabled it to cover a considerable number of subjects within its confines.[37] As William A. Wallace observes, natural philosophy seems to serve as the origin of the modern scientific disciplines.[38]

The revised curricula for the Iberian universities clearly reflect the attempt to promote a new hierarchy of knowledge, prioritising more practical subjects, just as in other European universities. As seen in Table 1, Coimbra and Salamanca offered a wide range of disciplines related to natural philosophy.

Table 1: Philosophy courses at Salamanca and Coimbra between 1800 and 1820.

Coimbra – 1772 statutes[39]	Salamanca – 1807 study plan	Salamanca – 1820 statutes
Rational and Moral Philosophy – ceased in 1801 to be replaced by Botany and Agriculture (since 1801)	Elements of Arithmetic, Algebra and Geometry	Second Course in Pure Mathematics
Natural History and Geometry (in Mathematics, as preparation for the following year)	Logica and Metaphysics	Natural History and Chemistry

---

[36] Janet Browne, "Natural History", in *The Oxford Companion to the History of Modern Science* (Oxford: Oxford University Press, 2003), 559–561.
[37] William A. Wallace, "Traditional natural philosophy", in *The Cambridge History of Renaissance Philosophy* (Cambridge: Cambridge University Press, 2008), 201–235.
[38] Wallace, "Traditional natural philosophy", 213.
[39] The philosophy course introduced in 1772 at Coimbra was maintained, with occasional changes, until 1820.

Table 1: Philosophy courses at Salamanca and Coimbra between 1800 and 1820. *(Continued)*

Coimbra – 1772 statutes[40]	Salamanca – 1807 study plan	Salamanca – 1820 statutes
Experimental Physics	Application of Algebra to Geometry	Rational Mechanics
Chemistry	Physics and Chemistry	Astronomy
————————	Moral Philosophy	Optics and Acoustics
————————	Astronomy and Natural History	Agriculture (bachelor's degree)
————————	————————	General History and Literary History
————————	————————	Medical Physiology and Spanish Constitution

The way in which the two governments understood natural philosophy was similar at Coimbra and Salamanca, and the two governments had similar goals, even though these materialised differently in the philosophy curricula.

At Coimbra, natural philosophy received more attention throughout the period being studied. According to the statutes, it was to include all disciplines aiming to study nature.[41] Described as a course in physics (*Curso da Fysica*), it was structured as a four-year course,[42] in which the first year, via natural history, would focus on the three *kingdoms of nature*[43] by means of demonstrations and experiments.[44]

The need for more concrete and detailed knowledge of nature and its products required a structured approach, progressing from hypothesis to experiment. The latter, known as the experimental part, involved two goals. The first, related to ex-

---

40 *Estatutos da Universidade de Coimbra (1772)*, 1972, Livro III: Cursos das sciencias naturaes e filosoficas, 229–230.
41 In the remaining years of the course, the students studied subjects related to moral and rational philosophy.
42 In the statutes consulted, the term *kingdoms of nature* refers to its three constituent elements, namely the animal, vegetable, and mineral components. It is often accompanied by expressions such as the *animal kingdom* (animals), the *plant kingdom* (plants), and the *mineral kingdom* (minerals).
43 *Estatutos da Universidade de Coimbra (1772)*, 1972, Livro III: Cursos das sciencias naturaes e filosoficas, 229–230.

perimental physics, consisted of identifying (and observing) the universal characteristics of bodies, while the second (chemistry), sought to identify their characteristics.[45] This more practical part, in which knowledge was acquired from close interactions with the material world, also led to the greater use of scientific equipment and infrastructures. At Coimbra, for example, new facilities were constructed, including the botanical gardens and a natural history cabinet. The aim was to supply first-hand knowledge of objects and products of various origins as well as to provide students with a place where they could conduct their experiments.[46]

At Salamanca, the division between the various components comprising (natural) philosophy did not emerge until the nineteenth century. In 1780, one professor (Martinez Nieto) still considered natural philosophy eclectic, as it complemented moral philosophy and theology.[47] This change in the understanding of philosophy on the part of the Spanish authorities differed from the process underway in Portugal. However, the initiative came in 1788, when a new philosophy course, more similar to the one already offered at Coimbra, was designed and sent to the Council of Castile.[48] Nevertheless, this proved to be a lengthy process, and it was only in 1820 that a broader change, in the form of the *Estudio de la Natureza* (nature study[49]), took hold based on Enlightenment ideas.

The new statutes prescribed a division focusing on all aspects in the study of nature and its products. Cosmography, natural history, zoology, botany, mineralogy, physics, and chemistry were all considered essential for understanding the natural world. The remaining disciplines, which included rational mechanics, astronomy, optics and acoustics, agriculture, and arts and crafts, ended up belonging to the category of natural sciences and useful arts.

However, this profound curricular change and the greater support provided by the governments for a certain type of knowledge resulted in internal conflicts at the universities themselves. The opposition came from already established knowl-

---

[44] *Estatutos da Universidade de Coimbra (1772)*, 1972, Livro III: Cursos das sciencias naturaes e filosoficas, 229–230.
[45] *Estatutos da Universidade de Coimbra (1772)*, 1972, Livro III: Cursos das sciencias naturaes e filosoficas, 229–230.
[46] Roberto Albares Albares, "La Filosofía, Siglos XVIII-XIX", in *Historia de la Universidad de Salamanca*, vol. III. 1: *Saberes y confluencias* (Salamanca: Ediciones Universidad de Salamanca, 2006), 611–612.
[47] Albares Albares, "La Filosofía", 605.
[47] *Informe de la Universidad de Salamanca. Sobre Plan de Estudios, ó sobre su fundacion, altura y decadencia, y sobre las mejoras de que es susceptible: con cuyo motivo presenta un proyecto de Ley sobre la Instruccion Publica*, XXIII.

edge, such as theology and canonical law. At the University of Salamanca, there was widespread opposition,⁵⁰ as illustrated by the following example.

In 1796, a meeting occurred at the University of Salamanca in which professors of theology, law, and even medicine opposed the curricular changes proposed by the professors of philosophy. This tension was only resolved by the new secretary of state and justice, Gaspar Melchor de Jovellanos, authorising the proposals of the philosophy professors.⁵¹

Further difficulties arose from the question of how this new philosophy course would relate to the medicine course. In 1801, the Portuguese regent, João of Bragança, expressed his concern to the rector of the University of Coimbra as follows:⁵² "the new Philosophical Faculty, comprising the particular object of the Faculties of Medicine and Mathematics, is, however, due to the importance of this great establishment, not merely a subsidiary course for the other Faculties, especially the aforementioned Faculties of Medicine and Mathematics".

A decade later, in 1811, José Bonifácio de Andrade, a professor of philosophy, again expressed a similar concern:⁵³ "I also know that the School of Philosophy ... the most highly esteemed today in Europe for its subject and the great benefits it brings to nations ... seems, by an inexplicable fatality, to be a mere subsidiary establishment of Medicine in Portugal". This coexistence was not easy, resulting in occasional interventions by the supervisory bodies. The struggle shows the importance of new knowledge for the Portuguese and Spanish governments, and an analysis of the valorisation of (natural) philosophical knowledge at the universities of Coimbra and Salamanca underscores Lorraine Daston's conclusions: the governments' new understanding of knowledge promoted a new hierarchy of knowledge, which resulted in a conflict of knowledge.⁵⁴

However, after the profound changes introduced in the eighteenth century, the Iberian reformers did not alter their understanding of natural philosophy and the

---

49 For an enlightening example of this type of problem see Addy, *The Enlightenment*, 193.
50 Archivo de la Universidad de Salamanca (AUSA), Actas de Claustros y Juntas de la Universidad, 1794–1796, Ausa 251, 419r–20, 430v–31, 448–50, 508r–508v; José Luis Peset and Mariano Peset Reig, *Carlos IV y la Universidad de Salamanca* (Madrid: Consejo Superior de Investigaciones Científicas, Instituto "Arnau de Vilanova", 1983), 119; Addy, *The Enlightenment*, 168–202; José Luis Peset, "La Nueva Ciencia, Siglo XVIII", in *Historia de la Universidad de Salamanca*, vol. III. 1: *Saberes y confluencias* (Salamanca: Ediciones Universidad de Salamanca, 2006), 452.
51 Arquivo da Universidade de Coimbra (AUC), Processos de Professores, Cx. 326. Original translated by the author.
52 Arquivo Nacional da Torre do Tombo (ANTT), Ministério do Reino. Instrução. Consultas do Concelho de Decanos da Universidade de Coimbra, 1779–1831, Mç 517. Cx. 643. Original translated by the author.
53 Daston, "History of Science", 145.

disciplines it included. On the contrary, at the dawn of the nineteenth century, these innovations were only reinforced.[55]

In 1801, for instance, the University of Coimbra received a royal letter demanding that the teaching of philosophy, especially its natural component, should be strengthened:[56]

> the investigation of the numerous and useful productions of almost all countries and parts of the world, which easily adapt to the happy climates and lands of Portugal and its colonies ... the observation and evaluation of the weak practices in Agriculture, and Arts, and the bad state in which the Factories and Manufactures find themselves ... it is convenient to reform and improve, to perfect the productions of Art, which can compete and enter into competition with foreign countries

The clearest consequence was the creation of a new subject – metallurgy – and the closure of the chair of moral philosophy in favour of the creation of a new chair of agriculture, taught together with botany.[57] In the same year, the regent D. João (the future King João VI) once again justified the need for this change to the rector, Francisco de Lemos, "as most of the kingdoms and states of Europe have already done ... to promote in every possible way their growth and prosperity, so that they may become as useful and important to my Royal Treasury and the general good of my people through their products and industry".[58]

In the case of Salamanca, several steps were taken, leading to the 1807 plan, which appears to approximate the ideas of the governments while including several disciplines associated with natural philosophy (see Table 1).

One crucial point to remember is that the innovations in the field of natural philosophy, which began in the second half of the eighteenth century and continued until 1820, strengthened the teaching of this subject for decades to come. The incentive for more practical teaching and constantly updating the philosophy curriculum was mainly due to the need to meet the objectives of the Spanish government.

---

54 This seems to have been a trend at several universities in Europe. From 1780 and onwards, the strengthening of philosophy faculties was a result of developments in the various disciplines. See Hammerstein, "O Iluminismo", 606.
55 Arquivo da Universidade de Coimbra (AUC), Legislação Académica, 1772–1824, IV-1° E 8, Tab. 3, n° 4, 127v–28. Original translated by the author.
56 *Actas das Congregações da Faculdade de Filosofia (1772–1820)* (Coimbra: Publicações da Comissão promotora das Comemorações do II Centenário da Reforma Pombalina da Universidade, 1978), 268–271.
57 Arquivo Nacional da Torre do Tombo (ANTT), Ministério do Reino. Instrução. Consultas do Concelho de Decanos da Universidade de Coimbra, 1779–1831, Mç 517. Cx. 643. Original translated by the author.

Two of the most important thinkers on educational reform in Spain, namely Benito Jerónimo Feijoo y Montenegro and Pablo de Olavide, already offer evidence of this.[59] Spanish historian Francisco Sanchéz-Blanco concludes that these thinkers introduced the notion of creating a new secularised university stripped of customs and traditions, whose mission was to train "men useful to the state".[60] This was to be achieved by valorising natural philosophy (and its constituent disciplines) as a tool for the rational exploitation of natural resources.

The creation of these new philosophy courses also shows how knowledge transcends spaces, as phrased by Lässig.[61] Although knowledge might not have circulated freely, it was disseminated in various fields and interacted in different contexts.[62]

3 The Core Subjects

The new philosophy courses included a variety of disciplines that could provide solid and correct training in the exploitation of natural resources, and the case of Coimbra is particularly instructive in this respect.[63] The reformers divided the teaching of philosophy into three branches: rational, moral, and natural. The first included subjects such as logic, ontology, and pneumatology. Thus, rational philosophy encompassed fields such as natural theology and psychology and metaphysics. Moral philosophy, in turn, was intended to instruct students in ethics.

However, natural philosophy received the most attention since the various disciplines dedicated to the study of nature and its products were to be found in this third branch of philosophy. It was designed to emphasise elements such as observation and experimentation involving different natural materials from various parts of the respective colonial empires. Among the subjects introduced by the reforms focusing on the study of nature and natural objects, the following appeared at both universities.

---

58 Francisco Sánchez-Blanco, *El Absolutismo y las Luces en el reinado de Carlos III* (Madrid: Marcial Pons. Historia, 2002), 106–109; Angela del Valle López, *La Universidad Central y su distrito en el primer decenio de la Restauración borbónica (1875–1885)* (Madrid: Ministerio de Educación, 1990), 435.
59 Sánchez-Blanco, *El Absolutismo*, 106–109. Original translated by the author.
60 Lässig, "History of Knowledge", 38–40.
61 Sarasin, "Was ist Wissensgeschichte?".
62 *Estatutos da Universidade de Coimbra (1772)*.

Table 2: Transversal subjects to philosophy courses at Coimbra and Salamanca.

Discipline	Year
Natural History	1772 (C)
	1807 (S)
Experimental Physics	1771 (S)
	1772 (C)
Botany	c.1790 (C)
	c.1799 (S)
Chemistry	1772 (C)
	1807 (S)

Although the discipline of natural history was introduced at different times at Coimbra and Salamanca, the material taught was similar. The subject underwent significant changes, although the advances in the discipline had a common goal: the physical and social improvement of the respective populations.[64] However, the evolution of the subjects included in natural history would also contribute to its fragmentation.[65] According to the Portuguese authorities, where the curriculum included knowledge related to zoology and botany, the aim was to produce exact descriptions of the various natural objects. The language used in the statutes at the University of Coimbra is revealing. In the case of zoology, students were expected to have full knowledge of the "Animals, which belong to Commerce, Agriculture, and other more sensitive and important uses of human life."[66] Introduced later at Salamanca, the same discourse can be found in 1820. Emphasising a stronger connection with medicine, the statutes stipulated that "The teacher of this sub-

---

[63] José Luís Cardoso, "Natural law, natural history and the foundations of political economy", in *The Elgar Companion to Economics and Philosophy* (Cheltenham: Edward Elgar Publishing, 2004), 14; Emma Spary, "The 'Nature' of Enlightenment", in *The Sciences in Enlightened Europe* (Chicago and London: University of Chicago Press, 1999), 179.

[64] Arquivo Nacional da Torre do Tombo (ANTT), Ministério do Reino. Instrução. Negócios diversos da Universidade de Coimbra, 1643–1831, Mç. 519, Cx. 645; Arquivo Nacional da Torre do Tombo (ANTT), Ministério do Reino. Instrução. Voto dos Decanos da Universidade de Coimbra Séc. XVIII, Mç. 516, Cx. 642; *Estatutos da Universidade de Coimbra (1772)*, 1972, Livro III: Cursos das sciencias naturaes e filosoficas, 27.

[65] *Estatutos da Universidade de Coimbra (1772)*, 1972, Livro III: Cursos das sciencias naturaes e filosoficas, 239–244. Original translated by the author.

ject will make known the natural substances that are used in medicine ... He will explain particularly botany".⁶⁷

But how was the interest in natural history justified? Two events may provide the answer to this question. The first involved both universities adopting the works of Swedish scientist Carl Linnaeus, which were studied in various disciplines, even though the knowledge that the reformers wanted to extract was very selective. While the taxonomic division proposed by Linnaeus was to be presented to the students, teachers were not allowed to spend too much time on this. Instead, they were expected to spend most of their time teaching students to identify the plants considered useful and the best ways of exploiting their properties.⁶⁸

The second was the appointment of Domingos Vandelli, an Italian naturalist, in 1772. The Italian naturalists found the chair of natural history important due to its ability to provide a "rigorous and systematic inventory of mineral, vegetable and animal resources and raw materials, with a view to their exploitation or economic use."⁶⁹ Accordingly, the statutes of the University of Coimbra for the first time promoted the work of naturalists to a discipline worthy of higher education.⁷⁰ Vandelli and his natural history syllabus thus highlight the valorisation of disciplines linked to physiocracy⁷¹ and a vision of natural history favouring knowledge that was of practical use to commerce and finance.⁷²

---

66 *Informe de la Universidad de Salamanca. Sobre Plan de Estudios, ó sobre su fundacion, altura y decadencia, y sobre las mejoras de que es susceptible: con cuyo motivo presenta un proyecto de Ley sobre la Instruccion Publica*, 53. Original translated by the author.
67 *Estatutos da Universidade de Coimbra (1772)*, 1972, Livro III: Cursos das sciencias naturaes e filosoficas, 242. Original translated by the author.
68 José Luís Cardoso, "Domingos Vandelli, a história natural e a economia política", *Memórias da Academia das Ciências de Lisboa, Classe de Letras*, n. Tomo XXXV (2003 de 2002): 101.
69 Ana Cristina Araújo, "O governo da natureza no pensamento da geração universitária de finais do século XVIII: os Estatutos Literários e Económicos da Sociedade dos Mancebos Patriotas de Coimbra", in *A Univeridade Pombalina. Ciência, Território e Coleções Científicas* (Coimbra: Imprensa da Universidade de Coimbra, 2017), 90.
70 Eduardo Escartín e Francisco Velasco Morente, "Quesnay y los conceptos generales de la Fisiocracia", in *Ilustración, ilustraciones*, vol. 3 (Real Sociedad Bascongada de Amigos del País: Sociedad Estatal de Conmemoraciones Culturales (SECC), 2009), 275–288; Ernest Lluch, "La Difusión del cameralismo y de la fisiocracia a través de Europa y en especial de España durante el siglo XVIII", *Sapere aude: el "atrévete a pensar" en el siglo de las luces*, no. 3 (1996): 17–26; Lars Herlitz, "Art and nature in pre-classical economics of the seventeenth and eighteenth centuries", in *Nature and Society in Historical Context* (Cambridge: Cambridge University Press, 1997), 163–75; Simon Schaffer, "The Earth's fertility as a social fact in Early Modern England", in *Nature and Society in Historical Context* (Cambridge: Cambridge University Press, 1997), 124–147.
71 Emma C. Spary, *Utopia's Garden: French Natural History from Old Regime to Revolution* (Chicago and London: The University of Chicago Press, 2000), 13.

In the case of experimental physics, there was a longstanding debate over its exact content. The position of the Spanish government was clear already from an early stage: a preference for approximation to the medical curriculum, focusing on the study of plants. Campomanes, still in 1771, reinforced this idea:[73] students of medicine could only enter the first year of the medical course after acquiring this knowledge.

The Council of Castile consulted several advisors who shared similar ideas. For example, physician and surgeon Antonio Fernandez Solano clearly voiced his preference: "the purpose of which is to provide students pursuing a career in medicine with the physical knowledge useful for the greatest progress in this Faculty [of medicine]".[74] Later, the Council of Castile reinforced this dependency, stipulating that the chair of experimental physics should be taught by a professor of medicine.[75] All these decisions would restrict the content of the experimental physics syllabus to the study of natural materials for medicinal purposes.

The content of experimental physics was similar at Coimbra, even though the range was wider and somewhat more varied. Containing a strong practical component, it required that experiments be carried out on a regular basis in the experimental physics laboratory. Since it had less of an explicit connection to medicine, students at Coimbra may have enjoyed greater freedom to perform experiments, aiming "to uncover the veil of Nature; and to ask the most hidden secrets of the operations, when Nature herself does not speak".[76]

The subject of botany appeared in philosophy curricula in the 1790s. In the case of Coimbra, this was due to the fragmentation of the chair of natural history. However, despite the changes to the chair of botany at both universities, the subjects lectured did not change significantly. In general, it always endeavoured to respond to the aims of the Portuguese government which, by the end of the eighteenth century, was to value what "has been discovered in the different species of Plants, which Nature copiously produces for the use of Man."[77] At Salamanca, the link botany and medicine was again clear, valuing plants mainly for medicinal

---

72 Archivo Historico Nacional (AHN), Consejos, Universidades, Legajos 5461-no23.
73 Archivo Historico Nacional (AHN), Consejos, Universidades, Legajos 5461-nº23, 46–46v. Original translated by the author.
74 Archivo General de Simancas (AGS), Secretaria de Gracia y Justicia. Instrucción Pública. Fechos de la Universidad de Salamanca, 1777–1788, Legajo 945.
75 *Estatutos da Universidade de Coimbra (1772), 1972, Livro III: Cursos das sciencias naturaes e filosoficas*, 245. Original translated by the author.
76 *Estatutos da Universidade de Coimbra (1772), 1972, Livro III: Cursos das sciencias naturaes e filosoficas*, 245. Original translated by the author.

and pharmacological purposes. The growing autonomy of botany changed the curricular structure offered at these universities.

In 1824, Félix de Avelar Brotero, a professor of philosophy at the University of Coimbra, justified this with some authority: "Zoology, Botany and Mineralogy did not cover such a vast scope of knowledge as today: since then there have been numerous discoveries in all of them, all of them have made extensive progress, and they are present in all of Europe and much cultivated due to their great utility in Medicine, Agriculture, Commerce, and Arts."[78]

Finally, it was important to understand transformation processes involving materials, focussing on the discipline of chemistry. In the nineteenth century, chemistry developed autonomously, even though its connection with philosophy, medicine, and mathematics remained clear in many university institutions. In Portugal, this subject was heavily influenced by the advances made in France, while at Coimbra, chemistry was compulsory for students of philosophy, medicine, and mathematics. They had one compulsory practical lesson once a week in the chemistry laboratory, which aimed to develop their knowledge in the preparation of different chemical substances.[79]

Once again, the significant difference in how this discipline was introduced at the two universities is found in its connection to medicine. At Salamanca, this tendency was the norm, partly limiting the variety of experiments carried out, which were always tied to the therapeutic nature of the materials used. At Coimbra, on the other hand, the practical classes offered students considerably more variety and depth. As students were to be taught to "separate the different substances that are part of the composition of a body; to examine each of its parts; to investigate their properties and analogies; to compare and combine them with other substances", they were encouraged to observe interactions with, for example, salty, metallic, and oily substances.[80]

Having analysed the contents of the various disciplines introduced at Coimbra and Salamanca, it is possible to identify their similarities and an obvious trend: the natural materials (regardless of origin) used by teachers and students in the classes were chosen according to their usefulness in terms of commercial, medical, and economic exploitation.

---

77 Arquivo da Universidade de Coimbra (AUC), Processos de Professores, Cx. 26. Original translated by the author.
78 *Estatutos da Universidade de Coimbra (1772)*, 1972, *Livro III: Cursos das sciencias naturaes e filosoficas*, 27.
79 *Estatutos da Universidade de Coimbra (1772)*, 1972, *Livro III: Cursos das sciencias naturaes e filosoficas*, 251. Original translated by the author.

This trend may be explained by the common aims bringing the Portuguese and Spanish reformers so close together. The economistic view of nature, championed by these governments and supported by several professors, adopted a logic of modernisation regarding the balance of trade.[81]

Conclusion

Based on the hypothesis that the valorisation of natural philosophy (and the disciplines it included) was a strategy adopted by the Portuguese and Spanish governments to increase economic productivity, this paper has shown how this rationale led to a preference for more practical knowledge. Consequently, this decision altered the hierarchy of knowledge at the university and led to disputes with professors working with the more established types of knowledge, such as theologians.

The Iberian reformers mainly agreed in their understanding of the knowledge of natural philosophy, although there were slight differences in how it was applied in terms of content and timing. In the late eighteenth century, Coimbra introduced a broad and more varied curriculum, whereas this only appeared in 1807 at Salamanca. This delay can be linked to a range of factors, even though, as this paper shows, one key problem concerned the philosophy curriculum's constant subordination to medicine.

Since natural philosophy was understood as offering knowledge fundamental to a more rational exploitation of natural resources, it clearly met the aims of the Portuguese and Spanish governments, which particularly valued the practical and utilitarian nature of the disciplines it included.

This tendency was clear in the obligation imposed on students to conduct a large number of practical experiments in classes, in which they interacted directly with the various products. This understanding led to a specific kind of idealisation of natural philosophy when creating the philosophy course. At Coimbra, for instance, the philosophy course was designed to teach several components individually, but in a complementary way. It started with natural history (in which the various products were introduced), to then move on to experimental physics (conducting experiments in order to understand and describe natural laws), and finally to chemistry (involving the chemical transformations of the products). This triple set of disciplines, which were compulsory subjects for students of phi-

---

80 Costa, "As Ciências Naturais", 181–184.

losophy and other courses, represented a great novelty in the new philosophy course.[82]

The study of these reforms contributes to the conclusion that knowledge interacts in different contexts and at diverse levels.[83] The creation of new philosophy curricula was not simply imposed from above, but often involved contacts and exchanges between the government and university authorities.

We may thus conclude that in the case of Catholic Iberian universities, the profound changes carried out from the eighteenth century and onwards were due to pressure from certain professors, but mainly from the central governments. The most obvious consequence was a greater concession to the direct concerns of the respective governments.[84]

About the contributor

Carlos Alves is a researcher at the Center for the History of Society and Culture, University of Coimbra, as well as a visiting assistant professor at the Faculty of Arts and Humanities, University of Coimbra, and the Faculty of Religious Studies and Philosophy, University of Saint Joseph, Macau. His main interest is the history of science, knowledge, and universities. His recent publications include the co-authored "The Study of Natural Law in Coimbra, Seville, and Santiago de Chile (Eighteenth and Nineteenth Centuries)" in *Comparative Legal History* (2022) and "The Teaching of Anatomy at the University in the South of Europe" in *The Spaces of Renaissance Anatomy Theatre* (2022).

---

81 Costa, "As Ciências Naturais", 185.
82 Lässig, "History of Knowledge", 38–40.
83 Hammerstein, "O Iluminismo", 607.

Carl-Filip Smedberg
Ordering the Social: The History of Knowledge and the Usefulness of (Studying) Social Taxonomies

Abstract: During the twentieth century, a number of actors and institutions across the global north set out to develop hierarchical social taxonomies of their national populations. Mainly used for the making of statistics, these divisions soon came to be influential in policy and public debates. Using mainly Swedish examples, this article offers new ways of understanding social taxonomies, thereby adding insights into an understudied research object within the field of history of knowledge. Social taxonomies connect mundane and practical aspects of knowledge in the making – in terms of how actors order empirical material to through these create statistics – with larger public debates on society. They are, moreover, linked to different epistemic and political projects. I argue that social taxonomies should be understood as difference technologies; that is, ways of ordering and studying the social by producing differences between and sameness within its classifications.

Keywords: knowledge technology, social classifications, taxonomy, knowledge production, twentieth-century Sweden

When the British Broadcasting Corporation (BBC) launched the Great British Class Calculator in 2013, they explained that the traditional categories of working, middle, and upper class were outdated.[1] In collaboration with a team of sociologists led by Mike Savage, the BBC invited the British public to take a digital test to find out which class they belonged to within a newly constructed taxonomy made up of seven groups. Taking aspects of ordinary life, such as cultural consumption and media habits, as well as social and economic factors into account, this division was supposed to reflect the complexities of the twenty-first century. Within a few weeks, millions had responded to the call, indicating a more than keen interest in understanding oneself through a social division. It was "one of the most successful pieces of popular sociology ever conducted," Savage concluded, even though it led to a deluge of emails in his inbox from people complaining that the calculator

---

[1] "The BBC's Class Calculator explained," *BBC News*, December 17, 2013, accessed January 3, 2023, https://www.bbc.com/news/av/business-25131283.

ə Open Access. © 2023 the author(s), published by De Gruyter. (cc) BY-NC-ND This work is licensed under the Creative Commons Attribution-NonCommercial-NoDerivatives 4.0 International License.
https://doi.org/10.1515/9783111078038-004

had placed them in the wrong class.² The quiz became a media event, discussed in newspapers, cafes, and staff canteens throughout the UK.³ Savage would later reflect that the project had resulted in the largest amount of political and academic criticism he had ever received throughout his entire career. The reason why, he thought, was because it had touched upon sensitive issues concerning inequality and societal progress.⁴

The Great British Class Calculator attempting to realign society by creating and promoting class knowledge can be placed in a lineage of other, similar ventures throughout the twentieth and into the twenty-first century. More specifically, the above example alerts us to a distinct but understudied phenomenon, namely social taxonomies. Prevalent current divisions sort the population according to gender, ethnicity, occupational status, place and function within production, education level, or place of living (i.e., the urban-rural divide). In this article, I argue for the theoretical usefulness of studying these types of technologies of knowledge. Social taxonomies are in this article analysed as difference technologies for producing, studying, and managing the population. The point is not to say that taxonomies such as the Great British Class Calculator are inherently incorrect – for example, they are needed in social science and social policy to measure inequality – but that they create reality effects in terms of how we view society and ourselves, or, to use Ian Hacking's phrase, they make people up.⁵ The article first discusses the theoretical underpinnings for how we may understand difference technologies and the research fields that this has bearings on, followed by discussing influential social taxonomies from the Swedish twentieth century up to the present time.

Social Taxonomies as Difference Technologies

The history of knowledge is a vibrant new research area concerning the transformation of knowledge.⁶ A main theoretical concept in the field has been circulation,

---

2 Mike Savage, "Concerned about the BBC's Class Calculator? Let me explain," *The Guardian*, April 13, 2013, accessed January 3, 2023, https://www.theguardian.com/commentisfree/2013/apr/10/bbc-class-calculator.
3 Mike Savage, *Social Class in the 21st Century* (London: Pelican, 2015).
4 Mike Savage, *The Return of Inequality: Social Change and the Weight of the Past* (Cambridge: Harvard University Press, 2021).
5 Ian Hacking, "The Looping Effects of Human Kinds," in *Causal Cognition: A Multidisciplinary Debate*, ed. Dan Sperber, David Premack, and Ann James Premack (Oxford: Clarendon Press, 1995).
6 For a good historiographic overview, see Johan Östling, "Circulation, Arenas, and the Quest for Public Knowledge: Historiographical Currents and Analytical Frameworks," *History and Theory* 59,

meaning how knowledge circulates between actors and contexts.[7] An ambition has been to focus on wider societal circulation.[8] As a result, a history of knowledge approach analyses knowledge actors and arenas in order to show how actors circulate knowledge and how arenas serve as sites of interactions between actors and their audiences.[9] What I want to propose is the fruitfulness of studying technologies of knowledge in general and social taxonomies specifically. Technologies such as sampling, classifying, or surveying have enabled the production of knowledge and are part of knowledge infrastructures. In this way, they connect the micro processes of knowledge in the making with larger phenomena and processes. More interestingly, these technologies often become public knowledge in themselves.

Studying technologies of knowledge has been done in other fields. Lutz Raphael has urged historians to research what he refers to as the scientisation of the social; that is, the (un)intended effects of the human sciences on society in the last 150 years. According to Raphael, one way of studying this process is by focusing on technologies.[10] Moreover, historians of the social sciences have investigated the cost-benefit analysis as a technology for mechanical objectivity, the invention of statistical sampling as a way to create the idea of an averaged citizen, and how economists think through models.[11] Peter Becker and William Clark refer to tables, reports, questionnaires, dossiers, and index cards as "little tools of knowledge" used for establishing bureaucratic and academic authority.[12]

---

no. 4 (2020); Joel Barnes and Tamson Pietsch, "The History of Knowledge and the History of Education," *History of Education Review* 51, no. 2 (2022).
7 Johan Östling et al., ed., *Circulation of Knowledge: Explorations in the History of Knowledge* (Lund: Nordic Academic Press, 2018).
8 Johan Östling and David Larsson Heidenblad, "Fulfilling the Promise of the History of Knowledge: Key Approaches for the 2020s," *Journal for the History of Knowledge* 1, no. 1 (2020).
9 Östling, "Circulation, Arenas"; David Larsson Heidenblad, *The Environmental Turn in Postwar Sweden: A New History of Knowledge* (Lund: Lund University Press, 2021); Johan Östling, Anton Jansson, and Ragni Svensson Stringberg, *Humanister i offentligheten: Kunskapens aktörer och arenor under efterkrigstiden* (Gothenburg: Makadam, 2022).
10 Kerstin Brückweh et al., "Introduction: The Scientization of the Social in Comparative Perspective," in *Engineering Society: The Role of the Human and Social Sciences in Modern Societies, 1880–1980*, ed. Kerstin Brückweh et al. (Basingstoke: Palgrave Macmillan, 2012).
11 Theodore Porter, *Trust in Numbers: The Pursuit of Objectivity in Science and Public Life* (Princeton: Princeton University Press, 1995); Sarah E. Igo, *The Averaged American: Surveys, Citizens, and the Making of a Mass Public* (Cambridge: Harvard University Press, 2007); Mary S. Morgan, *The World in the Model: How Economists Work and Think* (Cambridge: Cambridge University Press, 2012).
12 Peter Becker and William Clark, ed., *Little Tools of Knowledge: Historical Essays on Academic and Bureaucratic Practices* (Ann Arbor: University of Michigan Press, 2001).

Statistical tools for governance are well-explored in the science and technology studies (STS) literature regarding, for example, indicators for a worldwide human rights regime.[13]

Scholars have for a long time been interested in classifications and categorisations in the making of sameness in groups and differences between groups. The focus has often been on either informal folk classifications or state projects and practices of categorising the population, as if these are completely separate.[14] An important research tradition is centred on Michel Foucault's concept of governmentality. The rise of population statistics from the eighteenth century and onwards meant that new areas such as public health could be formed and become the subject of interventions. Statistics constitute an integral part of the practices and mentalities in how states govern.[15] In the words of James C. Scott, statistics make the population legible for those in power.[16] Moreover, numbers can then come to be part of how individuals come to understand and govern themselves.[17] This perspective especially informs the scholarship having developed with regard to racial classifications.[18] A similar research tradition on nationalism has understood statistics – following Benedict Anderson's term *imagined communities* – as a way of establishing notions of a common national community.[19]

---

[13] Richard Rottenburg et al., ed., *The World of Indicators: The Making of Governmental Knowledge Through Quantification* (Cambridge: Cambridge University Press, 2015); Rainer Diaz-Bone and Emmanuel Didier, "The Sociology of Quantification – Perspectives on an Emerging Field in the Social Sciences," *Historical Social Research/Historische Sozialforschung* 41, no. 2 (2016). See also Eli Cook's *The Pricing of Progress: Economic Indicators and the Capitalization of American Life* (Cambridge: Harvard University Press, 2017) on how economic indicators have led to the capitalisation of American life and how it thereby co-produced capitalism.

[14] A great deal of this research is summarised in Rogers Brubaker, Mara Loveman, and Peter Stamatov, "Ethnicity as Cognition," *Theory and Society* 33, no. 1 (2004).

[15] Michel Foucault, *The Birth of Biopolitics: Lectures at The College de France 1978–1979* (Basingstoke: Palgrave Macmillan, 2008); Mitchell Dean, *Governmentality: Power and Rule in Modern Society* (Thousand Oaks: SAGE, 1999).

[16] James C. Scott, *Seeing Like a State: How Certain Schemes to Improve the Human Condition Have Failed* (New Haven: Yale University Press, 1998).

[17] Nikolas Rose, *Powers of Freedom: Reframing Political Thought* (Cambridge: Cambridge University Press, 1999), 197–232.

[18] For example, Nicholas B. Dirks, *Castes of Mind: Colonialism and the Making of Modern India* (Princeton: Princeton University Press, 2001); Thomas S. Mullaney, *Coming to Terms with the Nation: Ethnic Classification in Modern China* (Berkeley: University of California Press, 2011); Mara Loveman, *National Colors: Racial Classification and the State in Latin America* (Oxford: Oxford University Press, 2014); Debra Thompson, *The Schematic State: Race, Transnationalism, and the Politics of the Census* (Cambridge: Cambridge University Press, 2016).

[19] For example, Benedict Anderson, *Imagined Communities: Reflections on the Origin and Spread of Nationalism* (London: Verso, 1991); Silvana Patriarca, *Numbers and Nationhood: Writing Statis-*

These research fields offer valuable insights while at the same time being quite focused on state actors. The study of classification systems, especially class taxonomies, as tied to knowledge production and as in movement between different actors is underdeveloped. A history of knowledge perspective offers a way of analysing these technologies in circulation between actors and contexts, as well as how actors come to use and attribute different meanings to them. The examples in this article mainly originate from twentieth-century Sweden, but they have a bearing on how to understand social taxonomies in other countries during the same period.[20]

Bruno Latour argues in his book *Reassembling the Social* that the way in which social scientists refer to the social reifies it as something external to us and urges us to look for the associations in how actors assemble the social.[21] Following Latour, STS scholars speak of the importance to study "the social life of methods"; that is, how methods from the social sciences create what they purport to map out by, for instance, establishing a language to imagine and delimit it.[22] This perspective is useful in understanding social taxonomies. They, I argue, all create and enact one vision of the social by tying together people and groups as belonging to a common but differentiated population. My term "difference technology" highlights what these social taxonomies do in terms of creating and establishing differences between their classifications and sameness within them. They standardise and quantify categories and bring them together in a taxonomic order, thereby turning them into statistical facts. The precise classifications allow for new ways of viewing and studying the population, which then creates knowledge that can be used as a basis for social interventions and debate.

---

tics in Nineteenth-Century Italy (Cambridge: Cambridge University Press, 1996); Henrik Höjer, *Svenska siffror: Nationell integration och identifikation genom statistik 1800–1870* (Hedemora: Gidlunds förlag, 2001); Bruce Curtis, *The Politics of Population: State Formation, Statistics, and the Census of Canada* (Toronto: University of Toronto Press, 2001); Tong Lam, *A Passion for Facts: Social Surveys and the Construction of the Chinese Nation State, 1900–1949* (Berkeley: University of California Press, 2011).

20 Scholars on social classification systems originating from national statistical bureaus have mostly studied the ideas behind their creation, not how they have been used. See Margo (Anderson) Conk, "Occupational Classification in the United States Census, 1870–1940," *Journal of Interdisciplinary History* 9, no. 1 (1978); Simon Szreter, "The Genesis of the Registrar-General's Social Classification of Occupations," *The British Journal of Sociology* 35, no. 4 (1984).

21 Bruno Latour, *Reassembling the Social: An Introduction to Actor-Network-Theory* (Oxford: University Press, 2005).

22 Thomas Osborne and Nikolas Rose, "Populating Sociology: Carr-Saunders and the Problem of Population," *The Sociological Review* 56, no. 4 (2008); John Law, "Seeing like a Survey," *Cultural Sociology* 3, no. 2 (2009); Mike Savage, "The 'Social Life of Methods': A Critical Introduction," *Theory, Culture & Society* 30, no. 4 (2013).

The Swedish Social Group Division

Most of twentieth-century Sweden was dominated by a specific social taxonomy, the so-called social group division (*socialgruppsindelningen*). This division served several functions and needs from its inception in the years around 1900 to its slow demise in the 1970s and 1980s. Here, I discuss some of the areas it came to influence the most: voter statistics and election campaigning, market research, opinion polling, and the post-war social sciences.

Historian and political scientist Pontus Fahlbeck (1850–1923), professor at Lund University between 1889 and 1915, was the one presenting taxonomy as an answer to "the social question" and the problems of his time. In his book *Estate and Class* (*Stånd och klass*) from 1892, he classified Swedes into three classes – manual labourers, middle class, and upper class – based on occupation. Fahlbeck wanted to attach ideological struggles to underlying social processes, and the goal of his taxonomy was to show why the present upper class should continue to exert power over society. It was a call against the labour movement. The starting point for the analysis was that Western culture needed to be sustained by a group that did not have to carry out manual labour, and his classification served as a tool used to verify that society was set up in this appropriate way.[23]

Timothy Mitchell and Mike Savage have argued that experts in modern times create categories to govern on a national scale, such as the economy, the political, and the social by a delocalising act.[24] Social taxonomies are based on distance; they take people from their locality and put them into collective categories on a national level, making them legible for different kinds of actors such as the state. Fahlbeck was quite explicit in the epistemic precondition for creating his vision of society. Societal phenomena such as class appear "only when you contemplate things at a distance and at large," he explained.[25]

The ironic dialectic is that this distance would transform itself into intimate self-knowledge during the span of the twentieth century, as Swedes started to make sense of themselves through these social group classifications. In 2008, sociologist Rosemary Crompton proposed three ways of understanding class: first, as structured inequalities – as in the ways in which statisticians and social scientists

---

[23] Pontus Fahlbeck, *Stånd och klasser: En socialpolitisk öfverblick* (Lund: Collin & Zickerman, 1892).
[24] Timothy Mitchell, *Rule of Experts: Egypt, Techno-Politics, Modernity* (Berkeley: University of California Press, 2002); Mike Savage, *Identities and Social Change in Britain since 1940: The Politics of Method* (Oxford: Oxford University Press, 2010).
[25] Fahlbeck, *Stånd*, 51.

create class knowledge – often found in classifications that the classified themselves would not recognise; second, class as lifestyle, status, and culture; third, class as social and political organisation.[26] Studying a difference technology such as the social group taxonomy shows how these ways often become enmeshed.

When the right to vote was to be extended to a larger portion of men in the 1911 national elections – the electorate more than doubled – Fahlbeck proposed that the Central Bureau of Statistics (SCB) should classify voters by class. In the span of a few weeks that summer, three officials at the SCB tried to manage the tricky boundary work arising when all occupations in the country were to be sorted into three distinct groups. Describing the principles they had worked on, the officials said that a "social" assessment had been the basis for the creation of social groups I, II, and III, which were from the outset described as synonymous with the "upper class," "middle class," and "working class". Senior civil servants and white-collar workers, professionals, major businessmen, and landlords were placed in group I. Minor businessmen, lower civil servants, craftsmen, and farmers were put in group II, while labourers, crofters, farmhands, and fishermen were classified as belonging to group III. A difference compared to Fahlbeck's classification was that the SCB moved the lower civil servants and white-collar workers from the upper class and placed them in group II.[27]

This type of social taxonomy was not unique to Sweden, and other countries soon followed. The state statistical bureau in the UK developed a social taxonomy in 1913 to map family sizes in different segments of the population, which became the standard in the twentieth century for how British statisticians and social scientists analysed the population structure.[28] It specified five "social classes" and this division migrated to the U.S. in the 1930s, where it was extended to six categories.[29] Both the British and U.S. taxonomies divided the people in social group III into several separate categories. One effect was that no single class could be said to constitute a majority of the population. However, the divisions were similar in their focus on occupation as the basis for a person's social position and in their arrangement of the population in a one-dimensional status hierarchy. These may be contrasted with the official French taxonomy of the population in the postwar period. There, six occupational groups were distinguished according to sector

---

26 Rosemary Crompton, *Class and Stratification* (Cambridge: Polity, 2008), Ch. 2.
27 SCB, *Riksdagsmannavalen åren 1908–1911* (Stockholm: SCB, 1912), 30–31.
28 Szreter, "Genesis."
29 Conk, "Occupational."

and occupational function, but without any clear and discernible hierarchy between them.[30]

In Sweden, those tasked with strategic voter questions, the so-called *ombudsmän* in the political parties, soon saw the usefulness of the social group statistics created by the SCB in terms of navigating representative democracy. This was at a time when nationwide political parties started to mobilise voters. Voter statistics gave the Liberal Party (Frisinnade landsföreningen), the Conservative Party (Allmänna valmansförbundet), and the Social Democrats (Sveriges socialdemokratiska arbetareparti) the tools to make representative claims on sections of the population as well as knowledge on how to design specific election campaigns (e.g., geared at particular voters). The Social Democrats, for example, laid claim to social group III as the basis of their party.[31]

During the post-war period, the social group division became influential in social scientific research, but also in Social Democratic policymaking as a tool for mapping out social differences. For instance, it was used to measure inequalities in higher education. The division was hereby translated and inserted into policymaking in the welfare state. Meanwhile, the SCB had discarded the taxonomy for being unscientific. By the end of the 1940s, they argued that it no longer reflected the social structure and stopped classifying voter statistics in accordance with it without offering something new to replace it.[32] However, many social scientists at the universities saw the usefulness of a well-tested taxonomy that also enabled comparing survey results with other studies, which is why they continued using it.[33] The taxonomy remained a difference technology for imagining and interven-

---

30 Simon Szreter, "The Official Representation of Social Classes in Britain, the United States, and France: The Professional Model and 'Les Cadres'," *Comparative Studies in Society and History* 35, no. 2 (1993). For an example of a Norwegian taxonomy, see Einar Lie, "Socio-Economic Categories in Norwegian Censuses up to about 1960," in *Nordic Demography: Trends and Differentials*, ed. Jørgen Carling (Oslo: Unipub Forlag, Nordic Demographic Society, 2002). On statistical bureaus, see Margo Anderson, *The American Census: A Social History* (New Haven: Yale University Press, 1988); Gunnar Thorvaldsen, *Censuses and Census Takers: A Global History* (London: Routledge/Taylor & Francis Group, 2018).
31 This is explored in my article "Klassriket: Klasskunskaper i den svenska partipolitiska sfären, 1911–1940," *Historisk tidskrift* 142, no. 2 (2022).
32 Statistiska Centralbyrån, *Riksdagsmannavalen åren 1949–1952* (Stockholm: SCB, 1953), 61.
33 For example Georg Karlsson, *Adaptability and Communication in Marriage: A Swedish Predictive Study of Marital Satisfaction* (Uppsala: Uppsala University, 1951); *Sociologi* (Stockholm: Forum, 1951); Edmund Dahlström, ed., *Svensk samhällsstruktur i sociologisk belysning* (Stockholm: Svenska bokförlaget, 1959); Gunnar Boalt, *Socialt beteende: Handbok i sociologi* (Stockholm: Natur och kultur, 1961); Gunnar Boalt and Torsten Husén, *Skolans psykologi* (Stockholm: Almqvist & Wiksell, 1964).

ing in higher education up until the 1980s. For the Social Democrats – who remained in government between 1932 and 1976 and who influenced much of Swedish society – this kind of classification was relevant and practical due to the fact that social group III could easily be translated into their main constituency and political subject: the working class. The statistics thus provided a basis for social reforms and were used extensively in political debates, such as in Social Democratic policies aimed at getting more people from social group III to apply for higher education. The Social Democrats could, moreover, evaluate the effects of their reforms by continuing to measure the social background of the students.[34]

Already from an early stage, not everyone was happy about how the taxonomy ordered the social. For example, Georg Andrén (1890–1969), a conservative politician and professor of political science, in 1937 presented his interpretation of what characterised modern Swedish politics: the balance of power between the "social classes," which, in turn, divided the political in a way that was desirable for the country's prosperity. Andrén used the division introduced by SCB for the 1930 census, mapping Swedes according to their function in the workforce: as business owners (a large group since farmers were also included here), as service personnel (basically white-collar workers), or as workers. In this vision of the social, no class was in a majority position.[35] However, the liberal newspaper *Dagens Nyheter* countered Andrén's conclusion. "The statistics Professor Andrén uses are hardly fit for purpose," their editorial pointed out, instead extolling the social group division as more accurate. "Nowadays, the working class in the broad sense, or social group III of the electoral statistics, constitutes a qualified majority of those entitled to vote." In fact, the class structure was constantly shifted in favour of the labour movement, meaning that there was no balance of power at all. The newspaper argued that conservatives and liberals needed to face this pressing reality.[36]

Others imagined new rational categories beyond class, thereby showing the importance of studying competing ways of ordering the social. For example, statistician Thor Andersson – publisher of *Nordisk statistisk tidskrift* in the 1920s – dreamed of a "higher order for society." The statistics of the future would no longer divide the population into "higher" or "lower" classes, but according to a "rational" point of view. Andersson envisioned population statistics divided into categories of "workers and parasites" – those who contributed to the welfare of

---

[34] See my article "Klass i begåvningsreservens tidevarv: Taxonomiska konflikter inom och genom svensk utbildningsforskning, c. 1945–1960," *Nordic Journal of Educational History* 8, no. 1 (2021).
[35] Georg Andren, *Tvåkammarsystemets tillkomst och utveckling*, vol. 9 of *Sveriges riksdag: Historisk och statsvetenskaplig framställning*, ed. Nils Edén (Stockholm: Victor Petterson, 1937), 608–612.
[36] "Balans: En klasspolitisk studie," *Dagens Nyheter*, March 14, 1937.

the nation and those who did not – social types who were represented in all occupational groups.³⁷

The social group taxonomy always overlapped with other social orders, both in the way that the statistics were constructed and how the statistics were subsequently interpreted. In voter statistics, for instance, women were placed in their husband or father's social group when lacking employment but were classified according to their own occupation in case of wage labour. However, in social scientific surveys, the social position of the household was often determined by the husband's occupation, as this was taken for granted to be decisive, even when the woman worked as well. During the late 1950s, this led to criticism in the Swedish press for making women invisible in social scientific and bureaucratic knowledge production.³⁸ Moreover, even though social group statistics could be presented in a gender-neutral way – as both men and women are included under a designation such as social group III – the figures were often used in gendered discourses. Various types of social group statistics were often seen as primarily concerned with the male part of the population, such as figures on which groups attended higher education.³⁹ Men were thus constructed as the norm for society. In other cases, social group statistics on women were highlighted. After women's suffrage was granted by the Swedish parliament in 1919, for example, the Social Democratic Party started to address women from social group III as a specific voter group, who were considered important to canvass in order not to let the upper or middle classes win the elections.⁴⁰

The social group division also influenced commercial actors in their statistical knowledge production concerning the consumer. The taxonomy came to structure knowledge regarding and enable interventions in advertising and consumption among Swedes from the 1930s and onwards. Ways in which to empirically survey the consumer and newspaper readers, with the promise of increased sales and more effective advertising, had been discussed before, but these notions were institutionalised and executed in the 1930s with the rise of market research compa-

---

37 Thor Andersson, "Folkregister och folkräkning i Sverge," *Nordisk statistisk tidskrift* 7, no. 1 (1928): 64.
38 Greta Liljefors, "Dagens frågor: Värre än sambeskattad," *Svenska Dagbladet*, October 25, 1958; Greta Liljefors, "Moder okänd," *Dagens Nyheter*, October 14, 1965; Kall, "Mamma har ingen betydelse när barnets socialgrupp avgörs", *Dagens Nyheter*, September 21, 1966.
39 See Lina Carls, *Våp eller nucka? Kvinnors högre studier och genusdiskursen 1930–1970* (Lund: Nordic Academic Press, 2004).
40 Olivia Nordgren, *Arbetarkvinnorna och höstens val* (Stockholm: Tiden, 1928). This emphasis on the equal value of all votes was not reflected in the party's organisation and political priorities. See Kjell Östberg, *Efter rösträtten: Kvinnors utrymme efter det demokratiska genombrottet* (Eslöv: Brutus Östlings bokförlag, Symposion, 1997).

nies. Depending on who signalled an interest in a product in a market survey, or which customer groups read a particular newspaper, it was possible to choose sales tactics and advertising locations. Here, the social group taxonomy became important as a proven technology for classifying and studying the consumption habits of Swedes, knowledge that was then used to market goods and services.[41]

Marketers embracing social grouping had a lasting effect on Swedish public life. In the early 1940s, an advertiser decided to import Gallup's opinion polling business from the U.S. The rhetoric surrounding the project presented the opinion polls as a democratic tool through which Swedes could understand themselves. Swedish Gallup sold the surveys to newspapers, which, in turn, could use them to attract readers. In her book *The Averaged American: Surveys, Citizens, and the Making of a Mass Public* (2007), Sarah Igo has shown how Gallup, together with the media, was part of creating a discourse concerning the average citizen.[42] In Sweden, however, opinion polls were just as much about locating differences within the population, in which case the social group taxonomy saw new uses. Swedish Gallup used it as a difference technology to discern and compare opinions. We cannot overemphasise the importance of this adoption for the public visibility and impact of the social group classification. Year after year until the 1970s, sometimes as often as weekly, Swedes were confronted with the opinions of the different social groups on issues ranging from foreign policy to film preferences.[43]

The circulation and translation of the social group division into all these spheres of society made it a common point of reference in public debate. Sociological interview surveys from the 1970s show that many Swedes used social group terms when asked to describe the structure of society.[44] "This division has become so firmly established in our country that many seem inclined to consider it more or less self-evident that it makes sense to divide [...] the contemporary Swedish population into social groups," the SCB noted in a report.[45] At the same time, how-

---

[41] See my article "En marknad för klass: Marknads- och opinionsundersökningar som skillnadsmaskiner 1930–1960," *Lychnos* (2021). On market research and the rise of similar consumer engineering in other countries, see Jan Logemann, Gary Cross, and Ingo Köhler, "Beyond the Mad Men: Consumer Engineering and the Rise of Marketing Management, 1920s–1970s," in *Consumer Engineering, 1920s–1970s: Marketing Between Expert Planning and Consumer Responsiveness*, ed. Jan Logemann, Gary Cross, and Ingo Köhler (Cham: Palgrave Macmillan, 2019).
[42] Igo, *Averaged*.
[43] Smedberg, "Marknad."
[44] Richard Scase, "Hur industriarbetare i Sverige och England ser på makten i samhället," *Sociologisk forskning* 13, no. 1 (1976).
[45] SCB, *Sociala grupper i svensk statistik: Ett förslag framlagt av en av Statistiska centralbyrån tillsatt arbetsgrupp* (Stockholm: SCB, 1967), 3.

ever, it was challenged and replaced by new ways of ordering the social, signalling a move away from class.

After Class: New Ways of Ordering the Social

In this section, I want to outline the establishment of new social taxonomies from the 1960s and onwards, all of which were based on statistical knowledge production and influenced political policy and public debates. These came from actors to the left of the Social Democrats, from within the SCB, and from the conservative and liberal opposition. These difference technologies were both part of producing social knowledge and enacting different social and political visions of Swedish society.

During the 1960s, the problem with poverty remaining in the Swedish welfare state was gaining a foothold in political discussions, egged on by a new generation of radical social scientists starting to research income inequalities and deep-seated social ills. This discovery of poverty was not unique to Sweden; a similar process can be seen in the United Kingdom and the United States.[46] As a result, the Social Democratic government appointed a commission to investigate the problems of low incomes, the so-called Low Income Inquiry (1965–1971). Its mission was to explore the remaining problems of low incomes in the Swedish welfare state – a kind of total survey of the Swedish population, which resulted in a dozen studies on everything from the health of Swedes, their political behaviour and cultural habits to working conditions.

The low-income earner was a new socio-political type created by the Low Income Inquiry – a classification uniting the unemployed, the long-term sick, pensioners, part-time workers, and low-wage earners into one group, previously scattered across different unions and social groups. The social group taxonomy often portrayed a social structure that was unequal in terms of people's resource distributions and life opportunities but with limited emphasis on antagonism between social groups. The radical Low Income Inquiry instead sought to revive a conflictual understanding of society, in which high-income earners grew at the expense of middle- and low-income earners, and where women, making up a majority of low-income earners, were described as oppressed by patriarchal structures. The media-active secretary of the inquiry, Per Holmberg, wanted the low-income earn-

---

[46] Felix Römer, "Evolving Knowledge Regimes: Economic Inequality and the Politics of Statistics in the United Kingdom since the Postwar Era," *KNOW* 4, no. 2 (2020); Alice O'Connor, *Poverty Knowledge: Social Science, Social Policy, and the Poor in Twentieth-century U.S. History* (Princeton; Princeton University Press, cop. 2001).

ers to join forces and fight the high-income earners across the work sectors. This difference technology highlighted new cleavages based on income instead of the social status of one's occupation. An effect of this knowledge production was that the Social Democratic government and the Swedish Trade Union Confederation tried to boost the economic situation of the low-income earners. Moreover, income inequalities became a key topic in Swedish politics throughout the 1970s. The figures of the low- and high-income earner have been part of the Swedish political debate ever since, although rarely involving as radical politics as when the Low Income Inquiry was operating.[47]

In official statistics, the SCB had since the 1950s sought to find a replacement to the social group taxonomy. They were looking for a new division with clear, theoretically grounded, and objective criteria that could be accepted by many stakeholders.[48] Throughout the 1970s, new taxonomies were evaluated internally without settling on a replacement – they had by now become so politically charged that they were difficult to tackle. They could always be accused of hierarchising the population while also suffering from boundary issues in the way they were constructed. "A polemical pincer operation can thus be deployed against socio-economic groups; they are morally-politically offensive, and they have serious technical shortcomings," a working group opined in 1974.[49]

The SCB finally launched – more than three decades after they phased out the social groups – a new taxonomy in 1982: *Socioekonomisk indelning* (SEI), which structured the population according to occupational skills. Workers were divided into skilled and unskilled; white-collar workers into three classifications – low, medium, and high positions – and, lastly, business owners as their own classification.[50] This reconceptualisation of social differences based on skills and education can be seen in other countries as well. In the United Kingdom, for example, the taxonomy of social classes dominating throughout the twentieth century suddenly changed the rationale behind these classifications for the 1980 census – from explicitly focusing on the perceived social standing of your occupation to the amount of skills and education needed for said occupation.[51]

We currently see how the tendency to categorise according to skills and education has been pushed even further. The "uneducated" and the "educated" are

---

47 Carl-Filip Smedberg, "Låginkomsttagarna. Expertis, politik och mediering i formandet av en ny kategori omkring 1968," *Scandia* 84, no. 1 (2018).
48 SCB, *Sociala grupper*.
49 Gösta Carlsson et al., "Socio-ekonomiska grupperingar," *Statistisk tidskrift* 12, no. 5 (1974): 382.
50 SCB, "Socioekonomisk indelning (SEI)," *Meddelanden i samordningsfrågor* 4 (1982).
51 Richard I. Brewer, "A Note on the Changing Status of the Registrar General's Classification of Occupations," *The British Journal of Sociology* 37, no. 1 (1986).

now recurring figures in Swedish (and global) public debates and in knowledge production regarding phenomena such as school success, career choice, and cultural consumption.[52] This becomes a way of talking about social differences by locating and explaining these by the amount of education an individual has accrued: what one may refer to as an ongoing educationalisation of the social.[53] One effect of this is that elite positions seem more "deserved" based on the knowledge, or in other words the "human capital," they possess. Those with low status, income, and power, on the other end, face this situation due to educational failures. This thus seems to sit quite well with neoliberal and conservative ways of looking upon society.

Liberals and conservatives also launched their own ordering of the social. Hans L. Zetterberg, a right-wing ideologue and leader of SIFO (Svenska institutet för opinionsundersökningar) – the largest opinion poll company in Sweden at the time – in the late 1970s introduced lifestyles as the best way to understand Swedish social life.[54] Closely related, a series of articles in the conservative daily *Svenska Dagbladet* in the 1980s discussed the new fluid lifestyles in contemporary Sweden, which had replaced the old social groups as the most important aspect of social identities. Psychologists and market researchers conceptualised Swedish society as made up of five lifestyle groups: *the traditionalist*, wanting to remain in the old society; *the conventional*, embracing the consumer society; *the moral* ones, living in a society of commitments; *the climbers*, people heading toward the society of the future; and, lastly, there were *the extremists*, who dreamed of a fairer system. This difference technology mapped out a new society of consumerism and careerism, and those stuck in the old ways opposing this society.[55]

---

[52] Skolverket, *Analyser av familjebakgrundens betydelse för skolresultaten och skillnader mellan skolor: En kvantitativ studie av utvecklingen över tid i slutet av grundskolan* (Stockholm: Skolverket, 2018); Myndigheten för kulturanalys, *Kulturvanor. Socioekonomiska analyser och tidstrender* (Myndigheten för kulturanalys, 2017).

[53] New perspectives in the history of education speak of an "educationalization of social problems" in the West since the 18th century (i.e., how social problems and how to solve them are increasingly described in terms of a lack of or need for education. See Paul Smeyers and Marc Depaepe, ed., *Educational Research: The Educationalization of Social Problems* (Dordrecht: Springer, 2008). In the last 60 years, I argue, we instead see an educationalisation of the social: the acceleration over the last 60 years of describing the very structure of society in educational terms.

[54] Hans L. Zetterberg: *Arbete, livsstil och motivation* (Stockholm: SAF, 1977). On Zetterberg's collaboration since the mid-1970s with Moderata samlingspartiet, the largest conservative party, see Lars Tobisson, *Främling i folkhemmet: Ett högerspöke ser tillbaka* (Stockholm: Atlantis, 2009), 200.

[55] Caroline Haux and Hedvig Hedqvist, "Grupper i dagens samhälle," *Svenska Dagbladet*, October 15, 1988.

In the mid-1980s, Zetterberg would warn against – but in doing so also create and diffuse – a divide in society between those in the private sector and those he called "the publicly supported" (*offentlighetsförsörjda*). By the latter category, he referred to people employed by the public sector as well as those depending on the state, such as retirees, long-term unemployed, and those on sick leave. The publicly supported had for the first time become a majority of the population (53.9 per cent according to Zetterberg and SIFO). This would, if not combated, lead to the inevitable rule of the Social Democrats since most of the publicly supported voted for them (as well as for the Left Party (Vänsterpartiet Kommunisterna) and the Liberal Party (Folkpartiet)). These parties would then continue to increase the public sector, leading to "spiralling taxes, spiralling inflation, spiralling interest rates, spiralling debt."[56] This theme came up in the Conservative Party's (Moderaterna) election campaigns, especially in party leader Carl Bildt's (1986–1999) rhetoric. His government between 1991 and 1994 introduced welfare cutbacks and neoliberal reforms such as school vouchers in a move to make the "backward" and state-dependent Swedish society more efficient and business-friendly.[57]

Later on, in 2004, an alliance of liberal and conservative parties launched the idea of a Sweden divided between the insiders of society and the outsiders (*innanförskap-utanförskap*). Those "outside," the 10–20 per cent of the population who were unemployed and on long-term sick leave, were "dependent" on and "passive" due to social benefits and should for their own good be forced to apply for jobs. This reconceptualisation remained important for these parties when in power between 2006 and 2014. Here, a large thriving society stood against those who had been placed on the outside. Lowering salaries and thresholds was key to letting them into society. This division is still very much present in contemporary political debates.[58]

At the same time, there are ongoing attempts to revive class-based language in the public debate, notably by the leftist think tank Katalys. They have published surveys of the Swedish class society in order to criticise inequalities and show the possibilities of a leftist revival if the working class were organised.[59]

---

56 Hans L. Zetterberg, "Försörjning och röstning," *SIFO indikator* 3 (1985).
57 Anders Ivarsson Westerberg, Ylva Waldemarson, and Kjell Östberg, ed., *Det långa 1990-talet: När Sverige förändrades* (Umeå: Boréa, 2014).
58 Tobias Davidsson, "Utanförskapelsen: En diskursanalys av hur begreppet utanförskap artikulerades i den svenska riksdagsdebatten 2003–2006," *Socialvetenskaplig tidskrift* 17, no. 2 (2010). See, for example, "Utanförskapet är Sveriges största utmaning," Svenskt näringsliv, accessed March 13, 2023, https://www.svensktnaringsliv.se/utanforskap/.
59 Daniel Suhonen, Göran Therborn, and Jesper Weithz, ed., *Klass i Sverige: Ojämlikheten, makten och politiken i det 21:a århundradet* (Lund: Arkiv förlag, 2021).

Conclusion

The (albeit selective) discussion on influential Swedish social taxonomies in the twentieth century up to the present time shows that difference technologies represent ways of ordering and studying the population by producing differences between and sameness within its classifications. Social taxonomies have been ubiquitous during the twentieth century, fulfilling an important role in the production of statistics and knowledge. Different actors and institutions needed social taxonomies to sort and structure data, and thereby create new knowledge, for their specific ends. In doing so, however, they also contributed to larger societal discourses, such as what the social structure looked like and, in some cases, what caused this stratification. These types of processes were not unique to Sweden. However, more thorough comparisons regarding the uses of social taxonomies in knowledge production and their presence in policy and public debates in different countries remain to be done.

The social group division, beginning with a conservative political scientist and the Central Bureau of Statistics in 1911, was soon used by the political parties, market researchers, opinion polls, the post-war social sciences, and welfare policymakers. It was thus part of fairly different projects, but they all enacted society as divided into three classes according to occupational status. As a result, the social groups became a common point of reference for how Swedes understood and debated society. The example shows the versatility and mobile character of these difference technologies, but also how actors, using them for their own political and epistemic ends, could unintentionally together create quite stable social worlds – in this case the Swedish class society. However, how this class society – co-constructed with the social group taxonomy – was understood and debated by different actors is the topic for another article.

From the 1960s and onwards, the social group division was challenged by actors from the left, the SCB, liberals, and conservatives. One dominant social taxonomy gave way to a plurality of technologies ordering the social in new ways. A tendency in these more contemporary social taxonomies is that those placed at the lower ends of society are passive and negative categories. The outsider and the uneducated, for example, are positions of deficiency. What is implicit here is a model saying that if only they can be brought into "normal" society, the inequalities and social problems facing them will dissolve. A hypothesis is that it is much harder to identify with and mobilise around a label of being uneducated or an outsider. These make it difficult to organise politically.

History of knowledge – which up to now has mostly focused on circulation, actors, and areas – has much to gain by studying difference technologies. Building on research from governmentality studies, the history of the social sciences, and the history of statistics, I show how social taxonomies connect mundane and practical aspects of knowledge in the making – in how actors order empirical material to through these create statistics – with political policy, public debates, and discourses regarding society. Difference technologies all order and produce different social worlds, highlighting some things while hiding other aspects of society. Through these, categories become statistical facts and thus more trusted, although at the same time possible to criticise on scientific, political, and moral grounds. Furthermore, social taxonomies are charged in the sense that people want to discuss and make sense of them – as seen in the example of the Great British Class Calculator – illuminating the struggles and complexities of ordering the social and the importance for historians of knowledge to study them.

About the contributor

Carl-Filip Smedberg is a researcher at the Department of the History of Science and Ideas, Uppsala University. His research focuses on social taxonomies, social identities, and the history of the social sciences. His present project studies the history of the knowledge society and debates concerning educational differences in post-war Sweden.

Section II: **Modes of Publication**

Charlotte A. Lerg, Johan Östling, and Jana Weiß

Modes of Publication: Introduction

Media, Practices, Structures

Modes of publication matter. As the media landscape diversifies technologically as well as in terms of formats and framings, our attention in the history of knowledge is drawn to the many ways in which knowledge is shared, circulated, and made available. In addition, different modes of publication shape and affect knowledge formation and its application.

Approaches informing the study of modes of publication and publication history include media studies, anthropology, or sociology. In addition, the practitioners' perspectives from library science or archival studies provide new insights. As Trevor Owens and Jesse Johnston have shown in the context of historical knowledge in digital archives, modes of publication have received renewed attention in the wake of the digital turn.[1] Marshal McLuhan's catchphrase about the medium being the message, which once enthused communication theorists in the 1960s, has since become a well-worn (over-worn?) slogan.[2] Nevertheless, it does have something to offer to the history of knowledge. How do we mediate and transmit knowledge? Does visualization, for example, always mean simplification or could there be more complexity?[3] Are we able to garner different kinds of knowledge from different types of materials?

Besides a media-centered approach, a focus on modes of publication may also shed light on practices in an innovative way. While cognitive and epistemic practices have been established as an object of critical inquiry in the history of knowledge,[4] thinking about the process of "doing knowledge" often remains confined to methodological and praxiological discourses. Already in 2002, however, Daniela Ahrens and Anette Gerhard argued that our understanding of knowledge is becom-

---

[1] Trevor Owens and Jesse A. Johnston, "Archivists as Peers in Digital Public History," in *Handbook of Digital Public History*, ed. Serge Noiret, Mark Tebeau, and Gerben Zaagsma (Berlin and Boston: De Gruyter Oldenbourg, 2022).

[2] Marshall McLuhan, "The Medium Is the Message," in *Understanding Media: The Extension of Man* (New York: McGraw-Hill, 1964).

[3] Gemma Anderson, *Drawing as a Way of Knowing in Art and Science* (Bristol: Intellect, 2017); Gillian Rose, "On the Relation between 'Visual Research Methods' and Contemporary Visual Culture," *The Sociological Review* 62 (2014).

[4] Simon Barker, Charlie Crerar, and Trystan S. Goetze, *Harms and Wrongs in Epistemic Practice* (Cambridge: Cambridge University Press, 2018).

ing more fluid and constructivist, resulting in a shift in attention from the question of *where* knowledge is accessed to *how* it is accessed; from how it is conserved or stored to how it is generated.[5] While this is not only a result of advances in digitized processes alone, and certainly predates them in some cases, new technologies raise our awareness when it comes to processes and force us to more consciously reflect on their ramifications. How does collaboration work? How may expertise be mobilized? What is the role of curating and categorizing research data?[6]

One thing that many practices have in common is that they provide some kind of reorganization, transposition, or translation, while in doing so indirectly adding to the content. This could mean turning data into narrative formats in articles and books or (re-)imagining abstract systems in visual representations, such as schematics or models. Similarly, this could apply to arranging information in networks of references using, once again, visual representation (for example, in network theory), traditional cross reference marginalia used especially during the Middle Ages, or their digital reincarnation – the hyperlink. It could also simply mean linguistic translation, which despite the best efforts of translation studies, is still often considered little more than a means to an end. The emphasis remains on a functional understanding of foreign idioms without paying sufficient attention to the cultural subtext and nuances. And yet, a multitude of special terminology, from *persona* or *esprit* to *folkhem* or, indeed, *Wissenschaft*, remain un-translatable and highlight the limits of literal translation.[7] Anyone who does not share in the globally dominant language community – at this point still mostly anglophone – can attest that language profoundly conditions modes of publication.

Critically interrogating structural contexts as part of understanding knowledge also involves extrinsic factors such as financial considerations, legal restrictions, and power hierarchies that impact the framework of publication practices. Imad Moosa, for example, has examined the rather problematic effect of the publish-or-parish culture in Western and now global academia and how this intersects with market-driven modes of publication.[8] The ongoing challenges of open access publishing with stakeholders among academics, publishers, policymakers, and society at large (i. e., taxpayers) links ideals concerning democratic access to – and

---

[5] Daniela Ahrens and Anette Gerhard, "'Doing Knowledge': Neue Formen der Wissensorganisation durch den Einsatz neuer Medien," *Medien & Kommunikationswissenschaft* 50, no. 1 (2002).
[6] Mark Tebeau, "Curation: Toward a New Ethic of Digital Public History," in *Handbook of Digital Public History*, ed. Serge Noiret et al. (Berlin and Boston: De Gruyter Oldenbourg, 2022).
[7] Barbara Cassin et al., ed., *Dictionary of Untranslatables: A Philosophical Lexicon* (Princeton: Princeton University Press, 2014).
[8] Imad Moosa, *Publish or Perish: Perceived Benefits versus Unintended Consequences* (Cheltenham: Edward Elgar Publishing, 2018), accessed May 2, 2023, doi.org/10.4337/9781786434937.00007.

participation in (!) – knowledge to restrictions related to copyright and intellectual property and needs to strike a balance between fair use and fair pay.

In short, relevant questions deal with material and social structures as well as traditions, ideas, and communication processes. Just like the history of knowledge generally, exploring modes of publication requires an interdisciplinary approach, which can draw productively on the new field of publication studies.

Publication Studies and the History of Knowledge

Publication studies have become a growing and multidisciplinary field. At some universities, it is a discipline in its own right, but it may also be conducted by researchers in a number of additional disciplines ranging from science studies, economics, and sociology to anthropology, communication studies, and literary studies. There is a strong focus on contemporary publishing practices and norms, often related to the digital transformation of the book market and the media landscape of the 21st century. Another important topic concerns critical investigations into contemporary production conditions in the natural and human sciences.[9]

Alongside contemporary studies, there is a significant current of historically oriented scholarship. Drawing on a well-established tradition of book history, other formats and modes such as encyclopedias, publishing houses, or the paper trade are examined in different periods and settings, often inspired by recent media history perspectives.[10] Lisa Gitelman's contribution to the first volume of *History of Intellectual Culture* may be seen as a manifestation of this approach. Being both historically concrete and theoretically sophisticated, she traces the changes in the rules for citation across nine editions of the *MLA Handbook* between 1977 and 2021, while relating them to the transformation of the media landscape at large.[11]

---

[9] Simone Murray, "Publishing Studies: Critically Mapping Research in Search of a Discipline," *Publishing Research Quarterly* 22 (2006), accessed May 2, 2023, doi.org/10.1007/s12109-007-0001-4; Alison Baverstock, "What Significance Does Publishing Studies Have Right Now?" *Learned Publishing* 33, no. 4 (2020), accessed May 2, 2023, doi.org/10.1002/leap.1319.

[10] See, for instance, Linn Holmberg and Maria Simonsen, eds., *Stranded Encyclopedias, 1700–2000: Exploring Unfinished, Unpublished, Unsuccessful Encyclopedic Projects* (Cham: Palgrave Macmillan, 2021); Daniel Bellingradt and Anna Reynolds, eds., *The Paper Trade in Early Modern Europe: Practices, Materials, Networks* (Leiden: Brill, 2021).

[11] Lisa Gitelamn, "Citation and Mediation: The Evolution of MLA Style," in *History of Intellctual Culture*, ed. Charlotte Lerg, Johan Östling, and Jana Weiß (Berlin and Boston: De Gruyter Oldenbourg, 2022), accessed May 2, 2023, https://doi.org/10.1515/9783110748819-002.

There is also clearly an increasing interest in scientific and scholarly publications. Recent examples include Alex Csiszar's *The Scientific Journal* (2018), a book on authorship and the politics of knowledge in the 19th century, and the edited volume *Science Periodicals in Nineteenth-Century Britain* (2020). In addition, it is easy to find detailed studies of the publication practices of individual scientists and discussions on different scientific sub-genres (e.g., scientific book reviews).[12] Many of these studies use publication patterns as entry points to analyze the orders, hierarchies, and structures of knowledge in a given chronological and geographical context.

These historically informed publication studies have in the last decade also served as a rich and critical source of inspiration for the emerging field of the history of knowledge. For instance, James A. Secord's work is an important point of reference for many historians of knowledge. He published key books like *Victorian Sensation* (2000) and *Visions of Science* (2014) that show how rewarding it is to study the book market and its changing conditions in order to understand how scientific knowledge was produced and circulated.[13] In a recently published article in *Isis*, moreover, he adopts a similar perspective to reinterpret how, when, and why "the scientific revolution" was established as a master narrative in the history of science.[14] Furthermore, book and media history perspectives have underpinned various recent studies in the history of knowledge, from discussions on early modern printed marginalia and analyses of how individual works served as sites in which knowledge circulated to the importance of paperbacks and book cafés for postwar popular education.[15]

---

[12] Alex Csiszar, *The Scientific Journal: Authorship and the Politics of Knowledge in the Nineteenth Century* (Chicago: The University of Chicago Press, 2018); Gowan Dawson et al., eds., *Science Periodicals in Nineteenth-Century Britain: Constructing Scientific Communities* (Chicago: University of Chicago Press, 2020); Jenny Beckman, "The Publication Strategies of Jons Jacob Berzelius (1779–1848): Negotiating National and Linguistic Boundaries in Chemistry," *Annals of Science* 73, no. 2 (2016); Sjang ten Hagen, "Evaluating Knowledge, Evaluating Character: Book Reviewing by American Historians and Physicists (1900–1940)," *History of Humanities* 7, no. 2 (2022).

[13] James A. Secord, *Victorian Sensation: The Extraordinary Publication, Reception, and Secret Authorship of Vestiges of the Natural History of Creation* (Chicago: University of Chicago Press, 2000); James A. Secord, *Visions of Science: Books and Readers at the Dawn of the Victorian Age* (Oxford: Oxford University Press, 2014).

[14] James A. Secord, "Inventing the Scientific Revolution," *Isis* 114, no. 1 (2023).

[15] Kajsa Weber, "Luther in Printed Marginalia: Reference Notes, Reading and Representations in Swedish Lutheran Prints 1570–1630," *Reformation & Renaissance Review* 24, no. 2 (2022); Helge Jordheim, "The Printed Work as a Site of Knowledge Circulation: Dialogues, Systems, and the Question of Genre," in *Circulation of Knowledge: Explorations into the History of Knowledge*, ed. Johan Östling et al. (Lund: Nordic Academic Press, 2018); Johan Östling, Anton Jansson, and Ragni Svensson, "Public Arenas of the Humanities: The Circulation of Knowledge in the Postwar Period," in *The Hu-*

Just like for many other contributions to the history of knowledge, these kinds of publication studies have the potential to put our present situation in perspective. While they arise from a scholarly interest in historical processes and phenomena, they may, at the same time, stimulate a more informed discussion and foster self-reflection regarding our own academic practices.

This thematic section has a similar ambition by opening up the diversity of aspects and approaches. From a media-centered perspective, **Chelsea A. Rodriguez** considers storage and retrieval in the analog-to-digital archive of the *New York Times*. In doing so, she interrogates the potential, limits, and methodological challenges of digitization in historical research, in particular when using large samples of newspaper sources. Modes of publication in the context of "doing knowledge" are at the heart of **Elena Falco's** analysis of the Wikipedian community. Her contribution traces how tensions arise in the context of the encyclopedia between ideals of Randian objectivism and growing calls for acknowledging identity and positionality. From a more historical perspective, **Elisavet Papalexopoulou** addresses a core issue in publication studies, namely the politics of translation. Looking at Greece in the Age of Revolutions, her contribution expounds on the ways in which women were able to mobilize and leverage their knowledge of language to participate in the philosophical and social discourse of the day, especially through the paratexts of translated works. Finally, in an overview of publication formats for university histories from a library science perspective, **Jean-Pierre Hérubel** ponders questions of genre within the structural framework of academic research, institutional representation politics, and popular publication markets.

Overall, in studying modes of publication, the contributions to this thematic section invite us to take seriously the many layers of presenting, sharing, and circulating knowledge. Reading these processes through the lens of media, practices, and structures, and in light of recent advances in publication studies, once again stresses the cultural formation of knowledge.

About the contributors

Charlotte A. Lerg is assistant professor of North-American History at Ludwig-Maximilian University Munich and managing director of the Lasky Center for Transatlantic Studies. She also serves on the board of the Bavarian American Academy. Her research focuses on the cultural history of knowledge, visual media, and historical theory. Publications include *Universitätsdiplomatie: Prestige*

---

manities and the Modern Politics of Knowledge: The Impact and Organization of the Humanities in Sweden, 1850–2020, ed. Anders Ekström and Hampus Östh Gustafsson (Amsterdam: Amsterdam University Press, 2022).

und Wissenschaft in den transatlantischen Beziehungen 1890–1920 (2019). She also edited *The Diary of Lt. Melvin J. Lasky* (2022).

Johan Östling is Professor of History, Director of the Lund Centre for the History of Knowledge (LUCK), and Wallenberg Academy Fellow. His research is mainly devoted to the history of knowledge, but he has a more general interest in the intellectual, political, and cultural history of modern Europe. His recent publications comprise *Circulation of Knowledge* (2018), *Forms of Knowledge* (2020), *Histories of Knowledge in Postwar Scandinavia* (2020) and *Knowledge Actors* (2023).

Jana Weiß is DAAD Associate Professor at the University of Texas at Austin. With a focus on U.S. and transatlantic history, her research interests include 19th and 20th century immigration, knowledge, and religious history as well as the history of racism. Her most recent publications include *The Continuity of Change? New Perspectives on U.S. Reform Movements* (co-edited with Charlotte A. Lerg, 2021), and (with Nicole Hirschfelder) "Overcoming Barriers: An Interdisciplinary Collaboration in a Transatlantic Research Network on the Black Freedom Struggle", in *Entgrenzungen: Festschrift zum 60. Geburtstag von Andrea Strübind*, ed. Sabine Hübner and Kim Strübind (Berlin: Duncker & Humboldt, 2023).

Chelsea A. Rodriguez

Digital Newspapers, Material Knowledge: Grappling with the TimesMachine Digital Archive as a Repository of Knowledge

Abstract: This article explores the functionality and character of the TimesMachine, the digital archive of the *New York Times*, as it relates to research in the history of knowledge and history of education. The TimesMachine was designed specifically to improve the accessibility and contextualization of digital newspapers. However, the fog of digitization still complicates how researchers can (and should) use these digitized newspapers as sources of knowledge. Using the TimesMachine as a case study, this article aims to contribute to current conversations regarding the possibilities and limitations of digital archives and to demonstrate the importance of digital literacy for historians. There are several takeaways from this article that can help researchers make informed methodological choices in their pursuit of history, including the recentering of materiality in the digital space and the integration of interdisciplinary and digital methods in the history of knowledge.

Keywords: digital archive, The New York Times, digital newspapers, sources of knowledge, digital methods

Introduction

The New York Times has played an instrumental role as a producer of knowledge and has served as the standard of authoritative journalism for its readership throughout the twentieth century.[1] In 2014, *The Times* developed its own digital archive, the aptly named TimesMachine, which was designed to be a utopia of digital newspaper archives and includes high-quality, full-page scans of its entire published body of work from 1851 to 2002.[2] Keyword searchable, creatively contextualized, and empirically rich, the TimesMachine and its unique immersive interface is

---

[1] For the sake of brevity, *The New York Times* is also referred to as *The Times* in this text.
[2] Jane Cotler and Evan Sandhaus, "How to Build a TimesMachine," The New York Times Open Blog, February 1, 2016 (archived), accessed April 13, 2023, https://open.blogs.nytimes.com/2016/02/01/how-to-build-a-timesmachine/. The TimesMachine is not a public archive but is accessible to subscribers of the *New York Times*, including academic institutions.

Open Access. © 2023 the author(s), published by De Gruyter. This work is licensed under the Creative Commons Attribution-NonCommercial-NoDerivatives 4.0 International License.
https://doi.org/10.1515/9783111078038-006

indicative of how digitization has shifted the outer bounds of what is possible for historians.³

However, while offering wide-ranging opportunities for research, untangling the forms and circulation of ideas through the prism of this digital database requires care and attention to the historical and material context of the newspaper as a cultural artifact. The value of newspapers as historical source materials is clearly established, owing to their rich historical context and unique periodicity, which makes them ideal for researching social continuity and change.⁴ However, as digitization continues to develop more user-friendly interfaces, the question still remains: how should historians best grapple with digital newspaper archives such as the TimesMachine, which aim to replicate the material experience of the newspaper within an abstracted digital space? There is a widely felt need to develop more historically informed understandings of digitized newspapers and to set standards to help researchers overcome both technical and philosophical challenges in digital archives.⁵

Scholarly debates concerning the digitization of newspapers and the ensuing implications of digitalization on historical research have kept pace with the proliferation of digital sources and archives over the last decade. The most consequential discussions for historians have concerned the impacts of source abundance and mass digitalization on the craft of history,⁶ the need for historians to develop

---

3 David Larsson Heidenblad, "The Emergence of Environmental Journalism in 1960s Sweden: Methodological Reflections on Working with Digitized Newspapers," in *Histories of Knowledge in Post-War Scandinavia: Actors, Arenas, and Aspirations*, ed. Johan Östling, Niklas Olsen, and David Larsson Heidenblad (London: Routledge, Open Access, 2020), 59.
4 Bob Nicholson, "The Digital Turn: Exploring the Methodological Possibilities of Digital Newspaper Archives," *Media History* 19, no. 1 (2013): 59–73, accessed April 13, 2023, doi:10.1080/13688804.2012.752963; John Tosh, *The Pursuit of History: Aims, Methods and New Directions in the Study of Modern History*, 6th edition (New York: Routledge, 2015).
5 Melody Beals and Emily Bell, *The Atlas of Digitised Newspapers and Metadata: Reports from Oceanic Exchanges*. Online resource (Loughborough: Oceanic Exchanges, 2020), 1, https://doi.org/10.6084/m9.figshare.11560059.v2.
6 Just a few of the most relevant examples include Richard Abel, "The Pleasures and Perils of Big Data in Digitized Newspapers," *Film History* 25, no. 1–2 (2013): 1–10, accessed January 31, 2023, https://doi.org/10.2979/filmhistory.25.1-2.1; Andreas Fickers, "Towards a New Digital Historicism? Doing History in the Age of Abundance," *VIEW Journal of European Television History and Culture* 1, no. 1 (2012): 19–26; Sarah Van Ruyskensvelde, "Towards a History of E-ducation? Exploring the Possibilities of Digital Humanities for the History of Education," *Paedagogica Historica* 50, no. 6, (2014), accessed January 31, 2023, doi:10.1080/00309230.2014.955511; and, most recently, Estelle Bunout, Maud Ehrmann, and Frédéric Clavert, *Digitised Newspapers – A New Eldorado for Historians?: Reflections on Tools, Methods and Epistemology* (Berlin & Boston: De Gruyter Oldenbourg, 2023), accessed January 31, 2023, https://doi.org/10.1515/9783110729214.

digital literacy and, accordingly, a new kind of source criticism skills,[7] and the effects of different design features and coding methods on the quality of digital archives and sources for historical researchers.[8] Essential work has also been carried out to establish interdisciplinary baselines concerning terminology, useability, and access related to digital newspaper archives, thereby allowing researchers from different disciplines and national contexts to better communicate and collaborate on digitized newspaper research.[9] However, most of these discussions about digital newspapers and archives have occurred outside the history of knowledge research field, meaning that there are few examples of scholarship explicitly focusing on the added value (or challenges) of using digitized newspapers to explore historical structures and circulators of knowledge.

One notable exception is the work of historian of knowledge David Larsson Heidenblad, who has recently used his research on the emergence of environmental journalism in Sweden to explore which considerations must be made when working with digitized newspapers.[10] In line with other scholars, Heidenblad points to issues of decontextualization, while also highlighting the positive aspects of expanded accessibility and the possibilities offered by digitization in terms of transnational research.[11] Digital sources are increasingly being used to craft complex and diverse histories in various disciplines, and there are many examples of

---

[7] See, for example, Helle Strandgaard Jensen, "Digital Archival Literacy for (All) Historians," *Media History* 27, no. 2 (2021): 251–265, accessed April 12, 2023, doi:10.1080/13688804.2020.1779047; Jon C. Giullian, "'Seans Chernoi Magii Na Taganke': The Hunt for Master and Margarita in the Pravda Digital Archive," *Slavic & East European Information Resources* 14, no. 2–3 (April 1, 2013): 102–126, accessed January 31, 2023, https://doi.org/10.1080/15228886.2013.813374; and Tim Hitchcock, "Confronting the Digital," *Cultural and Social History* 10, no. 1 (2013), doi:10.2752/147800413X13515292098070.
[8] Two of the most recent and relevant works are those of Sarah Oberbichler et al., "Integrated Interdisciplinary Workflows for Research on Historical Newspapers: Perspectives from Humanities Scholars, Computer Scientists, and Librarians," *Journal of the Association for Information Science and Technology* 73, no. 2 (February 2022): 225–239, accessed January 31, 2023, https://doi.org/10.1002/asi.24565; and Maud Ehrmann, "Historical Newspaper User Interfaces: A Review," Athens, Greece: IFLA (2019), accessed January 31, 2023, http://library.ifla.org/2578/.
[9] See, for example, Beals and Bell, *Atlas of Digitised Newspapers*; Lara Putnam, "The Transnational and the Text-Searchable: Digitized Sources and the Shadows They Cast," *The American Historical Review* 121 (2016): 377–402, accessed January 31, 2023, doi:10.1093/ahr/121.2.377; and Benjamin Charles Germain Lee et al., "The Newspaper Navigator Dataset: Extracting and Analyzing Visual Content from 16 Million Historic Newspaper Pages in Chronicling America," Cornell University [Cs] (May 2020), accessed January 31, 2023, http://arxiv.org/abs/2005.01583.
[10] Heidenblad, "Environmental Journalism."
[11] Ibid., 68–69.

quality research predicated on the analysis of historical, digitized newspapers.[12] However, unlike in digital history circles, where questions of digitization are frequently debated and circulated, most of these studies typically lack methodological reflections on the differences between material and digital newspapers in historical analyses.[13] Researchers are familiar with the challenges of digitization in general. However, it is valuable to explore these challenges within the specific space of the TimesMachine digital archive, which has not previously received a great deal of attention in academic circles.

In this article, I use empirical findings from my research into the history of post-war education news coverage to make a new contribution to the broader methodological discussions on digital source materials in the history of knowledge. Integrating concepts and methods from the history of knowledge into this project has allowed me to develop new perspectives on education news as a broad political, social, and cultural phenomenon. Particularly the notions of knowledge actors and circulation have allowed me to center *The New York Times* as a historical actor and arena of contestation that has set the limits on the circulation of knowledge about education for millions of readers throughout the twentieth century.[14] This type of in-depth institutional and historical research has been enabled by mass digitization, but there are drawbacks that need to be addressed.

The unique context and character of *The Times*, as it exists in the TimesMachine digital archive, is used as a case study to explore the potential and limita-

---

[12] A short selection of examples in different disciplines and national contexts include Jennifer L. Cohen, "Teachers in the News: A Critical Analysis of One US Newspaper's Discourse on Education, 2006–2007," *Discourse: Studies in the Cultural Politics of Education* 31, no. 1 (February 2010), 105–119, accessed January 31, 2023, https://doi.org/10.1080/01596300903465450; Joakim Landahl, "De-Scandalisation and International Assessments: The Reception of IEA Surveys in Sweden during the 1970s," *Globalisation, Societies and Education* 16, no. 5 (October 20, 2018): 566–576, accessed January 31, 2023, https://doi.org/10.1080/14767724.2018.1531235; Jani Marjanen et al., "A National Public Sphere? Analysing the Language, Location and Form of Newspapers in Finland, 1771–1917," *Journal of European Periodical Studies* 4, no. 1 (30 June 2019): 54–77; and Archie Thomas, Andrew Jakubowicz, and Heidi Norman, *Does the Media Fail Aboriginal Political Aspirations? 45 Years of News Media Reporting of Key Political Moments* (Chicago: Aboriginal Studies Press, 2021).

[13] See Alexandra Chassanoff, "Historians and the Use of Primary Source Materials in the Digital Age," *The American Archivist* 76, no. 2 (2013): 458–480, https://americanarchivist.org/doi/10.17723/aarc.76.2.1h76217m2m376n28; Donghee Sinn and Nicholas Soares, "Historians' Use of Digital Archival Collections: The Web, Historical Scholarship, and Archival Research," *Journal of the Association for Information Science and Technology* 65, no. 9: 1794–1809, https://asistdl.onlinelibrary.wiley.com/doi/full/10.1002/asi.23091.

[14] Based on the conceptualizations outlined in Johan Östling and David Larsson Heidenblad, "Fulfilling the Promise of the History of Knowledge: Key Approaches for the 2020s," *Journal for the History of Knowledge* 1, no. 1 (2020): 2, accessed January 31, 2023, https://doi.org/10.5334/jhk.24.

tions of analyzing digitized newspapers as sources of knowledge. This exploration is organized in four parts: first, I introduce *The New York Times* newspaper and its history in the post-war era. This section focuses, in particular, on how the newspaper viewed and structured itself and how its practices shaped a distinct reality and knowledge (about education). Second, I delve into the institutional, technical, and user-oriented aspects of the TimesMachine to explain how the medium of digital archives affects what researchers may find and perceive about the past.[15] I also focus on the archive's efforts to overcome common methodological limitations, particularly concerning historical and material contextualization, that came with previous digital newspaper archives.[16] While the design of the TimesMachine certainly addresses some of these issues, in the third section, I look more closely at which research prospects are still limited and how certain gaps between the digital and analog forms of the newspaper persist. Finally, in the fourth section, I present examples of how recentering the materiality of the newspaper in the archive can help researchers better navigate the fog of digitization. This article concludes with a discussion on how the case of the TimesMachine further illustrates the possibilities and limitations historians must grapple with when using digital newspapers and archives as sources of knowledge.

The New York Times as a Producer of Knowledge (about Education)

No newspaper in the United States has sought to establish itself with as much authority and influence in the lives of its readers as *The New York Times*. The very phrase used to describe an authoritative newspaper with a wide reach, "a newspaper of record," was actually created by *The Times* to describe itself, thus perpetually intertwining its practices and image with notions of objective, authoritative reporting.[17] While *The Times* is still an active and influential newspaper, many aspects of its organization, printing structure, leadership, and format have changed since the 1990s. This section explicitly concerns *The New York Times* during the

---

15 Inspired by Jensen's conceptualization of the archive, as elaborated in Jensen, "Digital Archival Literacy," 253, 257. Jensen equates the (digital) archive to other mediums of communication (e.g., radio or websites) as they channel cultural production (collections) in similar ways. A key thing to remember in the context of digital archives is the cybertechnical infrastructure, absent from analog archives, which mediates all interactions with users and the items they contain.
16 Nicholson, "Digital Turn," 60.
17 "The Newspaper of Record," Advertisement, *The New York Times*, October 26, 1924, p. S5, col. 5.

post-war era (1945–1990) and describes the character and nature of the paper as it is preserved in the TimesMachine, based on primary and secondary sources.

For most of its history, *The New York Times* provided daily local, national, and international news coverage to a predominantly middle-to-upper class readership, not only in the densely populated tri-state area (New York-New Jersey-Connecticut) or the metropolitan United States, but also across the globe.[18] Founded in 1851 and led by the Ochs-Sulzberger family since 1896, *The Times* has been described as "the fullest, most expensive daily record of history compiled by man," while the journalists responsible for the stories strewn across its grey pages "left their fingerprints on the first drafts of history."[19] Arguably, no other paper possessed comparable resources, esteem, or influence during the twentieth century, and certainly not in the post-war era: when *The Times* spoke, even the chancellors of Europe and the Kremlin took notice.[20] Every evening, hundreds of thousands of copies were printed and flown to all reaches of the world, and other major news outlets such as the Associated Press, Reuters, Agence France-Presse, and TASS would be transmitting chief dispatches by *The Times* by wireless and satellite before copies even hit the shelves.[21]

Its expansive staff and budget meant that *The New York Times* was always ready for the "next Titanic," and it would frequently send reporters to follow up on major stories weeks, months, or even years after an initial story broke.[22] *Timesmen*, a popular nickname for its journalists, strove for an almost "sociological" approach to news coverage, seeking to avoid sensational tabloid stories by framing their news coverage as investigative and authoritative.[23] While some Timesmen were credited with bylines during the twentieth century, a majority of stories in *The Times* were anonymous, reinforcing the illusion that the Grey Lady, not the journalists, was the one responsible for bringing knowledge of the world to its readership.[24] This notion was also reinforced by the paper's visuals, as its reserved

---

[18] Harrison Salisbury, *Without Fear or Favor: The New York Times and Its Times* (New York: Times Books, 1980), 4–5.
[19] Meyer Berger, "The Gray Lady Reaches 100," *Life Magazine*, September 17, 1951, 153; Seth Mnookin, *Hard News: The Scandals at The New York Times and Their Meaning for American Media* (New York: Random House, 2004), 4.
[20] Mnookin, *Hard News*, 4.
[21] Ibid.
[22] Ibid., 10–14; Edwin Diamond, *Behind the Times: Inside The New York Times* (Chicago: University of Chicago Press, 1994), 12.
[23] Diamond, *Behind the Times*, 11–12.
[24] Robert D. McFadden, "150th Anniversary: 1851–2001; 150 and Counting: The Story So Far," *The New York Times*, November 14, 2001, accessed January 30, 2023, https://www.nytimes.com/2001/11/14/news/150th-anniversary-1851-2001-150-and-counting-the-story-so-far.html.

use of large headlines and photo layouts presented an orderly, structured world for readers and became the standard by which the relative importance of events was judged.[25]

During the twentieth century, *The Times* was published in two formats: the *daily edition*, a two-section newspaper published Monday through Saturday, which ranged from 40 to 80 pages in length, and the *Sunday edition*, a multi-sectional news behemoth filled with upwards of 300 pages of content. The Sunday paper was perhaps the most prestigious, with its own dedicated executive editor and section-specific team of editors specializing in subjects such as Business and Finance, Travel, Local News, and Education. Besides extended news coverage, the extra volume on Sundays can also be attributed to the addition of *The New York Times Magazine, The New York Times Review of Books*, and extra advertising. The Sunday editor of *The Times* operated independently from the weekday managing editor up until the 1970s, meaning that news decisions made Monday through Saturday were different and often disjointed from the news decisions made for the Sunday edition.[26]

Counterintuitively, the presence of special sections on Sundays may actually have limited the circulation of knowledge and ideas regarding these subjects. Having a dedicated section on education in *The Times* provided the education editor with space for in-depth, nuanced coverage of education issues, but that education section only occupied half a page in the fourth section (Review of the Week) of the three-hundred-page newspaper. This means that most casual readers would likely not have encountered this education news section unless they intentionally sought it out. This demonstrates how the reach of certain policy and social ideas was often dependent on the placement of stories and topics within the paper.[27]

With the exception of a few months of strikes during the 1960s and 1970s, *The Times* has been shaping the contours of a *mediated* world for readers on a daily basis throughout the twentieth century. Mediated in this context refers to the power of the newspaper in communicating knowledge and information to readers, not only through the literal information it shares but also through the specific medium and prism of newsprint. Think here of media theorist Marshall McLuhan's assertion in media studies that "the medium is the message," as the material and cultural elements of a media artifact (newspaper) also influence the messages it aims to communicate.[28] Certainly at least since being purchased by Adolph Ochs

---

25 Ibid.
26 Mnookin, *Hard News*, 13.
27 Allen Bell, *The Language of News Media* (New Jersey: Wiley-Blackwell, 1991), 14.
28 Marshall McLuhan, "The Medium is the Message," in *Understanding Media: The Extensions of Man* (New York: McGraw Hill, 1964).

in 1896, *The New York Times* has been conscious of its image and influence on the worldview of its readers. Ochs and his daughter Iphigene would often share an anecdote with their staff about stonecutters and cathedral builders, which exemplifies the mentality of the newspaper: *The Times* does not employ stonecutters, who produce generic news stories with little care regarding their potential; *The Times* hires cathedral builders, who see their journalistic work as contributing to something greater, to building the kingdom of news and public knowledge that is *The New York Times*.[29] So, naturally, when the time came to digitize their newspaper archive, *The Times* "set out to reimagine the archive browsing experience" by developing an immersive, "more sophisticated" digital archive: the TimesMachine.[30]

What Can You Do with a TimesMachine? Exploring the Digitized Past

Until the creation of the online version of the newspaper in 1995, *The New York Times* was only available in print. As most text-based historical sources, archived editions could be found in select libraries and archives, mostly on microfilm.[31] The first version of the digital TimesMachine was launched in 2008 and consisted of full-page PDF scans spanning from 1851 to 1922.[32] Its launch coincided with the creation of many early digital newspaper archives, including the British Library of 19th Century Newspapers, Chronicling America, Hemeroteca Nacional Digital de México, and Delpher.[33] Sensing the limitations of full-page PDFs, notably the large file size and lack of internal metadata for keyword searches, the archive was redesigned in 2014 to expand its collection and improve the existing online interface.

---

[29] Gay Talese, *The Kingdom and the Power: Behind the Scenes at The New York Times: The Institution That Influences the World* (New York: Random House, 2007), 15–16.

[30] Evan Sandhaus, "Introducing the New TimesMachine," The New York Times Open Team Blog, July 11, 2013, accessed March 11, 2023, https://open.nytimes.com/introducing-the-new-timesmachine-e4686183261f

[31] Microfilm is obviously a different carrier medium involving different methodological and analytical challenges, even though it is not all that different from the initial full-page digital scans of *The New York Times* characterizing its first foray into digital archiving. An excellent overview of the history of microfilm and its challenges can be found in Ian Milligan, *The Transformation of Historical Research in the Digital Age* (Cambridge: Cambridge University Press, 2022). doi:10.1017/9781009026055.

[32] Cotler and Sandhaus, "How to Build a TimesMachine."

[33] Ten of these large-scale digital newspaper archives created between 2000 and 2012 are explored and analyzed in depth in Beals and Bell's *The Atlas of Digitised Newspapers and Metadata*.

Demonstrating its persistent ambition to establish itself at the forefront of journalism, *The Times* adopted a new method of structuring digital newspaper archives. By employing image tiling strategies from digital mapping software and combining this mapping with optical character recognition (OCR), the TimesMachine is able to display full-page, browsable scans of their newspapers in a keyword-searchable, but also page-turnable, interface.[34] This page-turning ability and full newspaper visualization features are what set the TimesMachine apart from other digital newspaper archives that typically retrieve individual articles and (unavoidably) conceal the context of the surrounding issue to which they belong.[35] The archive's interactive design sought to remove the barriers between users and the digitized newspaper by replicating the experience of holding a newspaper as close as the web permits, leveraging a vast collection of scanned images and metadata with accessibility and a user-friendly organization.[36] This immersive archive of 12.8 million articles and 4.1 million pages visually exemplifies the size and reach of *The Times* as a producer of knowledge.[37]

Perhaps the most relevant aspect for historians, however, is that the TimesMachine is intentionally structured to address a problem frequently plaguing (digital) archives: a lack of context.[38] Newspaper archives are often made up of scanned clippings or individual pages of newspapers, which are then retrieved for users via a search tool. As a result, the sources are presented as suspended in this digital space, stretched beyond the historical and material context in which they first appeared. For example, a researcher using keywords to search for information on Cold War student movements might find a front page story in the TimesMachine about the brutal suppression of student protestors by Warsaw police on October 5, 1957.[39] However, a contemporary reader absorbed in the newspaper that morning would have been considerably more interested in the headline story that the Soviet Union had successfully launched Sputnik, the first man-made satellite, into outer

---

[34] Both Google Books and the Barney Newspaper Collection from Gale use a combination of geographic mapping, image location, and OCR to enhance the user experience, although they stop short of replicating the experience of reading a physical book or newspaper in their software design.
[35] Ehrmann, Bunout, and Clavert, "Digitised Historical Newspapers," 4.
[36] Cotler and Sandhaus, "How to Build a TimesMachine."
[37] Ibid. and Salisbury, *Without Fear*, 5–8. The archive has not had a major update in terms of content since 2014, because articles written post-2002 are retrievable as archived webpages on NYtimes.com where the online version of the paper has appeared since 1996.
[38] Colter and Sandhaus, "How to Build a TimesMachine" and Sandhaus, "Introducing the New TimesMachine."
[39] Sydney Gruson, "Warsaw Crushes New Protest; Clubs, Tear Gas Rout Students," *The New York Times*, October 5, 1957.

space.⁴⁰ Knowing where the article on student protestors appeared (the bottom right of the front page), as well as what else occurred that day makes the source far more valuable to a historian, as it allows for the analysis of an article's content as well as the reach and social importance of that knowledge to contemporary readers in its time.

As with most digital databases, TimesMachine employs a digital search and retrieval engine based on OCR that prompts users to enter keywords to explore the collection. Keywords in the TimesMachine are words serving as categorical identifiers, which then link to relevant articles, headlines, and letters to the editor published between 1851 and 2002. A keyword may represent different subjects, people, and locations, depending on what the researcher is trying to find. A conceptual historian, for example, could use a particular concept such as "mediocrity" or "intelligence" as a keyword to trace its use and development in the news.⁴¹ Researchers interested in historical actors or networks can use names of individuals and institutions, such as "John F. Kennedy," "Ford Foundation," or "Harvard University," while historians hoping to follow the news coverage of particular regions can use the names of cities, states, and countries to gather comprehensive coverage from these regions at different times. However, it is not possible to search for articles written by specific journalists, which represents a major limitation of the archive for those hoping to research journalists as historical actors in the production of knowledge.

Most researchers want to follow the news coverage of a particular historical event or phenomenon and see those events in their original context, which is not always easy to synthesize into a single keyword. The TimesMachine search interface makes it possible to conduct searches with slightly more nuance and focus. These include allowing users to (1) simultaneously search multiple keywords, (2) delineate the time period of the search from one day of news coverage to news coverage spanning multiple years, and (3) add another layer of depth by keyword and category searches *within* each individual newspaper. While the collection search tool is not compatible with Boolean operators, it does allow for a combined search of keywords, names, and locations that might appear together, separated by

---

40 Walter Sullivan and William J. Jorden, "Soviet Fires Earth Satellite into Space; It is Circling the Globe at 18,000 M.P.H; Sphere Tracked in 4 Crossings Over U.S.," *The New York Times*, October 5, 1957.

41 Such an approach was employed in a recent article by Chelsea A. Rodriguez and Sarah Van Ruyskensvelde, "A Rising Tide of Discontent: Mediocrity, Meritocracy, and Neoliberalism in American Education, 1971–1983," *Paedagogica Historica* (2021), April 13, 2023, doi:10.1080/00309230.2021.1999276.

a semicolon.[42] The timespan of these searches can be set by the users, allowing them to search for keywords that appear on a particular day, or within any month, year, or number of years over the one-hundred-and-fifty-year span of content. While keyword searches and time-delineation do not constitute features unique to the TimesMachine, the multi-level organization and individual indexing of newspapers allow researchers to explore the continuity and change of social ideas, concepts, and policies more easily.

In a recently published study, I employed these methods of keyword cross-referencing and time setting together to trace the development of "mediocrity" as an educational concept in *The Times*. To trace the evolution of "mediocrity" leading up to the release of *A Nation at Risk*,[43] which warned of a "rising tide of mediocrity" in American schools, I had to collect every article using this concept to discuss U.S.-American education in *The Times* between 1971 and April 27, 1983.[44] Using the keyword "education" resulted in 71,652 articles in this time period, while "mediocrity" resulted in 958 hits. However, when combining "education" and "mediocrity," the collection whittled down to 187 results, a manageable amount for analysis. Close reading was still required to identify whether the categorization of education matched the research criteria for education news coverage, but these search features enabled me to easily collect source materials demonstrating how the concept developed as it moved between different school debates and policy discussions.[45] Keyword searches and delineating time periods are ubiquitous features in digital newspaper archives; however, this case illustrates how the mass digitization of newspapers has changed the ways in which we can apply mixed methods approaches in qualitative and quantitative analyses.

Perhaps the most crucial feature for researchers is that each daily paper in the TimesMachine is also individually indexed and searchable, a feature that is absent from most other digital newspaper archives. Users can use their own keywords to search the whole collection, but each digitized newspaper also contains an index with pre-coded categories created by the digital archivists. This allows readers to

---

42 Boolean operators are commonly used conjunctions (such as AND, OR, or NOT) used as directives to combine or exclude keywords in a search, thereby resulting in more focused and productive search results in digital archives and databases.
43 *A Nation at Risk: The Imperative for Educational Reform* (1983) was a report by the United States National Commission on Excellence in Education. Among other things, the report contributed to a discourse that American schools were failing and falling behind international competitors in terms of academic achievement and supremacy. While highly controversial and rhetorically charged, it set off a wave of local, state, and federal reform efforts that shaped education as we know it in the contemporary United States.
44 Rodriguez and Van Ruyskensvelde, "A Rising Tide," 4.
45 Ibid., 17.

quickly find important topics, individuals, and stories without having to manually read each page.[46] Having pre-set as well as custom keyword searches caters to both casual users of the archive and experienced researchers seeking more control in the search process.[47] The presence of multi-level organization in the archive may not seem all that groundbreaking, but for as-of-yet indiscernible reasons, there are often inconsistencies between what you can find using a whole-collection search and a within-paper search.[48] Within-paper keyword searches allow researchers to collect articles that are more relevant and contextualized to their needs.[49]

Each individual newspaper index is typically organized into five pre-set categories: *People, Organizations, Creative works, Places,* and *Descriptors. People* includes all named individuals appearing in an article in the paper. *Organizations* includes a broad range of collective groupings such as universities, businesses, non-profit organizations, government agencies, and more social categories, such as the use of "Negroes" as an organization throughout the 1950s and 1960s.[50] *Creative works* organizes all content related to the arts and creative expression, while *Places* lists all news by the locations discussed in the articles, ranging from local towns to nations across the globe. Finally, *Descriptors* refer to a range of concepts and categories, from "Education and Schools," to "Deaths" and relevant current events such as "The Presidential Election." These pre-determined categories are hyperlinked, thus making it easy for the user to jump to the results in the paper and see the stories in their original contexts. The results in these five categories are sorted first by prevalence in the paper and then alphabetically. For example, on Wednesday, May 6, 1970, the index for that day's paper reads as follows:

---

[46] As with many other archives, digital or otherwise, the methods used by the designers of the archive to create and organize these categories have not been disclosed.

[47] Adam Crymble, "Digital Library Search Preferences amongst Historians and Genealogists: British History Online User Survey" 10, no. 4 (2016), accessed January 31, 2023, http://www.digitalhumanities.org/dhq/vol/10/4/000270/000270.html.

[48] Perhaps the sheer volume of content and inconsistencies in metadata is to blame, but as a researcher, I have experienced these lapses and disconnections firsthand.

[49] It should be noted, however, that the within-paper indexes and keyword searches are also imperfect. For example, stories about certain universities or schools may not appear in a keyword search of "university" but will appear in the indexed categories as a specific organization (e.g., Kent State University).

[50] It is unclear how the index terms and categories were created in the archive. The use of now antiquated concepts as indexed categories suggests that, whether by AI or manual categorization, they were likely categorized based on terms and vocabulary originating from the historical newspapers themselves.

Index

Wednesday, May 6, 1970   See All

PEOPLE

Dickens, Charles John Huffam	2
Nixon, Richard Milhous	2
Abelson, Philip H	1
Alioto, Joseph L	1
Bauer, Yehuda	1

ORGANIZATIONS

Democratic Party	5
Kent State University	5
Congress	3
Black Panther Party	2
General Motors Corp.	2

CREATIVE WORKS

Chairs, The	1
Cherry Orchard, The	1
Endgame	1
Jeune Fille A Marier, La	1
Lacune, La	1

PLACES

United States	37
Vietnam	24
Cambodia	21
Cambodian Border Area	12
New York City	9

Continued

Index	
Wednesday, May 6, 1970	See All

DESCRIPTORS	
General Policies of Belligerents, Other Major Powers	18
Military Action	14
Deaths	13
Elections	10
Editorials	6

Even without any prior knowledge of U.S.-American history in this time period, the index presents the user with an inclination as to the dominant mood and most pressing concerns for readers. Someone familiar with this period in U.S.-American history would instantly recognize the links between the pre-selected categories: two days prior to the printing of this newspaper, four college students were killed by the U.S. National Guard at *Kent State University* while protesting the recent invasion of *Cambodia* by the *U.S. Military*, an action approved by newly elected *President Richard Nixon* as part of the ongoing *Vietnam War*. Thus, with some additional contextual knowledge, historians and researchers can with relative ease navigate the coverage of the events that shaped modern history.

Limitations of the Digital Space

While TimesMachine offers many possibilities for researchers, there are certainly noteworthy limitations. Some pitfalls include the limited reach and reliability of keyword searches, as well as the lack of transparency regarding why only certain editions of the paper are accessible in the archive. While these limitations do impact research in the TimesMachine in particular ways, they represent common limitations found in a majority of (digital) archives.[51] A more unique limitation is the lack of metadata for advertisements in the TimesMachine, which makes it difficult or nearly impossible to conduct research into advertisements as sources of knowledge.

---

51 Ehrmann, "Historical Newspaper User Interfaces," 15.

Keyword searches have limitations that most researchers are sorely aware of, as complex concepts cannot easily be distilled into searchable keywords and researchers must be creative and resourceful in how they choose their search terms. On top of this, while digital archives and search engines make it easier to mine data, the vast amount of data collected with keywords also makes it more difficult to frame and interpret this data and use it to write history.[52] For example, conducting a keyword search in the TimesMachine for all articles containing the keyword of "education" in the year 1957 will garner 5,723 results; yet, if you search for the keyword "school" in the same period, it garners over 15,000 results. Both concepts have multiple meanings and definitions, and AI or OCR systems cannot employ deductive reasoning or have a sense of what the researcher is searching for or hoping to find.[53] The search algorithm cannot differentiate between the subjective conceptual meaning and definitions of keywords, which is where the researcher must always come in.

Choosing the right keywords often requires researchers to possess perseverance and creativity, as well as an intimate knowledge of the culture and texts being studied.[54] It also requires researchers to distill the subject of their inquiry into a number of smaller, focused keywords to whittle down the thousands of hits and comb through the results by means of close reading: not a groundbreaking method, perhaps, but an effective one. Exactly how the metadata connects articles, categories, and keywords together in the TimesMachine is not public information. As with all archives (digital and otherwise), researchers are at the mercy of the unseen choices of these coders and archivists.[55] This means that we even more

---

[52] Abel, "Pleasures and Perils," 10.

[53] The strengths and limitations of AI and OCR, particularly with regard to how their algorithms impact the presentation of archival materials, are increasingly discussed in the fields of digital history and archival research. One notable example of this scholarship is that of Gregory Rolan et al., "More Human Than Human? Artificial Intelligence in the Archive," *Archives & Manuscripts* 47, no. 2 (2018): 179–203, https://doi.org/10.1080/01576895.2018.1502088.

[54] Adrian Bingham, "The Digitization of Newspaper Archives: Opportunities and Challenges for Historians," *Twentieth Century British History* 21 (2010): 231, as cited in Nicholson, "Digital Turn," 67.

[55] The mass digitization of source materials still does not resolve the issue that archives are curated, not just collected. They are comprised of artifacts and knowledge having been compiled through the choices of archivists motivated by professional, but also cultural and national inclinations. This means that minority voices and experiences are often silenced in archives, digital or otherwise, as explained in Rodney G. S. Carter, "Of Things Said and Unsaid: Power, Archival Silences, and Power in Silence," *Archivaria* 61 (September, 2006): 215–233, accessed January 31, 2023, https://archivaria.ca/index.php/archivaria/article/view/12541.

so need to recenter the material aspects of newspapers that persevere in and inform the digitized versions we grapple with.

Another major limitation is the lack of transparency as to which editions of the newspaper are actually included in the TimesMachine. Besides the daily and Sunday versions of the paper, *The New York Times* was also printed in different editions depending on its target audience, including the New Jersey Edition, the Tri-State Edition, and the most-circulated City Edition. Researchers can determine which edition they are reading in the TimesMachine by going to the front page of the paper and looking to the top right corner of the masthead, once again reiterating the value and importance of full-page scans. When using the digital archive, it is important to be aware of these different editions as the TimesMachine primarily includes scans of the Late City Edition.[56] Crucially, the Late City Edition is the de facto version of the paper, but the "Late" indicates that additional news updates or edits have been made to the paper after the initial printing and distribution.

Until the printing process was expedited at the end of the twentieth century, each edition of *The Times* was finalized and approved for printing at 6 pm the night before and distributed to newsstands by 4 am the next morning. If something major happened in the meantime, or if a mistake was found by an editor or journalist post-printing, they were added or fixed in the Late City Edition, which was printed and distributed later in the day. It is not possible to compare the different editions of the newspaper using the TimesMachine, as it typically only displays one copy of the paper for each day. Sometimes, the only edition available in the TimesMachine on a given day is an even more limited edition of the paper, such as the short-lived Western Edition (1962–1964) or the International Edition (1946–1967). This subtle but important decision to prioritize the Late City Edition in the archive to an even greater extent means that users are not really seeing the newspaper as it was originally experienced by its initial audience, an important consideration to keep in mind when using these digitized newspapers as windows to the past. These possible differences between the versions of these newspapers that have been digitized (and those that have not) can have major implications on the type of information you can glean from them.[57]

It matters which newspaper edition the article came from because the content of some articles changed depending on the edition and its target audience. For example, on December 18, 1975, *The Times* ran a three-column story in the middle of

---

[56] The masthead is the heading on the front page of the newspaper. *The New York Times* masthead features the name of the paper at the center top and is flanked by the paper's motto "All the News that's Fit to Print" on the left, and edition and daily weather information on the right.

[57] As explained in the research saga detailed by Jon C. Giullian in "Seans Chernoi Magii Na Taganke."

the Late City Edition titled "More New Jersey Parents Are Sending Children to Private Schools in the City." The scoop focused on some of the more prominent private schools in New York City, and the financial and time sacrifices New Jersey parents were making to help their children escape the "mediocrity" of their local public schools. However, the story changed when it appeared in the New Jersey City Edition, where it appeared on the front page at greater length, with a more negative tone, and more quotes from parents and evidence of failing local schools. While this certainly made it more attention-grabbing for the specific audience the story covered, the New Jersey version was likely seen by far fewer readers than the City or Late City editions.

Finally, advertising in the *New York Times* is not retrievable in the TimesMachine digital archive. When the archive was first launched, its developers assured that advertisements would be just as "legible, linkable, and shareable" as all other content in the archive.[58] However, the combination of different typefaces, complicated layouts, and the difficulty of algorithmically differentiating advertisements were later cited by *The Times* as reasons for the lack of metadata regarding advertisements.[59] This exclusion is significant, as a large number of ads in the paper were actually text-based, and special interest groups such as labor unions, political parties, and education associations often paid for advertised columns in order to target policy messaging to readers.[60] While they are visually similar to news stories and columns in the newspaper, these columns are classified in the same way as the more image-based (perhaps stereotypical) advertisements for travel, fashion, and food products. Crucially, these advertisements are not simply passive, isolated sources; readers often engaged in a dialogue with these targeted advertisements via letters to the editor, and those responses are findable via the keyword search tool.[61]

For example, Albert Shanker of the American Federation of Teachers (AFT) wrote an advertisement column "Where We Stand" in *The New York Times* for 27 years, offering "800 words of common sense, keen analysis and no-nonsense ideas about how to improve schools."[62] This column, classified as an advertisement

---

58 Sandhaus, "Introducing the New TimesMachine."
59 Ibid., also because the OCR used by the TimesMachine is not able to attribute metadata to images.
60 The exclusion of metadata for these paid columns might be due to the fact that the TimesMachine archive focuses on cataloguing content of which *The Times* takes ownership. Paid advertising content, while it did appear in the original paper, might be subject to different copyright rules.
61 Rodriguez and Van Ruyskensvelde, "A Rising Tide," 15.
62 Albert Shanker Institute, "Where We Stand," Archives Online, accessed January 30, 2023, https://www.shankerinstitute.org/resource/where-we-stand-archives-online. However, it should be noted that while this archive seems to exist, efforts by the researcher to access it were not successful.

since the AFT paid for this space in the paper, was frequently commented on by readers and generated a wealth of debate in the letters to the editor section of the paper over school privatization and teacher pay.[63] These letters allow researchers interested in these columns to track down the original advertisements, as the readers always refer to the date on which the original column appeared in their response. But, without a response letter, these advertisements can only be found by manually flipping through the digital pages week-by-week. *The Times* did develop a crowd-sourced archive of their advertisements called Madison, named after the famous avenue in New York City where a majority of advertising agencies have their offices.[64] However, for unclear reasons, Madison is no longer accessible to users, which means that researchers interested in the history and knowledge-producing potential of advertisements in *The Times* are essentially limited to manually searching page by page.

Making the Most of the Material: Recentering Context in the TimesMachine

If these digital limitations still persist, even in an archive designed to close the gap between digital and material, how then can we still make the most of databases like the TimesMachine? Here, I propose adopting a methodological approach to digital newspaper analysis that recenters the material aspects of the newspaper. I previously mentioned the Warsaw student protests and the Sputnik satellite launch, both of which made front page news on October 5, 1957. Both stories were newsworthy and touched upon similar Cold War anxieties, but their differing placement reveals a material aspect of newspapers that is often neglected or obscured in digital archives: the values and business motivations informing their placement.

When interpreting the knowledge produced by newspapers such as *The Times*, the placement of a story matters just as much as its content, if not more. Placement is a deliberate choice by the editor, and the location of a story within the paper can give us an indication of the perceived relevance and importance of a story to readers in comparison to other events. "News values," the often unspoken theoretical values in journalism that determine the newsworthiness of an event, can help researchers understand the mechanisms through which such news stories were

---

[63] Rodriguez and Van Ruyskensvelde, "A Rising Tide," 15.
[64] "Madison," *NYT R&D, The New York Times,* 2015, accessed April 11, 2023. https://nytlabs.com/projects/madison.html.

often selected, placed, and emphasized depending on how the audience's perception and the publisher's motivations intertwined.[65] The *proximity* of a story to readers, the *consonance* of the topic with their values and beliefs, and the *recency* of the event are just a few examples of news values that influence where a story will likely appear within a paper.

Beyond news values and wanting to publish impactful news, *The Times* (just like other newspapers) is a business, and its front page was designed to entice customers and sell copies to fund its expansive news empire. This means that news and market values greatly influenced the placement of stories, particularly the ones appearing on the front page. Here, however, we encounter another crucial material aspect of the newspaper that gets lost with digitization: how it *folds*. In the TimesMachine, users are presented with the full span of the front page in all its glory, but, crucially, in its *unfolded* glory. Readers in the past did not receive their newspaper this way, and while it may seem like a small distinction, it is a clear example of how digitization can change what we see and how we see our source materials.

It is important to remember how our sources were actually used and functioned in their context, particularly when researching the circulation of knowledge. When the morning copies of *The Times* arrived at the newsstand, they were stacked and displayed folded in half. Copies of the paper delivered to suburban doorsteps came similarly folded in half and rolled up. With this in mind, the front page of *The Times* for much of the twentieth century was organized so that the most relevant stories occupied the upper half of the front page, with the most important story typically occupying the top-right position under the masthead. That is not to say that stories appearing on the bottom half of the front page were not important – only, perhaps, less so in the eyes of the editor. We know that the student protest in Warsaw was featured on the bottom-right half of the front page on October 5, 1957, but by employing news values and material knowledge of the newspaper, it is easy to predict that the Sputnik story occupied the main headline and top-right position of the front page. Analyzing newspapers with these material inclinations in mind may sensitize researchers to the priorities of the newspaper, the values embedded in its organization, and the types of knowledge it sought to platform.[66] It further illustrates the importance of actually understanding the material context of the sources we use instead of solely relying on

---

65 Bell, *The Language*, 155–160; Michael Schudson, "The Sociology of News Production," *Media, Culture, and Society* 11 (1989): 263–265.
66 Simone Lässig, "The History of Knowledge and the Expansion of the Historical Research Agenda," *Bulletin of the GHI Washington*, no. 59 (Fall 2016): 31, accessed January 31, 2023, https://prae.-perspectivia.net/publikationen/bulletin-washington/2016-59/0029-0058.

keyword-retrieved articles. In other words, digital archives require us to focus not only on the contours of the knowledge map they present us, but also on the actual, original terrain those maps represent.[67]

In Conclusion

Above all, this case study demonstrates the value of incorporating digital history methods and perspectives into the history of knowledge and history of education. The aim of this article was to explore how historians of knowledge should best grapple with digitized historical newspapers and the archives that house them. The case of *The New York Times* TimesMachine archive was used to illustrate the possibilities and limitations of using digitized newspaper archives in historical research. There are several important takeaways from this article that can help researchers make informed methodological choices in their pursuit of history, particularly when grappling with sources such as newspapers which produce and circulate various mediated forms of knowledge.

Before entering the digital archive, it is vital to remember that every news institution has its own historical context, internal logic, actors, and values that inform its practices. Newspapers, like other institutionally produced source materials, have specific features that require researchers to zoom out and assess before zooming in on the archive. Researchers need to know if they are dealing with stonecutters or cathedral builders to better understand the sources of knowledge produced by those institutions. The TimesMachine presents searchable, full-page scans of one hundred and fifty years of news coverage and aims to recreate the experience of flipping through a newspaper to overcome the common problem of decontextualization in digital newspaper archives. The immersive interface and multi-level newspaper indexation open up a number of research possibilities for historians, but there are still distinct limitations that make some research approaches difficult to execute.

While the archive presents the contours of the newspaper as an arena of knowledge circulation and production, there are certain limitations regarding keyword searches, source selection, and advertisements. As in other digital archives, keyword searches represent an imperfect process, and the multi-level indexing of the collection still means that the researcher needs to think creatively and use historical knowledge to effectively choose keywords and navigate search results. Moreover, there is a lack of transparency regarding how the collection was

---

67 Beals and Bell, *Atlas of Digitised Newspapers*, i.

organized and which edition of the paper has been preserved. This has major implications for those trying to research the circulation of ideas in the paper, as some editions were distributed to a smaller number of readers. To alleviate these limitations, I advocate for a contextualized approach reemphasizing the material in this digital, abstracted space. Finally, advertisements, which serve as rich sources of social and cultural knowledge, are not indexed in the TimesMachine. This makes it very difficult to research advertised political columns and the circulation of political and social knowledge in advertising. However, I propose a few ways in which researchers may navigate around these limitations by cross-referencing letters to the editor that responded to certain advertisement columns. Just as is the case of traditional archives, users need to be aware of the logic of the digital archives they engage with and reflect on how digitization influences their sources and research.[68]

These findings and methods were developed in the context of a study on the history of education in the post-war era, but the integrative and generative capacity of the history of knowledge makes these approaches well-suited for studying the production of knowledge and circulation of ideas in several different news topics, themes, and contexts.[69] Similarly, while this study focuses on one unique digital archive, the main takeaways concerning how news content differed based on the days of the week, the edition of the paper, and the editor's inclinations and values are also relevant for research in all digital newspaper archives. Digital archives have undoubtedly expanded the possibilities for historians with regard to keyword searches and mass digitization, but the suspension of these newspapers in the digital space can still obscure key information on how the source material also informed the knowledge reproduced and circulated on its pages.

About the contributor

Chelsea A. Rodriguez is a PhD candidate in the history of education at the University of Groningen (Netherlands). She is interested in educational debates and the mediated communication of educational ideas in the public sphere. Her dissertation investigates the history of education news in the United States, specifically how the institution of *The New York Times* circulated particular forms of knowledge about U.S.-American education to readers during the post-war era.

---

68 Jensen, "Digital Archival Literacy," 252.
69 Östling and Heidenblad, "Fulfilling the Promise," 1; Lässig, "History of Knowledge," 32.

Elena Falco
How to Read Wikipedia: Design Choices and the Knowing Subject

Abstract: This paper describes a fruitful alliance between the fields of science and technology studies and the history of knowledge. Here, I present partial results from my ongoing research project, looking at how Wikipedia's web infrastructure operationalises epistemic values and virtues. I argue that competing epistemologies are negotiated through Wikipedia's website by coding artefacts expressing opposing ideals of testimony. The hardwired ideal, embedded from the beginning in the bones of the Wikipedia editing process, is that of a disembodied, detached, and autonomous knower. I am labelling this view the "clean channel ideal". Over time, however, members of the community have challenged this specific ideal by means of coding, by building artefacts purposefully highlighting the positionality of editors. In addition to describing this process as part of the design history of Wikipedia itself, I also relate the clean channel ideal to previous conceptions of the ideal knower, found in Ayn Rand's philosophy, and in the modern scientific subject.

Keywords: embedding epistemic values, Wikipedia epistemology, history of web design, testimony

Introduction

Objects and material culture represent crucial actors in the history of knowledge. They may serve as sources of information regarding practical, social, and tacit knowledge.[1] Objects facilitate the production and circulation of knowledge.[2] Closely related, one might argue that materiality is fundamental to all knowledge production, as knowledge is always and already situated.[3] Artefacts built to store and

---

1 Simone Lässig, "The history of knowledge and the expansion of the historical research agenda," *Bulletin of the German Historical Institute* (Fall 2016): 38.
2 Katherine M. Reinhart, "A Cyclops, a Stone, and a Four-Breasted Woman: Drawing Anatomical Knowledge," *KNOW: A Journal on the Formation of Knowledge* 6, no. 1 (1 March 2022): 47–79, https://doi.org/10.1086/718566. For some examples, see Johan Östling et al., ed., *Circulation of Knowledge: Explorations in the History of Knowledge* (Lund: Nordic Academic Press, 2018).
3 David N. Livingstone, "Keeping knowledge in site," *History of Education* 39, no. 6 (2010): 779–785, DOI: 10.1080/0046760X.2010.514343.

Open Access. © 2023 the author(s), published by De Gruyter. This work is licensed under the Creative Commons Attribution-NonCommercial-NoDerivatives 4.0 International License.
https://doi.org/10.1515/9783111078038-007

handle information are particularly important in this context: archives, for instance, embody specific ways of structuring and controlling knowledge.[4]

In this paper, I present some partial results from an ongoing project – an analysis of the English-language Wikipedia website, in the context of the community designing, using, and maintaining it. Others have interrogated Wikipedia in a similar vein, albeit with a different scope: Maria Karlsson has looked at the production of historical knowledge,[5] Maja van der Velden has analysed Wikipedia in terms of its compatibility with indigenous knowledge traditions,[6] and Heather Ford has analysed how Wikipedia's platform constrains and enables specific practices related to knowledge production.[7]

The general thrust of my work concerns analysing how the website, en.wikipedia.org, operationalises specific epistemic values. Work in science and technology studies and the philosophy of technology has shown that values may be embedded in technology.[8] Typically, these approaches concern moral, social, and political values. I extend my scope to epistemic values. In practice, this means asking which conception of knowledge and the knower is assumed through the design of Wikipedia. I take inspiration from recent work in the philosophy of technology, specifically concerning values in design relying on close readings to examine individual features of specific objects and interpreting these.[9] When this kind of philosophy of technology is applied to the production of knowledge, it often takes the form of the study of instruments.[10] Instead, I focus on a platform for the creation of knowledge.

Websites are not static. They evolve over time through updates and re-designs. In the case of Wikipedia, this process of updating is particularly complex: while the

---

4 Lässig, "History of knowledge".
5 Maria Karlsson, "Is there no one moderating Wikipedia?????," in *Forms of Knowledge: Developing the History of Knowledge*, ed. Johan Östling, David Larsson Heidenblad, and Anna Nilsson Hammar (Lund: Nordic Academic Press, 2020).
6 Maja van der Velden, "Decentering Design: Wikipedia and Indigenous Knowledge," *International Journal of Human-Computer Interaction* 29, no. 4 (2013): 308–316, https://doi.org/10.1080/10447318.2013.765768.
7 Heather Ford, *Writing the Revolution* (Cambridge, MA: MIT Press, 2022).
8 See, for instance, Langdon Winner, "Do artifacts have politics?," *Daedalus* 109, no. 1 (1980); Batya Friedman and David G. Hendry, *Value Sensitive Design* (Cambridge, MA: MIT Press, 2019).
9 See, for instance, T. E. de Wildt, I. R. van de Poel, and E. J. L. Chappin, "Tracing Long-term Value Change in (Energy) Technologies: Opportunities of Probabilistic Topic Models Using Large Data Sets," *Science, Technology, & Human Values* 47, no. 3 (2022): 429–458, https://doi.org/10.1177/01622439211054439.
10 See, for instance Davis Baird, *Thing Knowledge: A Philosophy of Scientific Instruments* (Berkeley: University of California Press, 2014) and Federica Russo, *Techno-Scientific Practices: An Informational Approach* (Lanham, MD: Rowman and Littlefield, 2022).

basic infrastructure of the website is only accessible to Wikimedia Foundation engineers, volunteers create additional coded objects and add them to the website. This additional code is known as bespoke code.[11] For the purposes of this article, Wikipedia's interface may be described as consisting of a hard-to-change bedrock of code existing below a more malleable space, the bespoke code, where interventions may occur. The different levels of intervention afforded by these two kinds of code define the space of negotiation I refer to in section 5.

My research project is interdisciplinary. I employ a mixed methodology, involving a close reading of the platform modelled on platform studies[12] and ethnographical methods involving interviews, analysing conversations, and documentation. So far, my body of data comprises 256 documents, including discussion pages, interview transcripts, technical documentation, email correspondence, branding guidelines, and primary sources on the history of Wikipedia. I have coded[13] 245 of these and performed a thematic analysis on a subset of 101.

While my overall research project is more wide-ranging, in the present paper I analyse a case study: I describe how a vision of the ideal knower and, consequently, of testimony was designed into Wikipedia's editing process and how, over time, members of the Wikipedia community have challenged this vision by means of coding. I argue that, at its core, Wikipedia's editing process embeds an ideal of the knower as autonomous, detached, and disembodied. I also argue that what I refer to as the "clean channel ideal" is rooted in the philosophy of Ayn Rand and a specific conception of the scientific subject. Over time, members of the community have challenged the clean channel ideal through interventions in the bespoke code that carry a different ideal of knower (i.e., as situated). I argue that en.wikipedia.org is a site for negotiating epistemologies while embodying a dialectic between opposing views of testimony.

---

[11] R. Stuart Geiger, "Bots, Bespoke, Code and the Materiality of Software Platforms," *Information, Communication & Society* 17, no. 3 (16 March 2014): 342–356, https://doi.org/10.1080/1369118X.2013.873069.

[12] See Nick Monfort and Ian Bogost, "Afterword on platform studies," in *Racing the Beam: The Atari Video Computer System* (Cambridge, MA: MIT Press, 2009). For an application, see Ilaria Moschini, "Social semiotics and platform studies: An integrated perspective for the study of social media platforms," *Social Semiotics* 28, no. 5 (2018): 623–640, https://doi.org/10.1080/10350330.2018.1504714.

[13] In this context, "coding" refers to a research tool used in social research, not to computer programming. Coding means organising a body of unstructured data by labelling and categorising specific parts of the data. See Virgina Braun and Victoria Clarke, "Using thematic analysis in psychology," *Qualitative Research in Psychology* 3, no. 2 (2006): 77–101. Despite what is suggested in the title, the applications of this paper go beyond psychology – it is a seminal paper in qualitative research and thematic analysis.

Wikipedia Essentials and the Birth of the "Clean Channel Ideal"

Wikipedia was founded by Jimmy Wales and Larry Sanger in 2001 as a way to support an already existing encyclopaedia (Nupedia), which just like traditional analogue encyclopaedias compiled articles written exclusively by experts in their respective fields.[14] The problem with Nupedia was that articles were produced at a slow rate. Wikipedia was started as a crowdsourcing project – lay editors would collect information for Nupedia authors. Eventually, however, Wikipedia became so efficient that it outgrew its older sibling.

Policies were introduced to regulate the work of a growing number of editors. Wikipedia's core policies to this day are "Neutral Point of View" (NPOV), "No Original Research" (NOR), and "Verifiability" (V). NPOV invites editors to adopt an impartial tone and perspective. If a topic is under debate, they should describe the controversies surrounding it rather than participating in these. NOR means that original research is not allowed: only information published in secondary sources is admissible on Wikipedia. Nor are personal experiences or direct observations admissible. V establishes that information should come from reputable sources, as defined in the policy itself.[15] This means that Wikipedians were (and still are) supposed to transfer information from a secondary source to the page, with as little intervention as possible.

Basic Wikipedia editing occurs through indirect interactions between Wikipedians. Editors decide what to edit, access the editing interface, and make changes to the article. If another editor disagrees with the edit, they can revert it – that is, restore the previous version of the page, thereby effectively invalidating the work of the first editor. However, the first editor is able to revert the revert, and so forth. This may lead to a long sequence of edits referred to as "edit warring".[16]

Sometimes, this indirect "edit warring" leads to verbal confrontations. Debates occur in public on discussion pages known as "talk pages". Other editors might weigh in at this point. Decisions are based on consensus, which is assumed in the absence of objections.[17] Discussions on "talk pages" are regulated by one of

---

14 Joseph Micheal Reagle, *Good Faith Collaboration* (Cambridge, MA: MIT Press, 2010), Ch. 2.
15 "Wikipedia: Verifiability," last modified April 2023, accessed 31 May, 2023, https://en.wikipedia.org/wiki/Wikipedia:Verifiability
16 "Wikipedia: Edit warring," last modified January 2023, accessed 31 May, 2023, https://en.wikipedia.org/wiki/Wikipedia:Edit_warring
17 "Wikipedia: Consensus," last modified January 2023, accessed 31 May, 2023, https://en.wikipedia.org/wiki/Wikipedia:Consensus

the most important policies: "Civility", which invites editors to be cooperative, avoid personal attacks, and treat "fellow editors as respected colleagues".[18] "Civility", combined with the basic editing process, establishes a space where conflict is necessary but needs to be contained in order for the process to function properly. This notion of knowledge production as regimented conflict is widespread on Wikipedia. Wikipedians themselves frequently use war metaphors: "edit warring" is one example, while other uses of similar metaphors may be found in comparing Wikipedia to a "battlefield of ideas" or "troll wars".[19] Adversarial knowledge production on Wikipedia may also be described as a duel, harking back to early modern models of justification in science, specifically to the idea of truth as a result of rational debate between gentlemen.[20]

Conversations on talk pages highlight the affective correlates of publicly defending one's own work, such as pride, embarrassment, defensiveness, hurt, and anger. Conflict on Wikipedia is widespread.[21] For the community to produce anything despite its foundational belligerence, however, affect needs to be disciplined – the CIvility policy invites detachment: "Avoid editing while you're in a bad mood".[22]

The process described above, together with the policies regulating the work of Wikipedians, frames the ideal editor (and hence, knower) as autonomous, disembodied, and detached. The importance of autonomy is apparent by noting significant absences: other systems of collective knowledge production, including earlier encyclopaedias, filter contributions through some form of review process and are supervised by an individual or group of individuals entrusting individual contributors with specific tasks. The process used by Wikipedia constitutes a radical departure from that model. Autonomy is embedded in the process by allowing editors to edit Wikipedia pages directly and at their own initiative. The ideal knower is also autonomous from other editors: collaboration is coordinated in

---

[18] "Wikipedia: Civility," last modified January 2023, accessed 31 May, 2023, https://en.wikipedia.org/wiki/Wikipedia:Civility

[19] "Wikipedia: Battlefield of ideas," last modified June 2018, accessed 31 May, 2023, https://meta.wikimedia.org/wiki/Battlefield_of_ideas; "Wikipedia: Troll war," last modified February 2014, accessed 31 May, 2023, https://meta.wikimedia.org/wiki/Troll_war

[20] Steven Shapin and Simon Schaffer, *Leviathan and the Air-Pump: Hobbes, Boyle, and the Experimental Life* (Princeton, NJ: Princeton University Press, 1985).

[21] Dariusz Jemielniak, *Common Knowledge* (Redwood City: Stanford University Press, 2014); Nathaniel Tkacz, *Wikipedia and the Politics of Openness* (Chicago and London: The University of Chicago Press, 2015).

[22] "Wikipedia: Civility"

an impersonal way through a process known as stigmergy,[23] a method of communication between members of a large group relying on each member making a change to a shared substrate (in Wikipedia's case, editing the article page), thereby leaving a trace for others to act upon (in Wikipedia's case, for instance, by reverting an edit).

The ideal Wikipedia editor is disembodied in relation to their role as an editor: when editing Wikipedia, the personal identity and experience of the editor are bracketed – they do not and should not matter. A common thread running through the three core policies is that expertise is not necessary for editing and that editors should keep their personal views private. The identity of editors is also concealed by the website's infrastructure: anonymous editing is the default option. Registration is possible, but it is customary to pick a username. While it is obviously possible to pick your own name and surname as a username, the common practice when Wikipedia was launched was to use a pseudonym.

Finally, detachment is rewarded by the editing process. Anonymity entails a modest notion of authorship. Looking at a Wikipedia article, it is impossible to tell who wrote it; the text appears uniform and is not signed. One has to access a separate page called "revision history" in order to see the work of editors. Furthermore, Wikipedia's process is informed by an ethos of radical collaboration as described above, where editors constantly undo each other's work. In such a context, having a feeling of ownership with regard to one's own edits is counterproductive. Further, emotional detachment is culturally encouraged (see the "Civility" policy), as behaving coolly in an argument makes one a more successful editor. In this manner, the editing process embeds a preference for detachment through a feedback mechanism: the edits of those who are able to maintain an emotional distance are more likely to remain on the page.

In sum, the ideal knower is defined, through Wikipedia's editing process, as a vessel of information, whose sole task is to transfer information from an external source to a Wikipedia page while keeping interference – in the form of experiences, relationships, and emotions – to a minimum. However, as I show in the next section, the clean channel ideal is not new and may be found in, for example, Ayn Rand's work and is rooted in the mid-20th century ideal of the scientific subject.

---

[23] Mark Elliott, "Stigmergic Collaboration: The Evolution of Group Work," *M/C Journal* 9, no. 2 (2006).

Roots of the Clean Channel Ideal and Technological Interventions: Userboxes and the Teahouse

Before explaining the ideological ties between the clean channel ideal and Ayn Rand's philosophy, I will briefly outline the historical significance of her work with regard to Wikipedia. Wikipedia's co-founders, Sanger and Wales, met through a mailing list named "Moderated Discussion of Objectivist Philosophy", which was moderated by Wales and centred around the work of Rand.[24] Wales invited Sanger to join the team developing Wikipedia's predecessor Nupedia due to Sanger's background in philosophy: "They saw the Nupedia project as turning objectivist theory into practice".[25] The early conversations between the Wikipedia co-founders, which I have read as part of my research, also show a familiar attitude towards Rand's work – her books are used as examples and some participants align themselves with her thought.[26]

In turn, Ayn Rand's influence is also visible when analysing Wikipedia's process and policies. Specifically, the "Neutral Point of View" policy and, more to the point, the ideals of detachment and autonomy that inform the clean channel ideal may be her philosophy, which she named Objectivism. Objectivist epistemology – the branch of Rand's system dealing with matters concerning knowledge acquisition and production – postulates that the world consists of a collection of entities and that knowledge is but a process of directly absorbing facts from the world without any active participation.[27] According to Rand, facts are found, not constructed: "'fact' is simply a way of saying 'this is something that exists in reality' – as distinguished from imagination or misconception or error".[28] This definition does not leave any room for points of view: it assumes that a univocal apprehension of reality is possible. Hence, aspiring to achieve a neutral point of view partly seems to be a result of the Wikipedia founders' engagement with Rand.

Closely related, Objectivism is consistent with the ideals of autonomy and detachment that inform the clean channel ideal: in Rand's view, the individual is the building block of society, selfishness is a virtue, and the role of government is sim-

---

24 Andrew Lih, *The Wikipedia Revolution* (London: Aurum Press, 2009), 32.
25 Lih, *Wikipedia Revolution*, 37.
26 Early conversations between Wikipedia founders can be accessed freely, accessed 31 May, 2023, https://lists.wikimedia.org/hyperkitty/
27 Ayn Rand, *Introduction to Objectivist Epistemology* (New York: Penguin, 1967).
28 Rand, *Introduction*.

ply to protect the individual's rights to life, property, and happiness.[29] Detachment, in Rand's view, is an epistemic virtue essential for achieving truth. In fact, she argued that truth may be accessed through the exercise of reason, while error is caused by the interference of emotions.[30]

Detachment has also been constitutive of the modern ideal of the scientist. Over the course of the 18th and 19th centuries, the idea of objectivity became attached to the body of the scientist, whose faculties of perception could be called into question. The scientist's detachment was, and is, considered a guarantee for truth:[31] "scientists aim to distance themselves from the values, vested interests, and emotions generated by their class, race, sex, or unique situation. By decontextualising themselves, they allegedly become detached observers and manipulators of nature."[32]

An implication of requiring editors to bracket their own identities is that positionality is not just irrelevant, when it comes to writing Wikipedia, but dangerous – a potential threat to the purity of encyclopaedic work. Accordingly, I here analyse two technological interventions designed to resist the clean channel model, specifically by highlighting positionality: "userboxes" and the "Teahouse". These are just two out of many possible examples. My aim here is to show how a dialectic in values has been reified in the practice of co-designing en.wikipedia.org.

The first case concerns the expression of one's identity and beliefs. In 2005, just three years after Wikipedia's inception, a controversy erupted known as the "Userbox Wars".[33] "Userboxes" are small banners that Wikipedians add to their own user pages to display personal features. They were intended as a way of conveying useful information, such as the languages spoken by the user and level of editing skill.[34] However, partially due to the fact that userbox code may be copied, pasted, and modified with relatively limited technical skills, userboxes evolved over time beyond displaying encyclopaedia-related information. They became ways in which users expressed themselves and their identity. Today, "userboxes" can be used to display the editor's adherence to a certain editing philosophy, political affiliation, sexuality, being left- or right-handed, and so on. The bone of contention during the "Userbox Wars" was the potential impact of userboxes on editing

---

29 Ayn Rand, "The Objectivist Ethics," in *The Virtue of Selfishness: A New Concept of Egoism* (New York: Penguin, 1961)
30 Rand, *Introduction*.
31 Lorraine Daston and Peter Galison, *Objectivity* (New York: Zone books, 2010).
32 Patricia Hill Collins, *Black Feminist Thought* (London and New York: Routledge, 2000), 255.
33 William Westerman, "Epistemology, the Sociology of Knowledge, and the Wikipedia Userbox Controversy," in *Folklore and the Internet*, ed. Trevor J. Blank, 123–158. (Boulder, CO: University Press of Colorado, 2009).
34 Westerman, "Epistemology ".

work. Were userboxes a sign of bias? Could editors displaying strong political leanings be trusted or could the diversity of points of view lead towards, as opposed to away from, neutrality?[35]

A compromise was reached at the time, but the debate regarding political userboxes continues. Some current Wikipedians seem unhappy with userboxes as markers of identity. A thread on the Village Pump, one of the community forums, dated September 2020 gathers the interventions of many Wikipedians who vehemently argue against userboxes and other kinds of political expressions, where the construal of what constitutes "political" expression encroaches more and more on personal matters, such as supporting the LGBTQIA+ community or abortion. One editor even argue for eliminating "all of such social media paraphernalia from this site and concentrate on building an encyclopedia rather than 'expressing ourselves'".[36] Regardless of how representative this quote is in terms of a widespread sentiment, it does touch on the heart of the debate: Wikipedians are discussing whether it is desirable, or even possible, to be clean channels.

The second case I discuss here is a forum where Wikipedians may discuss editing practices called the "Teahouse". This is the spiritual heir – or, according to some, the reincarnation – of a previous, now closed, forum called the "coffee lounge". The coffee lounge was part of "Esperanza", a project started in 2005 and closed in 2007, whose aim was to "support the encyclopedia indirectly by encouraging a sense of community" among Wikipedians.[37] Esperanza offered a support network for an atomised collection of supposedly clean channels of information, with practical initiatives supporting mental health (for those affected by "wikistress" – a concept that is not fully defined but, based on its usage, seems to point towards stress occurring as a result of editing Wikipedia) as well as support for newcomers.[38]

The ones wanting to close the project argued, among other things, that tending to relationships would be a distraction from editing the encyclopaedia. In addition, a concern was also raised that a small group might become too powerful, thereby hampering the decentralised, flat power structure of Wikipedia.[39] In this narrative, relationships are then akin to bias, as they represent an allegiance to a specific group, rather than the community as a whole – in contrast with the original ideals

---

35 Westerman, "Epistemology".
36 Quote from user. "Wikipedia: Village pump (idea lab)/Archive 33," last modified December 2020, accessed 31 May, 2023, https://en.wikipedia.org/wiki/Wikipedia:Village_pump_(idea_lab)/Archive_33
37 "Wikipedia: Esperanza," last modified October 2022, https://en.wikipedia.org/wiki/Wikipedia:Esperanza
38 "Wikipedia: Esperanza"
39 "Wikipedia: Esperanza"

of detachment and autonomy described above. In 2012, five years after Esperanza was disbanded, the Teahouse was born, seemingly to address similar needs.[40] However, the Teahouse is also a space for troubleshooting and guiding new editors, not simply to provide the kind of emotional support that the coffee lounge had focussed on.

Userboxes and the Teahouse are just two cases representative of a general trend of user-coded resistance against the clean channel ideal. In part, said resistance has taken the form of community building: nowadays, Wikipedians meet regularly in person at events such as the yearly Wikimania convention. In addition, edit-a-thons are organised to enrich coverage of underrepresented topics, such as women's biographies, Africa, or the LGBTQIA+ community.[41] Editors also give each other awards.[42]

By displaying their own identity through userboxes and reaching out for a sense of community, editors are challenging the notion that their bodies do not count. And they are effectively highlighting the impossibility of holding neutrality as a foundational ideal. They are attacking a tenet of the clean channel ideal while, contextually, bolstering a view adjacent to, for instance, feminist approaches placing identity at the core of testimony, such as standpoint epistemology and Black feminist epistemology.[43] Reintroducing affect in the knowledge production process also echoes valuing emotion in scholar activism.[44] Yet, as suggested by the resurgence of the controversy over userboxes, however, some editors still see value in the clean channel ideal.

Negotiating Epistemologies through Code

So far, I have argued that parts of the code that constitutes en.wikipedia.org embed conflicting views of the ideal knower. Creating – coding – artefacts then becomes a way to express one's views. In short, Wikipedia editors discuss by doing: in order

---

[40] "Wikipedia talk: Esperanza," last modified January 2023, accessed 31 May, 2023, https://en.wikipedia.org/wiki/Wikipedia_talk:Esperanza

[41] "Wikipedia: Edit-a-thon," Wikipedia, last modified December 2022, accessed 31 May, 2023, https://en.wikipedia.org/wiki/Edit-a-thon

[42] "Wikipedia: Awards," last modified July 2022, accessed 31 May, 2023, https://en.wikipedia.org/wiki/Wikipedia:Awards

[43] Sandra Harding, "Rethinking standpoint epistemology: What is wrong with 'strong objectivity'?," *The Centennial Review* 35; Patricia Hill Collins, *Black Feminist Thought* (London and New York: Routledge, 2014).

[44] See, for instance, Kye Askins (2009), "'That's just what I do': Placing emotion in academic activism," *Emotion, Space and Society* 2, no.1 (2009). I owe this observation to Jana Weiß.

to express a view, they create features that express it. These digital artefacts then become a space for negotiating epistemologies.

At this point, one might legitimately ask: why use code to counteract the structure? Why not advocate for a change in the policies or process? My provisional answer is: because bespoke code is accessible to volunteers, while policies and technical infrastructures are not. Since policies are written on Wikipedia pages, they could essentially be edited by anyone. In practice, however, doing this is not easy: as of March 2023, core policy pages are semi-protected, meaning that they can only be changed by a subset of editors, as signalled by a lock symbol on the actual policy pages. Banners on these pages also invite caution when editing on the grounds that policies are widely accepted standards. More fundamentally, the editing interface is essentially fixed. Bespoke code is not. Userboxes can be made and changed, forums can be created.

As well as constituting sites of negotiation by making, coded artefacts also become a catalyst for discursive discussions. The debate regarding these features is also a veiled debate concerning the epistemology of Wikipedia itself. Editors are supposed to maintain a neutral attitude towards their work on Wikipedia: as outlined above, sharing one's views is culturally frowned upon. But they may discuss features. For instance, the userbox controversy has sparked a conversation regarding the relationship between neutrality and identity: to some, situating oneself through userboxes represents a breach of neutrality, as this roots editing in a specific, as opposed to neutral, point of view. To others, who conceive of neutrality as the sum of many diverging points of view, userboxes are in the service of objectivity. In a community where neutrality is largely taken for granted, technology constitutes a safe venue and focus for self-expression.

Conclusion

In this paper, I have shown what can be gained from a historically informed close reading of Wikipedia. I have traced a rough outline of how conceptions of the knowing subject have been operationalised through Wikipedia's website. The core of Wikipedia's infrastructure embeds an ideal of the knower as detached, disembodied, and autonomous. Over time, this view has been questioned through coded interventions aimed at promoting a situated conception of testimony and, consequently, knowledge.

Adopting a broader view, the rough account outlined in this paper shows that digital objects may be sites of epistemic debate. Engineering can be read as a way of translating worldviews into matter. Indeed, as highlighted in the introduction, several areas of inquiry are based on the assumption that values may be embedded into objects. If that is the case, then multiple, competing epistemologies may be embedded into objects, thus transforming them into venues for debate. The Wikipedia example of epistemic negotiation by coding digital objects takes this conception to a new level.

However, these negotiations through objects can only become visible by adopting a historical view. We need to consciously acknowledge the challenges of analysing constantly evolving objects, such as digital artefacts. Freezing them in time would be like looking at a flattened concertina. It is only by extending it that we can start to understand how it works.

About the contributor

Elena Falco is a doctoral candidate in science and technology studies based at University College London. Her work is interdisciplinary and rooted in the philosophy of technology and STS. Her doctoral project analyses how epistemic values are embedded in Wikipedia's website. In parallel, she works on ageism in technology, having co-authored a chapter on "Digital Ageism, Algorithmic Bias and Feminist Critical Theory" that is forthcoming in *Feminist AI – Critical Perspectives on Algorithms, Data, and Intelligent Machines* (2023).

Elisavet Papalexopoulou

Women of the Word: Translation and Political Activism in the Age of Revolutions

Abstract: At the beginning of the nineteenth century, the age-old system of empires was beginning to crumble. People were trying to reimagine the political space, and geographies in Europe were shifting. In this intellectual landscape of upheaval, translation served as a powerful tool enabling vocabularies and ideas of revolution to travel from context to context. Translating texts into one's language was a scholarly activity permitted for women and it was frequently used by female writers as a space where they could unfold their ideas and influence their contemporaries. Although there has lately been a renewed interest in translators and translation, these aspects are still undervalued as a source by historians of knowledge and ideas due to a misconception that translation lacks originality. Yet, the expressive and intercultural potential of the translated word and the insights that paratexts surrounding translations have to offer tell an exciting story – a story of cultural mediation also existing outside the textual world and providing the promise of political participation, even under the dark shadow of gender power relations.

Keywords: translation history, women translators, age of revolutions

In April 1820, just a few months before the outbreak of the Greek Revolution, the translation of a French book on the manners of young women was published in Greek. It was Jean-Nicolas Bouilly's *Conseils à ma fille*, translated by twenty-year-old Evanthia Kairi (1799–1866).[1] The first book to be printed by the newly acquired press of the Kydonies (Ayvalik) academy would be remarkably successful. In the introduction, a text eight pages long in which the translator proclaimed with modesty that she was not worthy of having her work published, there was also a brief, but telling comment: "…I am in complete ignorance about the writer and how he is regarded in his own nation…"[2] She then went on to indicate that she was not particularly interested in either the writer or the original text. She had

---

[1] Jean Nicolas Bouilly, Συμβουλαί Προς Τη Θυγατέρα Μου Σύγγραμμα Ὑπο Ι.Ν. Βουΐλλου Μεταφρασθέν Εκ Του Γαλλικού Ὑπο Ε.Ν. Της Εξ Ἀνδρου, trans. Ευανθία Καΐρη (Kydonies: Τυπογραφείῳ τῆς τῶν Κυδωνιῶν Σχολῆς, 1820); Interfaces/fonds anciens Lyon, "Jean-NicolasBouilly, un auteur à succès pour la jeunesse," Billet, *Interfaces. Livres anciens de l'Université de Lyon* (blog), accessed December 29, 2022, https://bibulyon.hypotheses.org/5231.
[2] Bouilly, Συμβουλαί, 6.

published this translation as a pretext, as a way to reach Greek women in the Ottoman Empire and present them with a message: they should educate themselves. The entire "civilized world" was watching them, waiting to see if they could stand as tall as their ancestors. Their duty to their nation, Kairi continued, did not consist of reading this book by a European writer, but of getting acquainted with the important women of Ancient Greece and their accomplishments. She was too young and inexperienced to talk about this at length, she concluded, but she was using this translation to send a message to her readers. This tongue-in-cheek admission that the original text was just a foil for its translator's ambitious goals was hidden among her own proclamations that she would have never dared to publish anything herself were it not for the great men in her life. Kairi was careful to follow the rules of propriety most of the time, thus securing for herself the space to write her own thoughts about the Greek nation, its past and future, and the role of women in it.

This is but one example of how educated women in early nineteenth-century South-East Europe used translations as a vehicle to participate in the political debates of their turbulent times. It is also an indication of how, by examining translations and translators, we may gain a richer, more nuanced understanding of the intellectual worlds of the past. Translations have for a long time been viewed as a lesser type of text, plagued by the notion that they lack originality and thus merit less attention from intellectual historians and historians of knowledge.[3] However, the last thirty years have witnessed a renewed interest in translations and their history. Works such as those of Fania Oz-Salzberg have shown how translations in the eighteenth and nineteenth centuries served as the infrastructure through which ideas and vocabularies were circulated.[4]

To take this a step further, the story of Evanthia Kairi's translation, along with the other stories of female translators, shows us the need to "[h]umanize translation history," as the translation studies scholar Anthony Pym has so eloquently put it.[5] The effort to humanize translation history is not a strict methodological choice. Rather, it constitutes a commitment to ask questions about the people – the trans-

---

[3] On the ramifications of ideas of originality on intellectual history and women's history, see Berenice A. Carroll, "The Politics of 'Originality': Women and the Class System of the Intellect," *Journal of Women's History* 2, no. 2 (1990): 136–163.

[4] Fania Oz-Salzberger, *Translating the Enlightenment: Scottish Civic Discourse in Eighteenth-Century Germany* (Oxford: Clarendon Press, 1995).

[5] Anthony Pym, "Humanizing Translation History," *Hermes: Journal of Language and Communication in Business* 22, no. 42 (2009): 24–48; Bergantino, Andrea. "Translation History, Translators' Stories: Literary Translator Studies." Perspectives, 2022, 1–9. https://doi.org/10.1080/0907676X.2022.2059298.

lators – and not only the texts they produced. Instead of comparing the translated text to its source to identify differences and similarities between two clearly delineated languages and cultures, we ask biographical questions regarding the translators and seek their voices in their linguistic choices and the translation's paratexts (introductions, footnotes). As Pym notes, this "mode of questions may lead to unforeseen answers," mainly as it focuses on an intercultural space rather than a space defined by national historiographies and gender hierarchies.[6]

In this article, I explore how translation as a gendered literary activity gave women access to forms of political participation, even though it also reinforced nineteenth-century notions regarding women being lesser intellectuals. Carefully hidden behind this misconception that they were only good enough to be translators, that they were not important scholars, and that they did not have a say in political matters, women were able to express their revolutionary ideas without having to pay a high price for doing so. They became "literary activists" continuously negotiating the line between female modesty and public engagement.[7] I use the term "literary activists," which is more of a descriptive term than a normative one, as I believe that it highlights two main characteristics regarding the experience and intention of female translators. First, that this kind of activism was literary, meaning it was not linked to political or philosophical texts. Second, that it aimed to achieve political public engagement even if this was sometimes not clearly stated. Women used translations as a gateway to scholarly networks, used paratexts to boldly introduce their thoughts to the public, and gained access to the performative aspects of language at a time when the political and cultural boundaries of Europe were being redrawn.

A continuously growing body of historiography has discussed the importance of translation in Southern Europe in the eighteenth and nineteenth centuries.[8]

---

6 Pym, "Humanizing," 43.
7 To my knowledge, the term "literary activists" when referring to these specific actors was first used by Yanni Kotsonis in the introduction to the *Journal of Modern Greek Studies* special issue on the Greek Revolution, vol. 39, no. 1. The importance of "modesty" is ever-present when women writers are involved. See, for example, Susan Dalton, *Engendering the Republic of Letters* (Montreal and London: McGill-Queens University Press, 2003), 86.
8 Vicky Patsiou, "Μεταφραστικές δοκιμές και προϋποθέσεις στα όρια του Νεοελληνικού Διαφωτισμού," *The Gleaner* 19 (1993): 210–234, https://doi.org/10.12681/er.267; Fania Oz-Salzberger, "The Enlightenment in Translation: Regional and European Aspects," *European Review of History/Revue Européenne d'Histoire* 13, no. 3 (2006): 385–409; Stefanie Stockhorst, ed., *Cultural Transfer through Translation: The Circulation of Enlightened Thought in Europe by Means of Translation* (New York: Rodopi, 2010); Dimitris Tziovas, *Greece and the Balkans: Identities, Perceptions and Cultural Encounters since the Enlightenment* (London: Routledge, 2017); Anna Tabaki, *Ιστορία και θεω-*

Complex mechanisms in terms of relocating and adapting political ideas and vocabularies were at work. As revolutionaries were busy creating the ideological substratum of the new worlds they were imagining, these female literary activists constructed a scholarly experience of revolution. However, the expansion of translation activities not only occurred in early nineteenth-century Southern Europe. Nor was the gendered aspect of these activities limited to this area. The fervent translation activities offered a privileged platform for female scholars all across Europe.[9] It was considered an occupation that did not clash with feminine virtue as the translator represented herself as the conduit of someone else's assertions and maintained a demeanor of humility. This allowed women to publish and, in some cases, even receive remuneration for their intellectual labor. In other words, it was a significant factor with regard to fashioning women's intellectual personas, while also contributing to expanding their professional and political prospects.

I have chosen five women who published translated texts, focusing on those whose texts and lives offer us the most eloquent examples of how women weaved in and out of the discourses of femininity, erudition, and nationhood.[10] Not all of them are presented equally. For some, we have more information and access to personal documents such as journals, memoirs, and correspondence. For others, we rely solely on their own introductions, which thereby gain more significance by serving as a window to the lives of their writers.

ρία της μετάφρασης. 18ος αιώνας. Ο Διαφωτισμός [History and theory of translation. 18th century. The Enlightenment. (Athens: Kaligrafos, 2018).

9 Susanne Stark, "Women and Translation in the Nineteenth Century," *New Comparison: A Journal of Comparative and General Literary Studies* 15 (1993): 33–44; Luise von Flotow, *Translation and Gender: Translating in the "Era of Feminism"* (Ottawa: University of Ottawa Press, 1997); Rachel Lynn Williams, *Women Translators in Nineteenth-Century France: Genre, Gender, and Literary Creativity* (University Park: Pennsylvania State University, 2010), , accessed 31 May, 2023, https://etda.libraries.psu.edu/catalog/10483; Lisa Curtis-Wendlandt, Paul Gibbard, and Karen Green, ed., *Political Ideas of Enlightenment Women: Virtue and Citizenship* (London: Routledge, 2016), 3; Karen Green, *A History of Women's Political Thought in Europe, 1700–1800* (Cambridge: Cambridge University Press, 2014), 31, https://doi.org/10.1017/CBO9781316084496.

10 With the exception of Maria Petrettini, the women presented in this article have been present in the historiography of nineteenth-century female writers in Greece. Recently, Vasiliki Misiou published a book on female translators in nineteenth-century Greece. Unfortunately, this book was published after this article was finalized, which means that its insights and conclusions are not included. See Vasiliki Misiou, *The Renaissance of Women Translators in 19th-Century Greece* (New York: Routledge, 2023), https://doi.org/10.4324/9781003178279.

Literary Spaces of Freedom: Introductions to Translations

Introductions to published translations also represent a space where we can see the significance of women being able to get published. In most instances, we find introductions where, after the authoress has customarily purported her modesty, she herself makes bold claims regarding political and social issues. In the introduction to her translation of Goldoni's "La vedova scaltra" in Greek, Mitio Sakellariou (1789–1863) printed her father's letter of approval for the publication.[11] He stated that he had agreed to let his daughter publish this, "even though it was a comedy," only because she pledged that her next translation would be a more useful classical work promoting morality.[12] Sakellariou said that her father was right in his assessment and instruction. Yet, she then went on to extol comedy as a genre and stress its importance in discussions on morality, ultimately arguing for a position opposite to that of her father. All we know about Sakellariou comes from this introduction to her translation. She was a member of the up-and-coming Greco-Ottoman bourgeoisie and the daughter of a doctor. Women of higher classes were even bolder and sometimes were able to skip the fake modesty section. In her introduction to Gabriel Bonnot de Mably's *Entretiens de Phocion* (1819), the ar-

---

[11] Carlo Goldoni, *Η Πατρική Αγάπη ή η Ευγνώμων Δούλη και η Πανούργος Χήρα. Κωμωδίαι του κυρίου Καρόλου Γολδώνη εκ του Ιταλικού μεταφρασθείσαι παρά Μητιούς Σακελλαρίου* [Paternal Love or the Grateful Servant and the Devious Widow. Comedies by mister Carlo Goldoni translated from Italian by Mitio Sakellariou], trans. Sakellariou Mitio (Vienna: Ioannou Sneier, 1818). For more on Mitio Sakellariou, see Walter Puchner, *Γυναικεία δραματουργία στα χρόνια της Επανάστασης: Μητιώ Σακελλαρίου, Ελισάβετ Μουτζάν-Μαρτινέγκου, Ευανθία Καΐρη: χειραφέτηση και αλληλεγγύη των γυναικών στο εθνικοδιδακτικό και επαναστατικό δράμα* [Women's dramaturgy in the years of the Revolution: Mitio Sakellariou, Elisavet Mudzan-Martinengou, Evanthia Kairi: women's liberation and solidarity in national and revolutionary plays] (Athens: Kardamitsa, 2001); Eirini Rizaki, *Οι 'γράφουσες Ελληνίδες΄: σημειώσεις για την γυναικεία λογιοσύνη του 19ου αιώνα* [The "writing Greeks": Notes on female scholarship of the nineteenth century] (Athens: Katarti, 2007); Sofia Denissi, *Ανιχνεύοντας την αόρατη γραφή: γυναίκες και γραφή στα χρόνια του Νεοελληνικού Διαφωτισμού- Ρομαντισμού* [Tracing the "invisible ink": Women and writing in the years of the Neohellenic Enlightenment-Romanticism] (Athens: Nefeli, 2014); Paschalis M. Kitromilides, "The Enlightenment and Womanhood: Cultural Change and the Politics of Exclusion," *Journal of Modern Greek Studies* 1, no. 1 (1983): 39–61.

[12] Goldoni, *Η Πατρική*, 2.

istocrat Aikaterini Soutzou-Valeta (1795–1837) stated that she had translated and published this work to "mitigate men's bragging on political matters."[13]

In a very practical sense, working with translations allowed women to acquire the identity of a scholar. On the Ionian island of Zante, Elisavet Mudzan-Martinengou (1801–1832) wrote her autobiography, focusing on how she educated herself and how she had tried to avoid getting married.[14] Her goal in life was to become an intellectual, something she never achieved. Her father insisted on her marrying a man many years her senior and she died in childbirth without ever seeing her writings getting published. In her autobiographical text, she deployed translations from Italian, Latin, and Ancient Greek into Modern Greek as proof of her erudition. For her, the fact that she could move texts from one language to another was proof that she was a true scholar, regardless of her sex. Even though this is a story where knowledge did not prove to be a refuge from structures of oppression, it is telling of how a woman found a way to give herself agency through the practice of translation.

A different, more successful, case was that of Maria Petrettini from Corfu.[15] Born into one of the Greek aristocratic families of the Ionian Islands, she was given good home education. But when she wanted to continue her education in Italy, just like her brother, she was refused. Petrettini decided to translate and write historical works in Italian. If Greek language and literature had no place for a female scholar, then she would try a different place. Her scholarly work in Italian was what enabled her to get away from her island and live the majority of her life in Venice, pursuing her literary interests. She wrote her own works on women's literary history and translated Mary Wortley Montague's *Turkish Embassy Letters*.[16] She was able to fashion herself as a woman with two homelands.

---

13 Gabriel Bonnot De Mably, Διάλογοι Φωκίωνος Ότι Οικειότατον Το Ηθικόν Προς Το Πολιτικόν Υπό Μαβλή Μεταφρασθέντες Δε Υπό Της Νεάνιδος Αικατερίνης Σούτζης (Εν Ιασσίω: Θεοδώρου Νέγρη, 1819).
14 The autobiography was published much later, censored by her son Elisavetios Martinegos, Η Μήτηρ Μου. Αυτοβιογραφία Της Κυρίας Ελισάβετ Μουτζάν-Μαρτινέγκου. Εκδιδομένη Υπό Του Υιού Αυτής Ελισαβετίου Μαρτινέγκου Μετά Διαφόρων Αυτού Ποιήσεων [My mother. An autobiography of Mrs Mudzan-Martinegou. Published by her son Elisavetios Martinegos with some of his poems] (Athens: Korinni, 1881).
15 For some information on Maria Petrettini, see Mara Nardo, "Maria e Spiridione Petrettini" (Padova: Università di Padova, 2013); Elisavet Papalexopoulou, "Trans-Adriatic Enlightenments: Maria Petrettini's Italian Translation of the 'Turkish Embassy Letter'," in *Gender and Cultural Mediation in the Long Eighteenth Century: Women Across Borders*, ed. Mónica Bolufer, Carolina Blutrach, and Laura Guinot (London: Palgrave Macmillan, 2023).
16 Maria Petrettini, *Sulla educazione femminile scritto postumo di Maria Petrettini* (Padova: Company' tipi di A. Bianchi, 1856); Mary Wortley Montagu, *Lettere di lady Maria Wortley Montague* ...

"Venice," she said in one of her introductions, "I can call my second homeland, because of the time I have spent here and the literary friends who helped me regain my sanity."[17] On the other hand, she still signed all her literary works and translations as "Maria Petrettini, the Corfiot." She had acquired the freedom to self-determination through the networks she had built as a scholar and her choice to translate into a language other than her native one. She could choose to belong to two literary traditions: one Greek, the other Italian.

Maria Petrettini's story as a translator and scholar with two homelands is an example of how some thinkers dealt with rupture and dislocation in South-Eastern Europe at the beginning of the nineteenth century.[18] Petrettini was born in the Venetian republic, grew up in the French Empire, lived as a young adult in the Septinsular Republic – under Ottoman and Russian protection – and then in a protectorate of the British Empire.[19] All of this without ever leaving Corfu. When she was finally able to leave and pursue a literary career in Venice, she found more political and social stability as an émigré than she had in her place of origin. This experience of constant mobility was not an exception. This was a time of revolution and disruptions as empires redrew their borders. Nation states were emerging as a new type of political and cultural frame of reference. Women who worked as translators, adapting texts as they moved from one culture to another in a world of ever-shifting social and political contexts, often made decisions that shaped these very contexts.

Translation and Nation State Formation

Linguistic and cultural choices made by translators carried more weight at a time of nation state formation. In most of the cases examined here when the target was Modern Greek, a language that did not yet have an official form, many questions needed to be answered regarding morphological and grammatical features. Male scholars were engaged in endless debates on the "Greek language question," the relationship of the new language to Ancient Greek and to the Italian and Ottoman

---

durante i suoi primi viaggi in Europa, Asia ed Africa, tr. da M. Petrettini (Corfu: Nella tipografia del governo, 1838); Flavius Philostratus and Maria Petrettini, *Alcune immagini di Filostrato tradotte dal greco da Maria Petrettini corcirese* (Treviso: per Francesco Andreola, 1825).

17 Maria Petrettini, *Vita Di Cassandra Fedele* (Venezia: Stamperia Pinelli, 1814), 6.

18 Konstantina Zanou, *Transnational Patriotism in the Mediterranean, 1800–1850: Stammering the Nation* (New York: Oxford University Press, 2018).

19 Anthony Hirst and Patrick Sammon, *The Ionian Islands: Aspects of Their History and Culture* (Newcastle: Cambridge Scholars Publishing, 2014).

Turkish words it had acquired.[20] These were relentless debates between those who favored a "cleaner" ancient-like language supported by the Greek Orthodox Church and those who believed that Modern Greek should be the language spoken by Greek peasants. The latter would in many cases lose their careers and be forced to rearrange their lives due to their position. Meanwhile, female scholars who were not allowed to theorize on the subject were producing translations in a version of Modern Greek that was accessible to the less-educated Christian Ottoman population. They "cleaned" this version from words they considered being too foreign – using rather arbitrary criteria. In effect, they chose what would be later known as the "middle road" and maintained their position without ever being subjected to the rage of the linguistic debates of the time. After all, most of them addressed a readership of women who were expected to exhibit a lower linguistic level.

Choosing and translating a text from Greek into another language could also have significant political implications. The aristocrat Roxandra Stourdza (1786–1844) explained this in her introduction to her translation of an obituary for the Greek Patriarch Gregorios V from Greek into French.[21] The patriarch had been executed by the Ottoman Porte in June 1821 in its reprisals for the uprising of the Greek populations.[22] His body had been secretly carried to be buried in Odessa where there was a large Greek merchant community. The obituary written and delivered by an Orthodox priest-scholar was translated into Italian, German, and French by Stourdza. This was part of her effort to raise awareness among Europe-

---

[20] The "language question" permeated political debates in modern Greece until the mid-1970s. Its implications ran deep and defined a progressive and conservative side for 150 years. Indicatively, see Peter Mackridge, *Language and National Identity in Greece, 1766–1976* (Oxford: Oxford University Press, 2009); Peter Mackridge, "Katharevousa (c. 1800–1974): An Obituary for an Official Language," in *Background to Contemporary Greece I*, ed. Marion Sarafis and Martin Eve (London: The Merlin Press, 1990), 23–52; Gunar Hering, *Η διαμάχη για τη γραπτή νεοελληνική γλώσσα: Σύντομη ιστορία του γλωσσικού ζητήματος* [The controversy on the written modern Greek language: A short history of the Greek language question] (Herakleion: Cretan University Press, 2020).

[21] On Roxandra Stourdza and her diplomatic work during the Congress of Vienna and the Greek Revolution, see Stella Ghervas, "Le réseau épistolaire d'Alexandre et Roxandre Stourdza: une médiation triangulaire entre Occident, Russie et Sud-Est européen," *Revue des etudes sud-est européennes* 51, no. 1–4 (2013): 291–320; Stella Ghervas, "A 'Goodwill Ambassador' in the Post-Napoleonic Era," in *Women, Diplomacy and International Politics since 1500*, ed. Glenda Sluga and Carolyn James (London: Routledge, 2015), 151–166. There are no works on her translation and literary activities.

[22] Mark Mazower, *The Greek Revolution: 1821 and the Making of Modern Europe*, 1st ed. (London: Allen Lane, 2021), 33–34.

an courts and gain sympathy for the revolting Christian populations.²³ However, Stourdza saw another important function of this translation. She hoped that the translated text would "arouse general interest, not only from a moral and religious point of view but also as the product of a barely formed language."²⁴ She understood that, by using a language as the original text for a translation, she could bring this language into existence for the rest of the world. The historical study of translation sometimes presupposes rigidity. We try to understand how and why a text was prepared to move from one cultural/national context to another, but we often fall into the trap of supposing that these contexts themselves are immutable. Yet, women like Stourdza were conscious of the performativity of translation. They were conscious of the fact that it could also shape frames of reference both for the original source text and the target text. In this case, this could offer the political legitimacy required for constructing a national language.

Using language to legitimize the claims for a nation's existence as an autonomous entity was only one of a number of tools available to translators. Another was to explore the idea of the nation's space and territory. As some scholars were formulating the language they were translating to and from, others started delineating the location of its supposed origin. If there was such a thing as Modern Greece, where was it?

In 1816, a young woman from Wallachia, Aikaterini Rasti, undertook the seemingly unassuming task of translating a children's game into Greek. This was Étienne de Jouy's *Jeu des cartes géographiques*, a deck of cards with descriptions of all the different countries in the world, accompanied by a map.²⁵ The game promoted new forms of geographical knowledge and new conceptions of space, not only emphasizing the geomorphologic or climatic characteristics of countries, but also the achievements of each civilization. Rasti's choice to translate this

---

23 Konstantinos Oikonomos, *Discours pronocé en grec, a Odessa, le 29 juin 1821 pour les funérailles du Patriarche Grégoire, par Constantin, prêtre Grec, économe et prédicateur de la Maison du Patriarche. Traduit par Mme *** Grecque*, trans. Roxandra Stourdza Edling (Paris: Imprimerie de A. Bobée, 1821).
24 Konstantinos Papoulidis, *Τρία Ἀνέκδοτα Γράμματα Τοῦ Κωνσταντίνου Οἰκονόμου Τοῦ Ἐξ Οἰκονόμων Στή Ρωξάνδρα Καί Στόν Ἀλέξανδρο Στούρτζα* [Three unpublished letters by Konstantions Oikonomos to Roxandra and Alexandre Stourdza] (Thessaloniki: Patriarchal Instituition of Pateric Texts, 1979), 8.
25 Étienne de Jouy, *Jeu de Cartes Geographique, Orné de Figures Gravées Avec Soin et Représentant Le Différens Peuples de La Terre Dans Le Costume Particulier à Chacun d'eux; Destiné à l'instruction et à l'amusement de La Jeunésse de Deux Sexes* (Paris: Nicolie, Libraire, 1805); Etienne de Jouy, *Χαρτοπαίγνιον Γεωγραφικόν, Συγγραφέν Μεν Γαλλιστί Υπό Ε. Ζουΐ, Μεταφρασθέν Δε Εις Την Καθομιλουμένην Των Γραικών Γλώσσα Υπό Αικατερίνης Ραστή* [Geographical cardgame, written in French by E. Jouy translated in the everyday Greek language by Aikaterini Rasti] (Vienna, 1816).

game was much more radical than it may appear at first glance. In 1791, the appearance of a geographical book called *Modern Geography* caused great controversy, precisely because it tried to link countries to their cultural, political, and religious institutions. This resulted in the authors' careers as clerics being ruined.[26] The Orthodox Church did not look favorably upon geographical works departing from the Aristotelian model.[27]

On top of choosing a radical topic carefully disguised in the form of a children's game, Rasti made fundamental changes to the text itself. In her introduction, she pointed out the importance of learning geography for young people and explained that she had decided to translate the game to assist in the education of Greek girls and boys. She also explained that she had made some changes to correct "a few mistakes and misconceptions of the writer" and that she had replaced the first card, France, with that of her own homeland.[28] This was five years before the outbreak of the Greek Revolution. The developments that would lead to the creation of an independent Greek state were still far off in the future.

What was the homeland of a person understanding herself to be Greek at that time? For Rasti, it was what she called "European Turkey," which included the following regions: Thrace, Macedonia, Thessaly, Old Greece, the Peloponnese, Epirus, Albania, Bosnia, Serbia, Bulgaria, Wallachia, and Bogdania; in other words, the Christian Orthodox parts of the Ottoman Empire. In 1798, the idea that this region could be an autonomous political entity and the publication of a map presenting it that way was one of the things that led to the arrest and execution of the revolutionary Rigas Ferraios (1757–1798).[29] But Rasti, a young woman who was using the translation of an innocent children's game as "a way to improve [her own] knowledge of the French language," did not cause any such commotion, even if she did propose the existence of an autonomous territory within the Ottoman Empire. Her gender and her choice to work in a genre considered inherently apolitical allowed her to engage with radical ideas without paying the price for doing so.

---

26 Daniil Philippidis and Grigorios Constandas, *Γεωγραφία Νεωτερική ερανισθείσα από διαφόρους συγγραφείς* [Novel Geography gleaned from various writers] (Vienna: Thomas Trattnern, 1791).
27 Paschalis M. Kitromilides, *Enlightenment and Revolution: The Making of Modern Greece* (Cambridge, MA: Harvard University Press, 2013), Ch. 3.
28 Jouy, *Χαρτοπαίγνιον*, 4.
29 Roumen Daskalov and Tchavdar Marinov, *Entangled Histories of the Balkans. 1: National Ideologies and Language Policies*, Balkan Studies Library 9 (Leiden: Brill, 2013), 128.

Conclusions

Translation is often considered by historians as a movement of texts, vocabularies, and, hence, ideas.[30] In this article, however, I propose a focus on translation as part of scholars' experiences and political intentions. I argue that examining the motivations and material circumstances of translators results in more complex narratives. Following Anthony Pym's ideas on *humanizing translation history*, I examine the lives and work of women translators who self-identified as Greek at the beginning of the nineteenth century, focusing on how their translated texts fit into their own lives and goals of self-determination. In doing so, I show how people, otherwise marginalized due to their gender, could negotiate the tumultuous times they were living in to gain a voice and some elements of power.

Do we as historians have something broader to gain by focusing on the people who translated texts? We can avoid the binaries of source and target language and focus more on the negotiation between the two sides. We are no longer looking into two different textual forms, but into the mind laboratory of a person trying to negotiate the existence of an intercultural space. Thus, following translators, we are able to write about a past that was not just the predecessor of a monolingual present. We have access to the fluidity of contexts, languages, and canons. We can write a type of history that "retains the virtue of the local" but also categories of analysis broader than a single country.[31] The further study of translators allows us to "examine knowledge as an activity occurring in time and space," to use the words of James Secord.[32] Focusing on translators opens up a universe of exciting questions on knowledge and ideas of the past.

About the contributor

Elisavet Papalexopoulou is a PhD researcher at the European University Institute in Florence. Her research focuses on intellectual history with an emphasis on female thinkers and gender in the Age of Revolutions. Her publications include the artle "Tracing the Political in Women's Work" (2021) and

---

30 For an overview of methodological problems caused by a narrow understanding of translation studies and translation history, see Michaela Wolf, "Introduction: The Emergence of a Sociology of Translation," in *Benjamins Translation Library*, ed. Michaela Wolf and Alexandra Fukari, vol. 74 (Amsterdam: John Benjamins Publishing Company, 2007), 1–36, https://doi.org/10.1075/btl.74.01wol.
31 James A. Secord, "Knowledge in Transit," *Isis* 95, no. 4 (December 2004): 668, https://doi.org/10.1086/430657.
32 Secord, "Knowledge."

a forthcoming chapter on Maria Petrettini in the edited volume *Gender and Cultural Mediation in the Long Eighteenth Century: Women Across Borders*.

Jean-Pierre V. M. Hérubel

Higher Education Institutional Histories: Observations, Discussion, and Definitional Glossary of the Publication Genre in Canada and the United States

Abstract: Institutional histories present a unique phenomenon that institutions account for, as they project their past to their constituents and to posterity. Often, these works are books celebrating challenges and achievements. However, this form of institutional memory has a mixed reputation among professional historians. This observation and discussion offer an insight into this ecology of publication while framing the diverse nature of institutional histories. A sample of college and university histories are surveyed, and a typology of genres is discussed to better ascertain the value and nature of histories of higher education institutions, especially for the study of the academic history of higher education in Canada and the United States. Establishing a critical historiographic typology of genres is a necessary requisite for capturing the essence of institutional histories and publication. A definitional glossary for advanced students and historians in the field of the history of higher education is proposed, which categorizes institutional histories according to publishing and publisher formats to ascertain the relative values of institutional histories.

Keywords: college, university, genres, institutional histories, publishing

When historians of higher education examine individual colleges or universities, they encounter a diverse spectrum of institutional histories. For this reason, it is worthwhile gaining an efficacious recognition and appreciation of their scholarly status and value as historical scholarship. For academics, the history of professionalized academic knowledge occupies a complex scholarly ecology, and its professionalization is as old as the founding of Western European universities.[1] These

---

Acknowledgments: The author would like to thank the editors and anonymous reviewers for their helpful suggestions and observations.

[1] For a still relevant introduction, see Charles Homer Haskins, *The Rise of Universities* (Ithaca: Cornell University Press, 1965); William Clark, *Academic Charisma and the Origins of the Research University* (Chicago: University of Chicago Press, 2006).

∂ Open Access. © 2023 the author(s), published by De Gruyter. This work is licensed under the Creative Commons Attribution-NonCommercial-NoDerivatives 4.0 International License.
https://doi.org/10.1515/9783111078038-009

medieval institutions developed and were responsible for the professionalization of law, medicine, and theology. Since the 19th century, higher education institutions have forged a near monopoly regarding the generation and dissemination of knowledge and learning.[2] Accompanying this, academic disciplines have emerged and evolved into our present times. Intellectual, scientific, and ancillary disciplinary discoveries and advancements have perforce engendered distinctive disciplinary cultures within the academy.[3] Together with provincial academies and similar, higher education institutions have a stake in their respective histories. Therefore, it behooves historians of higher education and graduate students to examine institutional histories of higher education institutions to better understand their varied purposes with an additional critical eye toward their historiographic veracity. For these reasons, understanding, situating, and ascertaining the publishing practices observed in an examination of institutional histories and their various publishing formats is vital for addressing their significance to historians and graduate students of higher education. Without a classificatory framework for institutional histories, they remain an amorphous publication phenomenon.

Purpose and Methodological Approach

The following observations, discussion, and proposed glossary concerning institutional publication genres derive from experiences in university press publishing where the author serves as chair of the faculty review board for a university press. The question of institutional histories revolves around and is tied to their purpose, audience, sponsorship, authorship, and publication. The express nature of an institutional history is not easily defined without considering the nature of why they are undertaken. The following text attempts to frame institutional history as a publishing phenomenon within the context of its importance to higher education scholars, especially historians of universities and graduate students engaged in exploring and ascertaining the relative value for their research. To gain a historical context, this study examines the principal types of institutional histories written on American and Canadian higher education institutions in the period

---

[2] See Sheldon Rothblatt and Björn Wittrock, *The European and American University since 1800: Historical and Sociological Essays* (Cambridge: Cambridge University Press, 1993).

[3] For useful accounts of this, see Burton R. Clark, *Places of Inquiry: Research and Advanced Education in Modern Universities* (Berkeley: University of California Press, 1995); Burton R. Clark, ed., *The Research Foundations of Graduate Education: Germany, Britain, France, United States, Japan* (Oakland: University of California Press, 2021).

1700–1989, specifically focusing on four-year colleges and universities.[4] Two-year institutions are not included; however, for illustrative examples, departmental, graduate, professional, or disciplinary histories frame the general discussion. This examination utilizes historical sources offering data that enable a grounded discussion on bibliographic format, authorial context, and type of publisher.[5] For purposes of this observational examination, a listing of institutional histories was gleaned from these published bibliographic sources and categorized using spreadsheet software for tabulation and analysis. Each entry was examined for type of publication and categorized under the following headings: 1) University Press – Peer-Reviewed; 2) University Press, Illustrated and/or Commissioned; 3) Institutionally Commissioned, Non-University Press; 4) Celebratory Publishing; 5) Commercial Publisher; and 6) Private Printing. The categories were generated by the author based on publishing nomenclature.

These elements further contextualize histories of institutions within a historiographic frame of reference. Originating with and grounded in *de visu* bibliographically and textually examining institutional histories, a definitional glossary of genres was created as a template for identifying individual institutional histories within a genre category. Considering the fact that a comprehensive discussion of higher education institutional publishing is not feasible in this presentation, the following discussion focuses on a limited geographical and historical period concentrating on Canada and the United States. Its scope is to focus on those characteristics and qualities discerned and explicated for the North American experience. Developing an approach and definitional glossary offers a viable template applicable to the European context, especially institutional histories in the United Kingdom and Ireland, and may need to be adapted to non-Western institutional conditions.

---

4 There is a growing corpus of scholarship devoted to the writing of institutional histories, especially European institutions. The *History of Universities* annual journal provides a bibliography of major and minor studies of higher education institutions, attesting to the interest in examining institutional histories, accessed May 31, 2023, https://global.oup.com/academic/content/series/h/history-of-universities-series-hou/?cc=us&lang=en&.

5 Data were gathered from Arthur P. Young, *Higher Education in American Life, 1636–1986: A Bibliography of Dissertations and Theses* (New York: Greenwood Press, 1988); Linda Sparks, *Institutions of Higher Education: An International Bibliography* (New York: Greenwood Press, 1990).

The Phenomenon of Institutional Histories

A cursory perusal of a corpus of institutional histories will often leave the reader with the impression that an institutional history is more celebratory than a serious in-depth history adhering to standards of academic or professional historical approaches.[6] Indeed, this may initially be the case; however, the institutional history ecosystem is much more complex and varied, even though a discernible core exists that conforms to the celebratory approach.

Educational institutions, research institutes, and provincial and national academies all contribute substantially to the ecology sustaining and nurturing intellectual culture.[7] Public intellectual discourse and varied acknowledged contributions of discovery and dissemination aside, higher education institutions, especially universities and colleges, comprise a veritable intellectual ecosystem. Granted that tertiary institutions reflect more than research, teaching, etc., they are also sites of human interaction, at times ancillary to their professed objectives and justification for these objectives. Not devoid of contestations, they convey political, economic, cultural, and even religious overtones and connotations. Reflecting societal conditions at large, they are also isolated from these societal influences. Indeed, except for the public intellectual arena, higher education institutions in their varied guises constitute the mainstay and principle of advancing intellectual products and theoretical and methodological advances, as well as pure and applied research and instruction.

Professional history is not pursued ex nihilo – it is socially constructed and adheres to professionalized protocols and sets of consensus-driven methodologies, normative theories, and approaches.[8] Assuming that best practice procedural approaches are adhered to, academic historians of higher education, intellectual, or cultural history accede to the demands of historical scholarship. The history of intellectual effort and culture transcends the discrete history of ideas, expanding its purview to encompass the history of intellectual institutions. However, these are constructed over time and space and are open to the vagaries of human inten-

---

[6] The challenge to effectively writing an institutional history is expressed in John K. Bettersworth, "What's the Use of Writing College Histories?" *The Social Science Bulletin* 6 (1953): 24–27.

[7] Highly selective, celebratory, and cursory historical overviews point to the centrality of higher education institutions in human intellectual activities. See Carol J. Summerfield, Mary Elizabeth Devine, and Anthony Levi, *International Dictionary of University Histories* (Chicago: Fitzroy Dearborn, 1998); Blaise Cronin, *Cathedrals of Learning: Great and Ancient Universities of Western Europe* (Cambridge, MA: Chandos Publishing, 2016).

[8] For an insightful discussion of what constitutes historical research and writing, see Sarah C. Maza, *Thinking about History* (Chicago: University of Chicago Press, 2017).

tion and justification. This is especially true for institutions charged with the responsibilities of generating, shepherding, and imparting knowledge, old and new. Those who embark on and write histories dedicated to a singular higher education institution contribute to the history of intellectual culture in unique, distinctive ways. These histories become bellwether milestones in an institution's history; when taken together, they assume a critical mass of historical narrative framing the intellectual culture distinguishing the significance of higher education in human societies.[9] The relative importance of these histories depends on their veracity to convey, in a dispassionate way, the significance and gravity of their undertaking, without which an effective and trustworthy history can add to the intellectual history culture in all its manifestations. For these reasons, an effective introduction for historians and graduate students in the history of higher education fixes and clarifies this phenomenon.

The Archive in Relation to Historical Writing of Institutional Histories

A further consideration with regard to the historical usefulness of institutional histories to historians and graduate students in the history of higher education involves archival primary sources. Without archival sources, institutional histories cannot exist – they are, as rigorous historical research projects, substantially grounded in primary sources. Archives, especially institutional archives housed in higher education facilities, are absolutely critical to the writing of universities and college histories. Their availability, depth of primary materials, rationalized access procedures, and protocols for successful research are essential for the primary sources utilized for historical analysis. Constructing institutional histories is perforce grounded in the availability and veracity of what the institutional archive provides. Just as a higher education institution is a contested arena, the archive is also a contested site, rich in its own evolutionary construction.[10] The cen-

---

[9] For a thoughtful reading, see Pieter Dhondt, ed., *University Jubilees and University History Writing: A Challenging Relationship*, Vol. 13 (Leiden: Brill, 2014).

[10] For further reading on the nature of archives, see Irving Velody, "The Archive and the Human Sciences: Notes Towards a Theory of the Archive," *History of the Human Sciences* 11, 4 (November 1998): 1; Richard Harvey Brown and Beth Davis-Brown, "The Making of Memory: The Politics of Archives, Libraries and Museums in the Construction of National Consciousness," *History of the Human Sciences* 11, 4 (November 1998): 17–32; Marlene Manoff, "Theories of the Archive from Across the Disciplines," *portal: Libraries and the Academy* 4, no. 1 (2004): 9–25; Antoinette M, Bur-

trality of documents encountered in the archives with regard to historical memory and knowledge development also influences the historian's ability to ascertain their veracity. Several questions arise when confronted with the archival collection at a higher education institution: how extensive are the institutional documents, which lacunae are found, and what is the nature of the materials? Are metadata and search guides available, and most importantly, to what extent is the collection predicated upon an administration's prerogatives to direct or selectively sanitize what enters an archive? These tangled and labyrinthine questions also influence any possible institutional narrative. In recent years, institutions have confronted their own culpability during the period of slavery and are grappling with their respective histories[11] As shown in the case of Canada regarding indigenous unceded land and in the US with regard to acknowledging slavery and university fiscal aggrandizement, institutional archives may not present the required verisimilitude.

Since institutional histories constitute valuable information and context, derived from archival sources and often utilized as introductions for scholars pursuing research in higher education, the significance of institutional histories is their beneficial primary sources which they contain. Having said this, are they sufficiently grounded in recognized historical methodologies and historiographical knowledge according to professional historical consensus? Are they bone fide contributions to rigorous historical analysis? Is there a hierarchy of significance weighted toward the veracity of a critical historical approach and methodological protocols?

Are these histories peer-reviewed and do they generally adhere to best archival, historical, and historiographic practices? They owe their existence to the need to satisfy a specific interest, often adapted to the prerogative of the institution or alumni. The typology proposed below stipulates a hierarchization of historiographical valuation regarding the histories in order of historical importance from a high of 1 to a low of 6 (Table 1).

---

ton, ed., *Archive Stories: Facts, Fictions, and the Writing of History* (Durham, NC: Duke University Press, 2005).

[11] See, for instance, University of British Columbia Indigenous Portal, accessed May 31, 2023, https://indigenous.ubc.ca; Brown University, *Slavery and Justice Report* (2006), accessed May 31, 2023, https://slaveryandjusticereport.brown.edu

Table 1: Typology of Six Hierarchical Published Institutional Histories.

1	University Press – Peer-Reviewed
2	University Press, Illustrated and/or Commissioned
3	Institutionally Commissioned, Non-University Press
4	Celebratory Publishing
5	Commercial Publisher
6	Private Printing

Adhering to normative academic practices propounded by professional historians of higher education and publishers provides the lens by which institutional histories are ranked in terms of adherence to accepted scholarly historical scholarship. The most rigorous histories are peer-reviewed and must sustain critical scrutiny and evaluation, generally upheld by university presses, but not exclusively.

Considering the importance of archives for the writing of institutional histories, what is the nature of histories focused on American and Canadian higher education institutions? Specifically, what is the nature of institutional histories purporting to cover an institution's foundation, evolution, and key developments? This overarching question concerns the histories endeavoring to present an institution's raison d'être in whatever form the history takes.[12] Generally, these institutional histories present a holistic approach with regard to their subject; that is, they are not necessarily concerned with, nor particularly focused on, a singular facet of an institution's relationship to a set of givens or a specific topic (e.g., governmental relations, civil rights, student life, teaching conditions, gender issues, etc.).[13] Instead, they attempt to frame their narrative around the locus of an insti-

---

[12] For an introductory discussion and treatment of the varied and problematic nature of institutional histories pertaining to higher education institutions, see Jean-Pierre V. M. Hérubel, "University, College Institutional Histories, and University Presses: General Observations of a Unique Publishing Phenomenon," *Publishing Research Quarterly* 35 (2019): 352–361; Jean-Pierre V. M. Hérubel, "For Alma Mater: Publishing Institutional Histories of Higher Education and University Presses: Purposes, Genre and Scholarly Value," *Learned Publishing* 35 (2022): 288–291.

[13] For such historical studies, consult Susan Rumsey Strong, *Thought Knows No Sex: Women's Rights at Alfred University* (Albany: State University of New York Press, 2008); Stefan M. Bradley, *Harlem vs. Columbia University: Black Student Power in the Late 1960s* (Urbana: University of Illinois Press, 2009); Charles J. Holden, *The New Southern University: Academic Freedom and Liberalism at UNC* (Lexington: The University Press of Kentucky, 2012); Winton U. Solberg, *Reforming Med-*

tution's general life course. The historical and bibliographic complexities surrounding institutional histories present a variegated constellation of historiographic, if not, historical accuracy.[14]

Rationales behind Institutional Histories

There is a multitude of reasons for writing institutional histories, and these are not confined to higher education institutions. Museums, libraries, and publishing houses – just to mention a few – also have an interest in furthering their salience in society and have a concerted interest in furthering their own narrative.[15] These cultural foundations may be regarded as complementary, indeed instrumental, and constituent components of intellectual culture. Often, they represent critical contributing factors attached to higher education institutions, facilitating research, instructional pursuits, and programming. Individual centers engaged in research and teaching also have a vested stake in telling their story to insiders and outsiders, of which classical studies represents a firm exemplar.[16] Classical studies or any departmental disciplinary unit may wish to account for their longevity or significance. Generally, any cultural institution arrives at a juncture necessitating a projected narrative, often the subject of more than one history. Occasions such as jubilees or an institutional need to celebrate a watershed change in status (e.g., from

---

ical Education: The University of Illinois College of Medicine, 1880–1920 (Urbana: University of Illinois Press, 2009).

14 For an incisive discussion of historiographic concerns and similar, see Lester F. Goodchild and Irene Pancner Huk, "The American College History: A Survey of its Historiographic Schools and Analytic Approaches from the Mid-Nineteenth Century to the Present," in *Higher Education: Handbook of Theory and Research*, vol. VI, ed. John C. Smart (New York: Higher Education, 1990): 201–290. There are a number of schools of thinking concerning the writing of institutional histories. For an instructive introduction, consult Joel T. Rosenthal, "All Hail the Alma Mater: Writing College Histories in the U.S," *History of Universities* XXVII (2013): 190–222.

15 For instructive examples, consult H. Sarkowski, *Springer-Verlag: History of a Scientific Publishing House, Part 1: 1842–1945, Foundation, Maturation, Adversity* (Berlin and Heidelberg, Springer Verlag, 1996); H. Götz, *Springer-Verlag: History of a Scientific Publishing house: Part 2: 1945–1992. Rebuilding, Opening Frontiers, Securing the Future* (Berlin and Heidelberg, Springer Verlag, 1996); Maurice Hungiville, *From a Single Window: Michigan State University and Its Press, 1947–1997* (East Lansing: Michigan State University Press, 1998); Harry Carter, *A History of the Oxford University Press* (Oxford: Clarendon Press, 1975); Evan H. Turner, ed., *Object Lessons: Cleveland Creates a Museum of Art* (Cleveland: Cleveland Museum of Art, 1991).

16 Louis E Lord, *A History of the American School of Classical Studies at Athens, 1882–1942: An Intercollegiate Project* (Cambridge, MA: Published for the American School of Classical Studies at Athens by Harvard University Press, 1947).

being designated a college to being designated a university) prompt a desire to narrate the evolution of an institution.

Motivations leading to writing institutional histories represent a complex web not readily accounted for by historians of higher education.[17] When first encountering them, their appearance easily suggests that institutional histories constitute attempts to capture some kind of essence of a college or university – a simple but judicious effort to account for the principal historical heights that an institution has reached. Generally, received wisdom holds that institutional histories are less than bona fide historical analyses of higher education institutions; rather, they represent a particular celebratory genre. Institutional histories convey a sense of the institution, its major challenges, triumphs, and its general and specific mission over time. Most histories come into existence when a sufficient amount of time has elapsed, when there is a story to tell, and an audience is ready to receive and appreciate the institution's story.[18] Almost without qualification, the story told celebrates positive aspects and highlights, while at times also recounting challenges, but with a nod to a satisfactory denouement. It is not uncommon for academic historians to write the history of their own institution.[19] However, there are as

---

[17] An interesting selective survey of universities is Blaise Cronin, *Cathedrals of Learning: Great and Ancient Universities of Western Europe* (Hull: Chandos Publishing, 2016).

[18] Recently, a manuscript was discovered for Penn State University's first commissioned history, written but not published due to the board of trusties being dissatisfied with it, see Erwin W. Runkle, *The Pennsylvania State College 1853–1932: Interpretation and Record* (Nittany Valley, PA: The Nittany Valley Press, 2014). For a fascinating account of its discovery and subsequent publication, see http://www.statecollege.com/news/columns/the-first-history-of-penn-state,1467435/, accessed May 31, 2023. There have been two commissioned histories since then: Dunaway Wayland Fuller, *History of The Pennsylvania State College* (Pennsylvania State College, 1946) and Michael Bezilla, *Penn State: An Illustrated History* (University Park: Pennsylvania State University Press, 1985).

[19] For a stellar and illustrative example of commissioned histories, see Jonathan E. Helmreich, *Through All the Years: A History of Allegheny College* (Meadville: Allegheny College, 2005). For an excerpted description of its genesis, see "Through All the Years: A History of Allegheny College," a 560-page volume with almost 900 illustrations, which explores the evolution of the college from its beginnings in the frontier town of Meadville to the present day. The duties of college historian came about after he retired, when Allegheny president Richard J. Cook asked Helmreich if he would serve as college historian on a volunteer basis. Before he wrote Allegheny's history, Helmreich first had to decide for whom he was writing it. "Right or wrong, I decided to write a history of Allegheny primarily for current and future alumni and for past, current and future faculty and staff of the college," he said. "Secondarily, it is for residents of northwest Pennsylvania. If it is of passing benefit to historians of higher education in the United States that is an added bonus," accessed 21 May 2020, https://sites.allegheny.edu/news/2005/10/03/professor-emeritus-of-his tory-writes-history-of-the-college/. It is not uncommon that retired historians write the history of their institutions, see Phillip R. Shriver, *The Years of Youth, 1910–1960* (Kent: Kent State University Press, 1960); Walter Havighurst, *The Miami Years, 1809–1969* (New York: Putnam, 1969); David Stra-

many reasons for pursuing and publishing institutional histories as there are institutional histories to be pursued.[20]

The data reveal a spectrum of historical studies appearing in a variety of genres and publications. For American and Canadian institutions these histories appear in the following formats (figures 1 and 2):

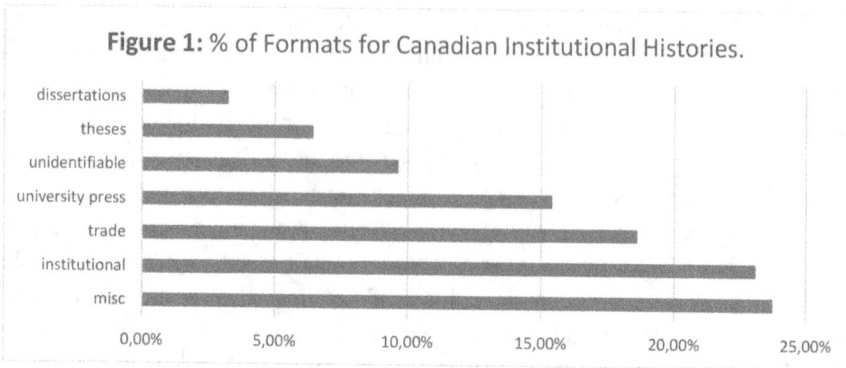

Fig. 1: Total institutional histories = 156.

The number of American institutional histories notwithstanding, both Canadian and American histories are heavily published by trade presses, while university presses capture a significant number of published histories. Canadian histories are likely to be published by their home institution, while theses and dissertations, even though they are not strictly speaking published, constitute a sizable amount. It should be noted that these types of histories conform to critical historical methodology and are generally informed by historiographic approaches. Thus, they are vetted within the protocols of historical practices and are accountable to best practices in historical research. The miscellaneous category of histories constitutes a grouping that includes private printing, alumni publications, institutionally sponsored works by interested groups, as well as a number of works emanating from non-scholarly interested parties, even governmental entities. They owe

---

dling, *In Service to the City: A History of the University of Cincinnati* (Cincinnati: University of Cincinnati Press, 2018), or trained historian archivist Michael Bezilla, *Penn State: An Illustrated History* (University Park: Pennsylvania State University Press, 1985).

20 A very anecdotal and entertaining narrative at times exercising tongue-in-cheek asides, comical vignettes, and yet an attempt to narrate a historical account is Christopher Redmond, *Water Under the Bridge: An Unofficial History of the University of Waterloo*, 1st ed. (Waterloo, Ontario: Publications Office, University of Waterloo, 1998); Andrew Schlesinger, *Veritas: Harvard College and the American Experience.* (Chicago: Ivan R. Dee, 2005).

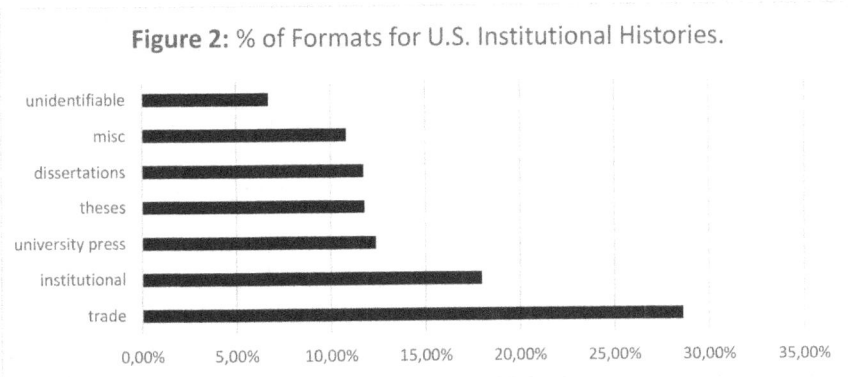

Figure 2: % of Formats for U.S. Institutional Histories.

Fig. 2: Total institutional histories = 2,803.

their very existence to the need to satisfy a specific interest, often orientating in the institution's or alumni's prerogative. Nostalgia, notwithstanding the drive to narrate significance, drives institutional history writing – many works in the category miscellaneous have been authored by alumni, former academics, presidents, or former administrators.

General Characteristics of Institutional Histories

Institutional histories comprise an ecology of histories occupying a range of narrative genres. Institutional histories fall under specific categories or genres under which most histories can be classified. Whether celebratory or not, most, if not all, exhibit readily identifiable characteristics. Chronological, rarely thematic, very positive in tone, and given to a sense of ever-achieving success, this normative practice is pursued in many institutional histories, often emulating the well-trodden chronicler's approach to laudatory storytelling. First, the majority of histories appear decades after their institution was founded. They adopt an overarching view rather than getting into the thickets and often emphasize an administrative-centric approach. Rarely concerned with micro-history (e. g., departmental history) or focused on professorial lives, activities, and achievements, they tend to favor higher administrators and institutional leadership as core values. Institutional governance especially favors institutional boards and top-down historical narratives, at the expense of more nuanced examinations. University archives tend to gather under their aegis of student records, departmental records, memoranda, marketing materials, administrative documents, and sundry documentation. The ways in which they are dealt with and accounted for, and how they may be subject to non-disclosure strictures, may present research complications or impediments. Of course, the ubiquity of student life, sports, and institutional accommodation also exerts a leitmotif. Commemorative in tone, many histories are celebratory publications specifically marking the institution's progress with semicentennial, sesquicentennial, or bicentennial milestones. Among these histories, more seasoned works appear, not expressly commemorative nor celebratory but informed by concerted scholarly examination.

For non-peer-reviewed histories, a particular finding is the marginalization of libraries and museums in institutional histories, in case they are even mentioned. The weight given to administrative history, key players within the upper administration, their efforts, failures, and successes looms large over the nuances of faculty participation in institutional activities. Great issues and instrumental pragmatic exigencies and concerns related to institutional progress generally overshadow individual accomplishments of researchers, teaching innovations, etc. Depending on the institution's relationship to collegiate sports and/or physical facilities, student life and other concerns for detailed narrative often eclipse a balanced and analytical treatment. A major caveat is the use of statistics and photography to highlight the narrative. Moreover, agency, external forces, influences, or pressures treated through this lens occur within the context of the weight of administrative responses.

Published Institutional Histories, Theses, and Dissertations as Historiographical Resources

Beyond the typology of published institutional histories, graduate student degree research constitutes a valuable source of institutional history complementing the published corpus available to historians of higher education. It is critical to note the existence of these other institutional histories emanating from master's theses and doctoral dissertations, albeit in manuscript form. Products of sustained research effort, additionally vetted by a committee of academic historians, such as theses (shorter unpublished studies) and dissertations (unpublished original and substantive analytical research) conform to the rigorous requirements of graduate school history standards, sustained by the professionalization of historical research and final approval by the committee of historians. Moreover, theses and dissertations must embed their institution's history within the context of historiographic knowledge and research execution.[21] An additional value pertaining to

---

21 For sound examples of institutional histories, see Albert Lawrence Biehn, "The Development of

theses and dissertations concerns their bibliographies and methodological foundation upon which their historical subject is grounded, making these histories especially conducive as analytical history. While not entirely free from institutional influence, they tend to achieve a more scholarly examination. As pedagogical experiences, graduate students benefit from exposure to sustained evaluation, careful examination of archival methods, and historiographic framing as they experience proficiency in systematic historical research. Selective *de visu* examination of theses and dissertations reveals preliminary but foundational usage of rich archival sources, which might be mined by graduate students and seasoned historians alike.

Institutional histories as primary source material provide critical evidentiary sources for further research. They also provide digestible accounts ascertaining key themes confronting a given institution's position within the wider context of studies of institutional adaptation and evolution. When discernible and feasible, curricular changes may be identified and mapped for greater analysis. Programmatic emphases responding to intellectual, pedagogical, scholarly, and research initiatives, as well as administrative direction and caveats, may be explored in a sample population of institutional histories. Critically, moreover, indicators of changes in degree structure, attrition and graduation rates, or substantive evidence of institutional culture vis-à-vis regional, state, national, and societal influences may be gleaned from these histories. The old chestnut of vocational versus humanistic education is particularly well-suited for examination. Longitudinal studies of institutional responses to institutional concerns, among others, may be broached within the larger context of socio-economic conditions, contingencies framed by the purpose and raison d'être of higher education. Cohorts of institutional histories by year of publication, region, state, etc. (whether public or private foundations) may elucidate specific or common pressures affecting institutional missions. Four-year regional liberal arts universities or national research-intensive institutions may be effectively examined for salient characteristics either individually or within a specific category of institutional morphology. Comparative studies in particular may contribute to identifying general preoccupations absorbing institutional energies and resources. As institutions are not the ivory towers they sometimes propose to be and do not exist in splendid isolation, internal and external

---

the University of Nebraska" (Master's thesis, University of Nebraska, 1934); Melvin R. George, "Northeastern Illinois University: The History of a Comprehensive State University" (Ph.D. diss., University of Chicago, 1979); Mildred Bernice Gaalot, "Grambling State University, 1901–1977" (Ed.D. diss., Louisiana State University and Agricultural & Mechanical College, 1982). For a departmental history, see Ralph Joseph Clark, "A History of the Department of Extension at the University of Alberta, 1912–1956" (Ph.D. diss., University of Toronto, 1986).

forces and institutional responses constitute an essential avenue of historical investigation.

Definitional Glossary

A critical and advisory component of the discussion on institutional histories of higher education institutions is the conceptualization and formulation of a definitional glossary for this unique phenomenon in the history of higher education publishing and scholarship. As an effective approach for situating institutional histories, this glossary offers additional context for institutional histories assessed for historiographic veracity and content analysis.

1 University Press – Peer-Reviewed

This type of publication is rarer as it generally adheres to the observed principles and normative research characterizing critical historical scholarship.[22] Such histories follow the historiographic protocols of historical research and attempt to frame the institution's narrative within the context of critical archival work. Verisimilitudes, problems, challenges, and unresolved concerns are framed along with achievements. These histories are informed by a concern for a critical and disinterested account. It is not uncommon that an institution's history is published by another university press, as this provides a more concerted scholarly approach.[23] Reliance on an institution's archival resources normally grounds the pri-

---

[22] For an outstanding example, see Paul Keith Conkin, *Gone With the Ivy: A Biography of Vanderbilt University* (Knoxville: University of Tennessee Press, 1985); David B. Potts, *Wesleyan University, 1831–1910: Collegiate Enterprise in New England* (New Haven: Yale University Press, 1992); Robert A. McCaughey, *Stand, Columbia: A History of Columbia University in the City of New York, 1754–2004* (New York: Columbia University Press, 2003); Martin L. Friedland, *The University of Toronto: A History*, 2nd ed. (Toronto: University of Toronto Press, 2013); John W. Boyer, *The University of Chicago: A History* (London: The University of Chicago Press, 2015).

[23] Testimonial from a Research-1 university press director, "While the genres differ, my preference is for a historical approach rather than laudatory. Integrity demands transparency. A couple of reasons come to mind as to why university presses are a good fit: first, such a venture would give the press a visibility on campus that it probably previously did not enjoy. Second, a university press would hold the publication to research and editorial standards that may or may not be held by another unit capable of producing such a volume (e. g., university marketing and communication). Third, a university's institutional history would require true interdepartmental cooperation and expertise." Email correspondence with author, 19 March 2019.

mary materials, from which interpretative responses may follow. Lastly, but crucially, these histories undergo a peer-review process by readers conversant in higher education history and the like, further legitimizing the historical scholarship represented by these works. As historians, they tend to use a broader source base that does not exclusively stem from the university archive.

Ex.: Martin L. Friedland, *The University of Toronto: A History*, 2nd ed. (Toronto: University of Toronto Press, 2013).

2 University Press Publication, Illustrated and/or Commissioned

Sometimes, a university press is approached to consider publishing a commissioned history of their affiliate institution. This is frequently an administrative suggestion carrying a concerted interest with a stake in a successful telling of the institution's narrative. The writing may be either a team effort or an individual effort, quite often a retired administrator with writing or scholarly acumen or a retired former faculty historian. These works can be highly and critically informative, albeit with the caveat that administrative interests may trump historiographical veracity. Yet, these tomes are often grounded in the institution's archival sources, replete with pictorial layouts and illustrations that enhance the narrative drive to a more positive historical account. An important caveat is that these histories do not necessarily undergo peer-review by experts in the field of the history of higher education.

Ex.: University of Illinois administration, *Illini Years: A Picture History of the University of Illinois, 1868–1950* (Urbana, IL: University of Illinois Press, 1950).

3 Institutionally Commissioned History, Non-University Press

Commissioned histories constitute a unique form of institutional publication. These tomes are artifacts directly emanating from administrations, governing boards, or alumni interested in accounts that are more hagiographic in nature. Their historiographic veracity is adventagous only by their usefulness to these agencies wishing to aggrandize their position in institutional memory. Few of these histories can match a well-rounded, penetrating, and historiographically sophisticated study. Their purpose is to maintain a feel-good, self-congratulatory frame of historical reference. Frequently, these publications are predicated upon archival primary sources originating almost exclusively from within the institution.

Ex.: James P. Walsh, *San José State University: An Interpretive History, 1950–2000* (San José, CA: San José State University, 2003).

4 Celebratory

This genre anticipates and captures the institution as a celebration of everything that the institution has achieved, with little regard for seasoned, articulated research. Moreover, it frames the institution's milestones with peppered vignettes and grand achievements with little regard for framing the institutional history within a scholarly context. All forms of historiographical discussion are absent, as is any attempt to contextualize the narrative within the scholarship of the history of higher education. Often accompanied by a plethora of illustrations, campus photography, and reputation-enhancing highlights, these histories are welcomed by institutional administrations and alumni. Celebratory histories are what they purport to be – an unbridled account free of trials, concerns, or the sticky issues concerning an institution's position with regard to a dispassionate historical examination. And yet, some of these narratives offer a chronological development replete with data and, at times, hard-won primary sources.

Ex.: John Norberg and Purdue University, *Ever true: The Campaign for Purdue University: Celebrating 150 Years* (Lafayette, IN: Purdue University, 2015).

5 Commercial Publisher

This type of history is often written and published for a wider readership, broaching a more generalized institutional account. Commercial publishers will publish these accounts, especially if their appeal captures a market interested in an institution's past, while highlighting grand and compelling themes that drive and illustrate easily accessibly written narratives. A concern for historiographical matters generally does not appear in these publications, while illustrations and institutional mythologies prevail. Concern for educational missions, research, scholarly achievements, as well as intellectual position in the larger higher education landscape is less demanding. The staples of student life and administrative triumphs complement an emphasis on sports and overall institutional guiding figures. Institutional archival sources often serve as the basis for formulating the narrative.

Ex.: Verna A. Stadtman, *The University of California, 1868–1968* (New York: McGraw-Hill, 1970).

6 Private Publication

The privately written and published institutional history stands alone among the possible types available in the institutional history publication ecology. Indeed, it may take many forms and appear as limited editions, pamphlet-like works, illustrated histories, or focused on key figures and bellwether moments in the evolution of an institution. More importantly, subsidies originating from the institution itself or interested parties finance the publication. Generally, these accounts do not follow strict historiographical protocols, nor academic historical research procedures. However, a dependence on primary sources, even if occasionally a very specific selection, buttresses these histories.

Ex.: Daisy Woodward Beck, *Once Over Lightly: An Indiana University Story* (privately printed, 1962).

The Unique Case of the Illustrated History

In terms of palatable history, the illustrated history replete with photographs, maps, and visual asides is the photographic history.[24] For many institutions and institutional authors, it offers a ready-made potpourri of easily digestible and identifiable nostalgic cheesecake. Often uncritical, these works offer a narrative of carefully orchestrated storytelling with the advantage of hindsight and purposeful narrative drive. A quasi-cinematic tableau offers the reader a visual introduction into the life of the institution, its architecture, snapshots of student life, selected professorial lights, administrative notables, as well as daily activities selected to capture the spirit, if not the essence, of the institution's life course. Generally, accompanying this visual feast is the proverbial coverage of sports. Aside from the propagandistic nature of these histories, their importance for archival primary photographic and visual presentation may be valuable as primary source materials for historiographic study or inroads into larger collections of visual material available.[25]

---

[24] For examples, see Christina M. Consolino and Michael Chmura, *Historic Photos of University of Michigan* (Nashville: Turner Publishing Company, 2017). For short vignettes and heavy illustrations, see Kim Clarke, *Always Leading, Forever Valiant: Stories of the University of Michigan, 1817–2017* (Ann Arbor: University of Michigan Press, 2017). This book was published by the University of Michigan Bicentennial Office. See also John T. Bethell, *Harvard Observed: An Illustrated History of the University in the Twentieth Century* (Cambridge, MA: Harvard University Press, 1998).

[25] The primarily photographic histories published by Arcadia Publishing offer an invaluable primary source for historians of individual institutions and should be consulted, accessed May 31,

The Phenomenon of Specific Institutional Unit Histories

Unlike a history dedicated to an entire college or university, histories dedicated to a single academic unit provide a wide spectrum of genres. In the past thirty years, there has been a growing number of distinct histories focused on a single unit in an institution, such as a college at a university, a medical school or pharmacy school, law school, engineering, or a specific department. However, departmental histories pertaining to the humanities have rarely been broached or published as books. Professional schools are more likely to pursue their respective histories than a humanities entity.[26] They are frequently commissioned by the respective unit, authored by the unit, by a faculty member, or retired faculty member. Alumni have also authored such histories. These histories tend to follow similar trends in terms of format as proper institutional histories. They may be celebratory, often reminiscent, offering personal vignettes, and so on, besides presenting the evolution of a particular unit.[27] Some institutions have garnered a number of publications, works authored via commission or not.[28] Yet, these are more likely published

---

2023, https://www.arcadiapublishing.com/Navigation/Subjects/Schools-Education. As of 12 May 2020, 252 photographic books have been published by authors generally associated with these institutions. These histories include professional schools, universities, flagship campuses, as well as branch or affiliated campuses, liberal arts colleges, and community colleges.

[26] A notable exception is the University of Toronto – there have been a number of such studies published for the University of Toronto: R. Helmes-Hayes, ed, *A Quarter-Century of Sociology at the University of Toronto, 1963–1988* (Toronto: Canadian Scholar's Press, 1988); Maddalena Kuitunen and Julius A. Molinaro, *A History of Italian Studies at the University of Toronto: 1840–1990* (Toronto: Department of Italian Studies, University of Toronto, 1991); C. D. Rouillard, *French Studies at the University of Toronto, 1853–1993* (Toronto: Department of French, University of Toronto, 1994).

[27] For illustrative American and Canadian examples, see Kristen A. Yarmey, *Labors & Legacies: The Chemists of Penn State 1855–1947* (University Park: Pennsylvania State University, 2006); Karamjit S. Rai, *Four Decades of Vector Biology at the University of Notre Dame: A Scientific Perspective* (Notre Dame: University of Notre Dame, 1999); R. S. Fraser, *Cardiology at the University of Alberta, 1922–1969* (Edmonton: Department of Medicine, University of Alberta, 1992); Roche Duval, *Les Cheminements Educatifs de l'Orientation et de la Pédagogie de 1943 à 1993 à la Faculté des Sciences de l'Education de l'Université Laval* (Sainte Foy: Université Laval, 1995); John W. Steele, *History of the Faculty of Pharmacy 1899–1999* (Winnipeg: Faculty of Pharmacy, University of Manitoba, 1999); Eric Damer, *Discovery by Design: The Department of Mechanical Engineering of the University of British Columbia: Origins and History, 1907–2001* (Vancouver: Ronsdale Press, 2001).

[28] See Willie M Reed, *Celebrating a Continuum of Excellence: Purdue University School of Veterinary Medicine, 1959–2009* (West Lafayette: Purdue University Press, 2009).

by the unit or by the university press by special arrangements with or without the university press *imprimatur*.[29]

Concluding Observations, Institutional Narratives, and Scholarly Considerations

As with any historical account, the need to minimize overt bias is imperative for an academic historian. To some degree, institutional histories reflect the nature of writing a history of a singular institution without sufficiently situating it within the larger spectrum of the history of higher education. However, each history does represent the attempt to provide an accounting of its raison d'être as well as provide a comprehensible and valuable picture of its value to its constituency and society. Given their mixed reception and value to a scholarly history of higher education, individual histories offer the professional historian a roadmap that may be traced and utilized for their provision of first-order history – this is, their value as secondary, if not primary sources in furthering rigorous historical scholarship. Indeed, some set an institution's position within a given context in situ but few do. Their true value lies in their attempt to mine primary archival sources, provide vignettes, first-person accounts and testimonies, and to provide a useful framework of what has been pursued. For historians and graduate students of higher education, they provide a treasure trove of information.

Scholarship devoted to the history of intellectual culture, in its different approaches, includes the histories of higher education institutions in their myriad forms. The attempt to establish a viable and efficacious approach for ascertaining the different types of institutional histories provides an approach that can be pursued among other possibilities. Limited to the United States and Canada, this approach offers insights into the nature of the established and growing corpus of such histories as they manifest themselves within the framework of publication types and trends. The salient purpose of this approach is to readily identify and

---

29 According to a Research-1 university press director, "In these cases, it's far more appropriate the books be celebratory. The sponsoring group gets something they can use to engage alumni, drive fundraising, bolster their department's standing, use as gifts, etc." "But the higher ups do care that we provided this service to make these departmental histories possible—every institutional administrator is constantly reviewing every aspect of the institution and asking university press directors, how does this advance and help our immediate community," and "It really depends upon the author or sponsoring group to get their facts right." Email correspondence with author, 4 June 2020.

situate the historical veracity of various individual institutional histories as they appear in publication.

This discussion has focused on the phenomenon of singular histories of higher education institutions, specifically Canadian and American. Their content and different purposes are as varied as their historical veracity and usefulness as historical narratives, especially scholarship. The approach developed to ascertain their characteristics, predicated upon a definitional model and glossary identifying various approaches, provides an efficacious introduction into this variegated primary and historiographic corpus. With necessary qualification and modification, it may be applied to other groups of institutions prone to writing their histories.

Since their inception, institutional histories have been and continue to be published and provide foundational material for further historical scholarship.[30] The history of higher education institutions is all the more richer due to their presence among distinct historical scholarship. Moreover, these histories provide valuable insights into individual institutional conditions as well as bibliographic and archival references and practices of self-presentation. They visually contribute to an institution's quotidian activities and built environment; illustrations alone can offer additional critical knowledge beyond textual treatments. Future research into institutional histories as a pragmatic approach for understanding the historiographic conditions characterizing individual institutions will add to articulating an informed historiography of higher education. Indeed, the spectrum of publishers and their relationship to institutions, authors, and authorial intent constitute a complex ecology inhabited by the historian, the institution, and the publisher. These histories alone cannot provide the necessary knowledge required to develop a historiographically grounded collective history of higher education, but they serve as a necessary component in the intellectual vitality and significance of that history of higher education.

---

[30] Some institutions have published more than one history or type of history, see Phillip Raymond Shriver, *The Years of Youth: Kent State University, 1910–1960* (Kent: Kent State University Press, 1960); William H. Hildebrand, Dean H. Keller, and Anita Dixon Herington, *A Book of Memories: Kent State University, 1910–1992* (Kent: Kent State University Press, 1993); William H. Hildebrand, *A Most Noble Enterprise: The Story of Kent State University, 1910–2010* (Kent: Kent State University Press, 2009). Other institutions have garnered more than nine individual histories, including Harvard (30), Michigan (14), Oberlin (13), Princeton (21), Rutgers (10), Stanford (11), Pennsylvania (14), UNC-Chapel Hill (18), Notre Dame (12), Virginia (17), Wisconsin (10), UC-Berkeley (17), Tuskegee (11), U.S. Military Academy (14); McGill (11), Laval (10), Saskatchewan (10), Toronto (17).

About the contributor

Jean-Pierre V. M. Hérubel is Professor of Information Studies in the Libraries and School of Information Studies, Purdue University. His interests include historiography and theory, history of scholarly publishing, history of academic disciplines, and mapping historical scholarship. He has published studies on disciplinary cultures, bibliometric analysis, and scholarly communication.

Section III: **Engaging the Field**

Bennet Rosswag and Christoph Schmitt

The Objectification of Meaning: A Systems-Theoretical Approach to (the History of) Knowledge

Abstract: While the history of knowledge often understands knowledge in the same way as this term is understood in the sources, the literature claims a lack of precision when defining the term. Operationally, knowledge is seen as a moveable entity, with research focusing on the effects of the environment on said entity and vice versa. The article uses systems theory to add to this perspective by focusing on the social production of knowledge. This allows to conceptualize objectivity and subjectivity, as well as definitions of validity and pseudo in their functionality within the social production. Following this path, knowledge can be defined as 'Objectified Sense/Meaning', the result of a process of interaction with the environment, previous existing knowledge, and our expectations.

Keywords: systems theory, social production of knowledge, sociology of knowledge, definition of 'knowledge,' truth and objectivity

Looking at the field of the history of knowledge, one notices, paradoxically, that the definition of the term 'knowledge' appears to be a blank spot – a fact that is noted institutionally, in practice, and in the accompanying research. In a notable article in the journal *Merkur*, Daniel Allemann argued for replacing the term knowledge with that of information, as the former had become too unclear. Similarly, in a review of two books on the 'historicity of knowledge,' Thomas Mohnike referred to the existing concept of knowledge as being mainly integrative and regretted the lack of a deeper definition and theorization. Michael Hagner has offered comparable reservations with regard to the term and its role in historical research.[1] Many

---

Acknowledgments: We would like to thank our colleagues Simon Götz, Maria Tauber, and Senta Terner for their motivation, help and discussions, as well as both reviewers for their fruitful comments.

[1] Daniel Allemann, "Die Wiederkunft der Information," *MERKUR* 870 (2021): 68–73. Michael Hagner, "Anstatt einer Einleitung. Rückblick auf die Wissensgeschichte," *Nach Feierabend. Zürcher Jahrbuch für Wissensgeschichte* 15 (2021): 35–47. Thomas Mohnike, "Über die Historizität des Wissens," review of *Forms of Knowledge: Developing the History of Knowledge* by Johan Östling et al. and *Knowledge in Motion: The Royal Swedish Academy of Sciences and the Making of Modern Society* by Karl Grandin et al., *H-Soz-Kult*, 4 February 2022, <www.hsozkult.de/publicationreview/id/reb-29755>.

Open Access. © 2023 the author(s), published by De Gruyter. This work is licensed under the Creative Commons Attribution-NonCommercial-NoDerivatives 4.0 International License.
https://doi.org/10.1515/9783111078038-010

analyses in the history of knowledge define knowledge as what contemporaries viewed and understood as knowledge.[2] This approach enables the history of knowledge not to be limited to a history of science and its conclusions, thus making it possible to look at, for example, practical day-to-day or subaltern knowledge as equally valid. Nevertheless, it does not allow for tracing societal negotiations that are part of knowledge production, which inevitably leads to the question of how people came to define something as knowledge.

So, how does something become knowledge in the interaction of societies or groups? We define this process as the social production of social knowledge, which means that knowledge is not a closed entity but the product of societal interactions and an objectification of what Niklas Luhmann refers to as *Sinn* (i.e., sense/meaning). In doing so, it is crucial that we distinguish and define various categories that are part of the production of knowledge by means of communication: facts, information, meaning, and opinion. In the following, we first explore the existing definitions of knowledge within the history of science and history of knowledge, as well as their predecessors. In the second part, we discuss systems theory and its uses in historiography as well as, specifically, when it comes to knowledge. Thirdly, we explain our proposed definitions and approach to knowledge production based on systems theory. Finally, we try to illustrate our approach through a brief empirical example – the 'scientification' of yoga in early 20th-century Germany.

Definitions in the History of Knowledge and of Science

The history of knowledge and the history of science are both vital fields within the landscape of historiography. Even though knowledge is the central object of the history of knowledge, it seems difficult to arrive at a precise definition of the term.[3] It deserves to be said that both fields seem to be extremely close to the point of being indistinguishable from one another, as they are heavily influenced

---

2 Cf. Harald Fischer-Tiné, *Pidgin-Knowledge: Wissen und Kolonialismus* (Zürich and Berlin: Diaphanes, 2013), 11. This does not refer to a conceptual historical approach. Here, 'knowledge' constitutes an analytical category and not the word itself used in the sources, which of course can lead to issues of translation and meaning.

3 Cf. Suzanne Marchand, "How Much Knowledge is Worth Knowing? An American Intellectual Historian's Thoughts on the Geschichte des Wissens," *Berichte zur Wissenschaftsgeschichte* 42 (2019): 126–149, 139; Lorraine Daston, "The History of Science and the History of Knowledge," *KNOW: A Journal on the Formation of Knowledge* 1 (2017): 131–154.

by cultural studies. Both approaches analyze the production of knowledge in a specific environment, thus circumventing a general definition.

The history of knowledge finds another basis in the field of postcolonialism and colonial history. A good example of the aforementioned definition of knowledge being what people perceive as knowledge is the concept of "pidgin-knowledge," which is part of a post-colonially informed history of knowledge and was developed in Harald Fischer-Tiné's essay of the same title. In opposition to previous ideas in which knowledge more or less successfully trickles down from the Global North or is even transferred unchanged,[4] his approach highlights the entanglement of knowledge and its production by addressing contact zones and exchanges between different "knowledge systems" and their role in the local colonial production of knowledge as well as that of the colonizers. This concept aims to take those forms of knowledge seriously that may seem unscientific from a 'modern', Global Northern view, and were therefore sometimes portrayed as an opposite of and even an obstacle to *true* knowledge production.[5]

Fischer-Tiné's essay makes it clear that pidgin-knowledge constitutes an open concept of knowledge that is constantly subject to change. According to the text, this fluid body of knowledge is composed of equally changeable knowledge elements. However, these *Wissensinhalte* are not explained further.[6] The nature of knowledge is also addressed by Donna Haraway's essay "Situated Knowledges," which, adopting a feminist approach, discusses conditions and localizations of knowledge.[7] The text argues that knowledge should be situated, dependent on embodied and social conditions: "Situated Knowledges are about communities, not about isolated individuals."[8] Both approaches argue for knowledge as a social construct and a perception of knowledge that cannot be defined once and for all as it is dependent on its surroundings. To break down the hierarchies, both approaches take off from an open concept of knowledge, in which knowledge is everything considered as such. We agree that knowledge is dependent on place and time but would stress that knowledge is not an entity in itself. The focus should not be on the effects of the surroundings on a preexisting entity of knowledge but on the role of these surroundings in the production of knowledge.

---

4 Cf., for instance, Richard Bauman and Charles L. Briggs, *Voices of Modernity: Language Ideologies and the Politics of Inequality* (Cambridge: CUP, 2003).
5 Cf. Fischer-Tiné, *Pidgin-Knowledge*, 9–10.
6 Cf. Fischer-Tiné, *Pidgin-Knowledge*, specifically 12–13.
7 Cf. Donna Haraway, "Situated Knowledges: The Science Question in Feminism and the Privilege of Partial Perspective," *Feminist Studies* 14, no. 3 (1988): 575–599.
8 Cf. Haraway, "Situated Knowledges," 590.

The literature is quick to point out that these approaches have their downsides. Historian Marian Füssel cautions that "it may be morally questionable if every historical claim to scientificity were accepted unquestionably, as the study of science in totalitarian systems will show."[9] This shows the normative nature of knowledge and, in the minds of many, the close relationship between this term and truth and science, as well as the notion that knowledge is seen as "justified true belief."[10]

Consequently, Füssel's caution is only relevant if one equates knowledge and truth. If, on the other hand, one tries to look at the *function* of knowledge in historical society, we believe that this issue will not arise. On the contrary, it is precisely the claim of scientificity with regard to science in totalitarian systems that legitimized the horrors of these regimes in the eyes of many contemporaries. If one takes a cue from the sociology of knowledge, for example, following sociologists Peter Berger and Thomas Luckmann, knowledge is understood through the lived acceptance of common realities: "'knowledge' is defined as the certainty that phenomena are real and have certain properties" while "reality" is defined as "the quality of phenomena that exist regardless of our will."[11]

The history of knowledge distinguishes between different practices and functions of knowledge as a finished product. The outputted knowledge can be differentiated conceptually and functionally, depending on the theory and discipline used, via the practices of knowledge, the actors, the localities of knowledge production and validity, or even the mediality of knowledge. What all these approaches have in common is that they adopt a praxeological approach, recognizing the existence of knowledge through its recognition within a group.

Systems Theory and History (of Knowledge)

The use of Niklas Luhmann's approach to Systems Theory can help define what knowledge is and what it is not, tracing how it comes into existence, and how it

---

[9] Cf. Marian Füssel, *Wissen: Konzepte – Praktiken – Prozesse* (Frankfurt am Main and New York: Campus Verlag, 2021), 10.
[10] Cf. Edmund L. Gettier, *Is Justified True Belief Knowledge? / Ist gerechtfertigte, wahre Überzeugung Wissen?*, trans. Marc Andree Weber and Nadja-Mira Yolcu (Ditzingen: Reclam, 2019 [1963]).
[11] Cf. Peter L. Berger and Thomas Luckmann, *Die gesellschaftliche Konstruktion der Wirklichkeit: Eine Theorie der Wissenssoziologie* (Frankfurt am Main: Fischer Taschenbuch Verlag, 2016), 1.

affects communication and society as a whole.[12] Systems theory, in general, is an epistemologically driven approach to the world, understanding the world as created through and made up of systems with various functions and their interactions. Luhmann's Systems Theory has contributed to the sociology of science, especially with regard to the role of truth as a code in science[13] and subsequently, in this capacity, been touched upon in the history of knowledge.

Sociological systems theory uses the 'system' as a metaphor to describe actors, such as persons or institutions, as well as to explain their societal interactions. Sociological theorist Talcott Parsons, who along with social scientist Gregory Bateson may be seen as foundational for Luhmann's approach, defines a system as "a stable set of independent phenomena," which exists in opposition to an "ever-changing external environment."[14] These "phenomena" are held together by the function that the system serves and by the "not-serving" of the functions of other systems. Using this logic, it is possible to organize the world into different systems, containing various subsystems. These systems set themselves apart from their environment containing an infinite number of other systems, by distinctions that matter to the system and its function.

Using this approach leads to a focus on communication between said (social) systems as the driving force within society. It is through these interactions that everything social is created. The epistemological questions inherent in systems theory also allow for a deeper understanding of knowledge and its production, meaning that this appears to be a productive approach to the history of knowledge.[15] This approach prevents tautological narratives of progress and direct causality by stressing the processes of adaption and idiosyncratic interaction, while not ignoring elements of power and inequality (be they hierarchical, social, or material) that may affect the outcome.

While also criticized, especially in German-speaking historiography and cultural studies, the historiographical use of systems theory following Luhmann has been productive. For example, it has informed the works of Rudolf Schlögl, Elena Esposito, or the conference on systems theory and antiquity organized in

---

12 Niklas Luhmann, *Vertrauen, Ein Mechanismus der Reduktion sozialer Komplexität* (Stuttgart: Enke, 1989). Niklas Luhmann, "Die Unwahrscheinlichkeit der Kommunikation," in *Niklas Luhmann: Aufsätze und Reden*, ed. Oliver Jahrhaus (Ditzingen: Reclam, 2001), 76–93.
13 Cf. Claudio Baraldi, Giancarlo Corsi, and Elena Esposito, *Unlocking Luhmann: A Keyword Introduction to Systems Theory* (Bielefeld: BiUP, 2021), 205–207.
14 Sandro Segre, *Talcott Parsons: An Introduction* (Lanham, MD: UPA, 2012), 7.
15 Cf. Frank Becker and Elke Reinhardt-Becker, *Systemtheorie: Eine Einführung für die Geschichts- und Kulturwissenschaften* (Frankfurt am Main and New York: Campus Verlag 2001), 9–10.

Berlin in 2022.¹⁶ These examples all show us how the models of systems and functionality, as well as the baseline issue described by Parsons regarding so-called "double contingency" (the fact that we cannot know what others are thinking, only what we understand out of their communication),¹⁷ allow for a better and deeper understanding of history. By understanding the world through a systems theoretical lens, Schlögl shows, among other things, the effects of communication and media on the organization and functioning of society. In her book, *Die Fiktion der Wahrscheinlichen Realität* [The Fiction of Probable Reality], Esposito demonstrates how written fiction and concepts of probability and their development in the 17th century may be seen as linked processes affecting contemporary ideas on reality and the future that still affect us today.

The history of knowledge sometimes brings systems theory and its contributions to the sociology of knowledge into its analyses, such as in Marian Füssel's book on knowledge and knowledge production, *Wissen: Konzepte – Praktiken – Prozesse* [Knowledge: Concepts – Practices – Processes], while mostly using it to explain the specific code of "truth" in the field of science as well as the field's function in society, in contrast to and interaction with other fields/systems such as "politics, religion or the economy," before moving on.¹⁸

This is particularly important for the history of knowledge and, subsequently, the history of science. In these two perspectives, interrelationships often come into play as a starting point. For example, Timothy Lenoir's renowned work *Politik im Tempel der Wissenschaft* [Politics in the Temple of Science] addresses the interrelations between material conditions and the production of science.¹⁹ Focusing on interaction/communication would allow one to complement this material approach by looking at other (systemic) influences on science.

We would argue for an understanding of a production of knowledge within a system through processes of coding and decoding in communication with the environment as well as other systems within it. We try to explain both of these processes in the following paragraphs. Some of the following categories, such as envi-

---

16 Rudolf Schlögl, *Anwesende und Abwesende: Grundriss für eine Gesellschaftsgeschichte der Frühen Neuzeit* (Konstanz: KUP, 2014); Elena Esposito, *Die Fiktion der wahrscheinlichen Realität*, trans. Nicole Reinhardt (Frankfurt am Main: Suhrkamp, 2019). Moritz Hinsch, "Tagungsbericht: Systemtheorie und Antike Gesellschaft," H-Soz-Kult, accessed August 17, 2022, <www.hsozkult.de/conferencereport/id/fdkn-127979>.
17 Cf. Niklas Luhmann, "Vorbemerkung zu einer Theorie sozialer Systeme," *Niklas Luhmann: Aufsätze und Reden*, ed. Oliver Jahrhaus (Ditzingen: Reclam, 2001), 7–30, 11.
18 Füssel, *Wissen*, 20.
19 Timothy Lenoir, *Politik im Tempel der Wissenschaft: Forschung und Machtausübung im deutschen Kaiserreich* (Frankfurt am Main and New York: Campus Verlag, 1992).

ronment, information, and meaning, are linked to systems theory, which is why we use the definitions of Luhmann and the translations of Esposito et al. while adapting them to knowledge and its production, as well as supplementing specifically knowledge-oriented categories, such as data, opinion, and facts.

The Social Production of Knowledge in the System

Outside a system (e. g., a person or an institution), there is an *"environment,"*[20] which describes everything that is not the system. This environment may be accessed in a variety of ways. As part of this interaction, *information* – statements about the (outer) world that "make a difference"[21] – about the environment is generated, decoded, and processed by the system. This interaction, typically understood by Luhmann as communication, can be the perception of the world directly via our senses, such as sight, hearing, or touch, but also more indirectly via media, such as through writing, other symbols, rituals, or even recordings. These interactions, like any form of communication, are not to be understood as simple processes of perception but as acts of decoding and interpreting the elements of the environment, influenced by the system's preexisting expectations and knowledge regarding it.[22] A major influence here is the specific "situation" the system finds itself in, this being a certain repeated and repeatable combination of structures, expectations, roles, and behaviors.[23] As these patterns are recognizable by systems, they result in the behavior and expectations of the other systems in a particular situation becoming more predictable, thus influencing the process of decoding and thereby easing communication.

Data is a special expression of such an information-creating interaction with the outer world. Data can be understood as images of the world filtered by certain media and thus constructed by said media. These may include figures in tables, outputs of measuring instruments, or the like. As Allemann notes, this data may be wrong. Defective equipment, errors during measuring, or other human errors may lead to incorrect data.[24] Furthermore, this data, true or false, does not repre-

---

20 Baraldi, Corsi, and Esposito, *Unlocking Luhmann*, 235–237.
21 Baraldi, Corsi, and Esposito, *Unlocking Luhmann*, 109–110. Luhmann refers to Bateson for this definition.
22 Luhmann, *Unwahrscheinlichkeit der Kommunikation*, 80.
23 Segre, *Talcott Parsons*, 7.
24 Cf. Allemann, *Wiederkunft der Information*, 72–73.

sent the world or reality itself, but only what the instrument measured. Depending on methods of measurement, this image may differ and is therefore strongly influenced by said method. Nevertheless, it is possible to derive information from said data; for example, by comparing it with other results collected using the same method or with aforementioned expectations, as well as by contextualizing its method and the organization/individual responsible.[25] A single temperature measurement, for example, shows us nothing, as it represents a pure and singular unit of data. However, using a series of measurements or physical perceptions (given that they are comparable due to similar means of production), this data can be turned into information by making the difference it represents clear, meaning that it can be used to describe developments and make predictions.

However, from a system-theoretical point of view, information itself cannot be grasped, since it is deeply encoded in the media and needs to be decoded within a kind of black box inside the system using existing knowledge, expectations, and other information. This process then creates "sense" or, following Esposito et al., "meaning" [Luhmann's German term here is *Sinn*]. This allows us to perceive connections, similarities, and differences in the world. Using this meaning, we can then decide if data and the information gained from it is trustworthy or if one might be mistaken. Since these processes of 'making sense' only occur within the system itself, both information and meaning must be considered subjective, dependent only on the individual system's perception and process of decoding.[26]

Arguably, the system (e.g., the human being) is aware of this subjectivity. It knows that its view of the world is not necessarily shared by everyone, which is why systems differentiate between different forms of truth and why the categories of facts and knowledge exist. *Facts* are statements about the world believed to be objectively true. More precisely, these are statements of which we assume and trust that other systems have received the same or at least similar information, or, more accurately, that the other systems have constructed the same by decoding and interpreting the world in similar ways. If, furthermore, we can expect others to expect similar things and further contextualize these shared, objectified facts in similar ways, we arrive at a shared sense, a shared meaning, which we call *knowledge*. The answer to the question of what knowledge is would therefore be: knowledge is meaning that we believe others have arrived at as well; knowledge is objectified meaning.

---

[25] Uwe Schimank, "Reputation statt Wahrheit: Verdrängt der Nebencode den Code?," *Soziale Systeme* 16, no. 2 (2010): 233–242.

[26] Cf. Oliver Jahrhaus, "Zur Systemtheorie Niklas Luhmanns," *Niklas Luhmann: Aufsätze und Reden*, ed. Oliver Jahrhaus (Ditzingen: Reclam 2001), 306–309; Baraldi, Corsi, and Esposito, *Unlocking Luhmann*, 137–139.

The assumption that the information one has decoded can be treated as facts and that the generated meaning can be treated as knowledge facilitates interactions and communication in society. This is not least due to the opposite: the perception of infinite possibilities serves to paralyze by creating insecurity regarding the validity of our statements on the world. The reduction in the number of possible interpretations that have to be taken into account in every situation is referred to as "complexity reduction" in systems theory[27] and is seen as an important element driving societal changes. In everyday life, we inevitably trust that we will not permanently deceive ourselves until we are convinced otherwise. We expect our behavior to be connectable and to be connected to the environment, as well as that others will act on similar knowledge and facts, and that therefore our expectations as well as our expectations of others' expectations are right. If we are unable to do so due to habitual, linguistic, or cultural barriers, we lose this sense of security, especially if we are unaware of barriers interfering with our smooth interaction with the outer world.[28] As meaning and information are not directly observable, we can only identify these categories indirectly through communication and interaction, and then through the processes of comparison with preexisting facts (for information) and knowledge (for meaning). Facts and knowledge are thus the result of social negotiations and require constant confirmation, through which humans make sure that they can trust their view of the world in practice.

When comparing our own information and meaning with those communicated by other systems, we can find that they coincide or that they do not. If we accept them as shared, as objective or objectified, and therefore as *truth*, they become facts and knowledge as described above and will be treated as such by the system in future interactions (e. g., informing future decoding processes). Information and meaning that we do not share can be dealt with in two ways: Either they (those of others or one's own) can be categorized as objectively untrue, which in some way makes them 'negative' facts or knowledge, or they can be categorized as subjective *opinions*. To do so, the production of said meaning or information is looked at and compared, keeping in mind that the system, thus the process itself, is a black box. This means that everything going into the system – all the data, the context of perception, the meaning and knowledge of uninvolved other systems, etc. – is analyzed to look for differences that may have influenced the diverging outcome. Admittedly, in day-to-day life, this process is often outsourced to institutions we trust due to their reputation and past examples of fact-checking.[29] If the reason for the

---

27 Cf. Baraldi, Corsi, and Esposito, *Unlocking Luhmann*, 49–52.
28 Cf. Luhmann, *Vertrauen*, 1.
29 Cf. Schimank, "Nebencode."

difference can be found outside the systems, such as a lack of data or perception or the use of other pieces of information or meaning deemed to be untrue in the production, the difference is objectified, which leads to the categorization of true and untrue, respectively.

If, on the other hand, the differences are found within the systems, such as a legitimate difference in expectations and experiences, (e.g., taste or one's past), it becomes an opinion, or worldview if it is more fundamental. These differences can be tolerated within a society as long as they do not affect or negate other productions of meaning too much. Harmless examples of such hard-to-accept effects on other productions of meaning include optical illusions. They may lead to the system questioning the validity and objectivity of its own perception and thus its production of knowledge, which, in turn, shakes the foundation of our trust necessary for interacting with society, as discussed above. Take, for example, the image of a dress from 2015, which went viral online, in which viewers perceived the dress as either blue and black or white and gold.[30] We assume the colors in our environment to be objective, so it is difficult to digest the realization that this is not the case. However, even while there was a lot of discussion and everyone felt they had to be right in their perception of the color of said dress, in the end it was quite harmless in the end.

Things get much more serious when objectifying information that is important for the functioning of society. A suitable example would be a stance against vaccinations. While it can be, and often is, tolerated as a wrong minority opinion as long as it only affects a few individuals deciding for themselves, in cases where this stance affects the health of a sufficient number of additional individuals, the difference is less socially tolerable. The same is true of conspiracy theories. While some may be quite harmless, the claims of widespread fraud in a democratic election are more complicated. This is due to the fact that the legitimacy of a government as an objectified fact, especially one accepted by the opposition, is crucial for the state to function in democracies. If one needs to depend on a shared basis upon which to act, dissention creates difficulties as it weakens the validity of our expectations and our trust in them. This consequently may impede the functioning of whatever processes may be reliant on this shared basis.

This importance of dependable and therefore objectified knowledge applies to science in particular. "Truth" is the central "code," the difference maker and object of scientific interaction, at least in the self-image of said system.[31] This rings true if

---

[30] Cf. Julio Gonzáles Martín-Moro et al., "Which are the colors of the dress? Review of an atypical optic illusion," *Archivos de la Sociedad Española de Oftalmología* (English Edition) 93 (2018): 186–192, accessed February 7, 2023, doi: 10.1016/j.oftale.2018.02.003.

[31] Schimank, "Nebencode," 233.

one looks at the fact that "the history of science was and is at the same time always a history of the struggle against the unscientific, of defensive rhetorics and strategies, of defining and marking divergent practices as non- or pseudoscientific."[32] This is also done by bringing the aforementioned normative and moral perspective on science into the equation. Hence, pseudoscience, being excluded from the accepted sciences, represents an interesting object within the history of knowledge. The aim of pseudoscience is not to be unscientific, quite the opposite. Its practitioners see themselves as following the same goal, which is the pursuit of truth. The differences are fundamentally in the perception of the methods and concepts used, which, in the eyes of pseudoscience are seen as unjustly dismissed by mainstream science, drawing historical comparisons to approaches and their developed knowledge that were at first ostracized before being accepted and included into the scientific canon.

It is striking that we know the term pseudoscience, but there seems to be no such thing as *pseudo-knowledge*. The term pseudo-science, although not strictly defined, refers to a pejorative classification of another system and is to be distinguished from the terms protoscience or emerging science. The ambiguity of this term, as a source and descriptive term, testifies to a relative uncertainty of research.

The subject of pseudo-science is an important object of study within the histories of science and knowledge. It allows a closer look at the "question of the inclusion and exclusion of knowledge and its carriers," which is more or less inherent in science.[33] The analysis of pseudo-knowledge may illustrate the attempts to find dependable common ground between cultures of knowledge that are, or are at least perceived to be, different. The validity of knowledge is assessed by its results and methods, with this assessment being embedded in social situations and standards, as well as scientific expectations. Our example of yoga shows the interaction of simultaneous, and somewhat different, productions of knowledge. Through comparisons of the methods and results of the other with one's own expectations and practices, knowledge is generated through communication between systems: What fits and works in the system's knowledge production is validated as 'true', while things that do not are either defined as false – if it is contradictory – or as a difference of opinion or even worldview if it does not interfere with said production itself.

---

32 Dirk Rupnow et al., "Einleitung," *Pseudowissenschaft: Konzeptionen von Nichtwissenschaftlichkeit in der Wissenschaftsgeschichte*, ed. Dirk Rupnow et al. (Frankfurt am Main: Suhrkamp Verlag 2008), 7.
33 Rupnow et al., "Einleitung," 7.

Empirical Illustration: The Scientification of Yoga in Interwar Germany

When 'yoga' became of interest to society in Europe and the West in general at the beginning of the 20th century, we observe an interaction of different knowledge systems. Western systems of science, in this example mostly German-speaking, had to deal with this at first seemingly foreign and differently produced knowledge.[34] It goes without saying that because of its origin in the Global South, 'yoga' had a more difficult path of 'scientification' and possible acceptance as knowledge compared to Global Northern knowledge. This makes it a prime illustration of our suggested approach.

Next to a variety of integration attempts, three very different groups sought ways of *scientificating* ("*Verwissenschaftlichen*") yoga in their own ways. The first group was the Theosophical Society, founded in 1875 and, according to the literature, serving as a "flow heater" of esoteric ideas, led by Annie Besant.[35] The second group approached yoga from psychoanalysis, namely represented by Carl Gustav Jung, who addressed occult topics in his doctoral thesis in 1902 and was not only interested in yoga but also in various forms of mysticism with regard to psychoanalytical research.[36] Finally, there was a loose group of Indologists, religious scholars, and medical doctors around Jakob Wilhelm Hauer. Together, they wanted to popularize yoga in a 'western-scientific' understanding, founding the journal *Yoga. International Journal for the Scientific Investigation of Yoga*, which, for various reasons, was discontinued after one issue.[37]

One thing all three groups had in common was that they had the same initial conception of yoga and the same initial expectations of its orientalized practices and ideas, at the same time as all three claimed to be scientific. However, they all had some somewhat differing ideas on the subject, and while some of the differences could be tolerated, especially between Jung and Hauer, others were not and could not be. By examining these clashes and their absence regarding the

---

[34] This section is based on Christoph Schmitt's master's thesis, submitted to the University of Konstanz.
[35] Kocku von Stuckrad, *Was ist Esoterik?: Kleine Geschichte des geheimen Wissens* (Munich: C.H. Beck, 2004), 197.
[36] Cf. Kris Manjapra, *Age of Entanglement: German and Indian Intellectuals across Empire* (Cambridge, Mass.: HUP, 2014), 233.
[37] Cf. Helmut Palmié, ed., *Yoga: Internationale Zeitschrift für wissenschaftliche Yoga-Forschung* 1, no. 1 (1931). For more, compare Anne Taylor, *Annie Besant: A Biography* (Oxford: OUP, 1992); Horst Junginger, "Jakob Wilhelm Hauer," *Handbuch der völkischen Wissenschaften* 1 (2017): 274–279.

ideas around yoga and the communication between these groups, we can observe the processes of how knowledge is produced.

Jung and Hauer organized a series of lectures on the subject of psychology and Kundalini Yoga in Zurich in 1932.[38] They agreed on the scientificity of the practice and that yoga could be experienced practically and was a means of "getting the machinery of the body in hand, so to speak" or that "yoga, in its healing path, addresses the whole of the soul's transmission."[39] Jung saw the possibility of medicinal healing through the study and practice of yoga and spoke, albeit not uncritically, of opportunities for doctors to use "Eastern healing systems."[40] They agreed on certain facts (thereby making them such), and they both saw yoga as a different path to the same ends as Western science. This leads to the validation and reinforcement of both Western medicine and the practice of yoga as *truth*. Their knowledge production of yoga was capable of integrating the facts, data, and previously produced knowledge, which they perceived as being of Indian origin, with little contradiction.

Besant's approach, however, differed fundamentally – in terms of perception – from that of Jung and Hauer and was vehemently rejected by both. The differences were so fundamental that they could not be tolerated and accepted due to the inner logics of Hauer's and Jung's knowledge construction. Besant, who valued mysticism equally as science, spoke of a "psychological science of India," thus opposing the idea of Western superiority, while also describing events in which practitioners could live up to 150 years or even control their body through mental effort. Neither the nature of the events described nor the equivalence of Western scientists with Indians could be accepted[41] as they endangered the Western production of knowledge by questioning its methods or claiming results too different from the Western approach, denying this information the classification of fact. Besant's description of Indian results, her data, and information had to be classified as false and her knowledge of yoga as being pseudo- or unscientific to allow the other approaches to continue as true and valid, and therefore scientific.

---

38 Cf. Carl Gustav Jung, *Die Psychologie des Kundalini-Yoga: Nach den Aufzeichnungen des Seminars von 1932*, ed. Sonu Shamdasani (Ostfildern: Patmos-Verlag, 2019).
39 Annie Besant, *Hâtha-Yoga und Râja-Yoga oder Geistige Entwickelung nach altindischer Methode* (Leipzig: Theosophisches Verlags-Haus, 1909), 7.; Jakob Wilhelm Hauer, "Der Yoga im Lichte der Psychotherapie," Bericht über den V. Allgemeinen ärztlichen Kongreß für Psychotherapie in Baden-Baden, 26–29 April 1930: 1–21, 9. Here and in the following, our own translation of the German original.
40 Karl Baier, *Der Yoga auf dem Weg nach Westen: Beiträge zur Rezeptionsgeschichte* (Würzburg: Königshausen & Neumann, 1998), 239. Cf. Jakob Wilhelm Hauer, "Yoga und Zeitwende," *Yoga: Internationale Zeitschrift für wissenschaftliche Yoga-Forschung* 1, no. 1 (1931): 5–8, 6.
41 Besant, "Hâtha-Yoga," 1, 9–10.

As Hauer wrote: "But the journal could also become of some importance for the East. The knowledge of real yoga and yoga experience is quite rare in India today, according to my observations of several years." One problem for Hauer was primary sources not being used or being interpreted incorrectly.[42] Hauer and Jung were united as they both worked according to their common scientific approach and ensured their common facts and information in this approach through comparison.[43] In Hauer's *Der Yoga als Heilweg* [Yoga as a Healing Path], which was dedicated to Jung, the similarities were emphasized:

In particular, however, it seems to me to be an imperative of the hour to approach yoga from the point of view of psychological problems, from which the religious and philosophical spheres will again receive new light, and in this connection, a relationship must be established with Western science and healing methods, which in some areas have of themselves come to surprisingly similar results as yoga, namely with psychoanalysis and with the psychotherapy based on it.[44]

It made no difference, or rather it was a tolerable difference, whether Jung, unlike Hauer, thought that the psychoanalytical concept of driving forces was the same as the concept of "kleshas" and assigned their treatment to the field of psychology: "A medical psychology has developed among us [...] which deals specifically with the kleshas. We call this the 'psychology of the unconscious'."[45] Likewise, it was bearable for Hauer that "C. G. Jung [...] wrote a lengthy introduction to it [which] contains a number of thoughts very noteworthy for our subject, but, as it seems to me, mixed with all sorts of problematic things."[46] The important thing was that these opinions did not affect the production of meaning too much, while still leading to similar results at the level of information and meaning. These differences could be tolerated as opinions as they did not endanger the others' production of knowledge.

---

42 Hauer, "Yoga und Zeitwende," 8.
43 For the relevance of synchronization and socialization, see also: Armin Nassehi, *Muster: Theorie der digitalen Gesellschaft* (Munich: C.H. Beck, 2019), 271–273. Here Nassehi makes the argument, building on Luhmann, that a narratable world requires a common ground.
44 Jakob Wilhelm Hauer, *Der Yoga als Heilweg: Nach den indischen Quellen dargestellt* (Stuttgart: Kohlhammer, 1932), VIII.
45 Cf. Baier, *Yoga auf dem Weg nach Westen*, 248. Baier here refers to C. G. Jung, *Gesammelte Werke, Bd. XI*, ed. Marianne Niehus-Jung et al. (Zürich: Rascher, 1963).
46 Hauer, "Der Yoga im Lichte der Psychotherapie," 2.

Conclusion

Our example addressed the arguments of Besant, Hauer, and Jung, each of whom had their own ideas about yoga and tried to construct and match them with their environment. It is crucial that these constructions came from within the respective productions and were not mere copies of external discourses. In doing so, we can show how the boundaries of what is considered science and knowledge are constructed by contemporaries, what is considered true and why, as well as the function of truth for society and knowledge itself.

In this essay, we attempted to show how a systems theoretical approach can help to understand knowledge and science more deeply in the past as well as in the present. It allows one to further the understanding of knowledge production and helps with the definition of what knowledge is, functionally. The classical approaches assume that knowledge exists within its surroundings (e.g., laboratories, colonial power relations, material conditions, and so on), which influence it. These approaches can examine knowledge in terms of the negotiation and struggles of interpreting existing forms of knowledge and their hybridization. But these texts frequently do not address what counts as knowledge, instead introducing new terms to pinpoint the object of the investigation. Our intention is to augment this by focusing on the internal logic and processes of said production through communication. By stating the social, procedural differences of knowledge, information, fact, and opinion, we were able to outline a model of (social) production processes, based on agreement or tolerable differences, and define knowledge as objectified sense.

The article defined knowledge as objectified sense or meaning, something we expect others to believe to be true and which will affect how they interpret the world in future interactions. This expectation is based on comparisons of the production of said meaning by comparing methods, facts, and held opinions and worldviews with our own as well as commonly held positions. This leads to the creation of a common basis of knowledge in a society, which is needed to enable interactions by reducing complexity through the resulting shared expectations. However, to reach this common basis, knowledge production involves mechanisms of inclusion and exclusion. This does not just involve external motivations, the interpretative or discursive sovereignty over knowledge, but also the systemic contexts of knowledge production and construction. To reach this position of objectivity and truth, knowledge must constantly be compared and questioned. However, these challenges, if fundamental enough, must lead to one side being excluded and delegitimized as unscientific or wrong.

We believe that this systems theoretical approach may prove helpful in addressing the difficulties of defining the object of the history of knowledge as well as understanding knowledge, science, and society in general in the past as well as in the present. We also feel it shows the importance of shared knowledge for the functioning of society as a whole and how one can and does reach this point: By the comparison of the production of knowledge.

About the contributors

Bennet Rosswag is a research assistant at the chair of early modern history at the University of Giessen. He is interested in trans-epochal media history, the construction, legitimization, and function of early modern power, bureaucracy and states, as well as the application of sociological theories in historiography. His PhD project focusses on the role of media in the administrative reform in territories of the Holy Roman Empire around 1800.

Christoph Schmitt is an academic assistant in the History Department at the University of Education Schwäbisch Gmünd. His research interests include theory and methodology of history, social history, and social mobility. His doctoral thesis deals with the epistemic construction and formation of social history in the FRG (1960–1990) in exchange with different systems, using the example of social rise and social mobility.

Anton Jansson
Review Essay: The History of Atheism, Secularism, and Humanism: Recent Works and Future Directions

Abstract: In this review essay, the author presents and discusses current research on the history of atheism, secularism, and humanism, specifically focusing on seven recent monographs. Based on these works, he paints a picture of where this research field stands today while also offering some suggestions regarding in which direction research on this topic ought to move in the future. The author stresses that even though the research discussed spans many geographical areas and time periods, it constitutes a coherent research field. He underlines how context matters, stressing the importance of paying attention to specific religious contexts. He emphasizes the need for more English-language research on cases other than the US and the UK and the need for more comparative, entangled, and global histories. He welcomes the trend of 20th-century topics in a field dominated by earlier centuries. Finally, he points out how research on this topic could enrich nearby fields, specifically discussing which synergies may be found in relation to the history of knowledge.

Keywords: atheism, secularism, humanism, freethought, intellectual history

---

Victoria Smolkin, *A Sacred Space is Never Empty: A History of Soviet Atheism* (New Jersey: Princeton University Press, 2018).

Christopher Cameron, Black *Freethinkers: A History of African American Secularism* (Evanston: Northwestern University Press, 2019).

Nathan G. Alexander, *Race in a Godless World: Atheism, Race, and Civilization, 1850–1914* (Manchester: Manchester University Press, 2019).

Alec Ryrie, *Unbelievers: An Emotional History of Doubt* (London: William Collins, 2019).

Kimberly A. Hamlin, *Free Thinker: Sex, Suffrage, and the Extraordinary Life of Helen Hamilton Gardener* (New York: W.W. Norton & Company, 2020).

Stephen P. Weldon, *The Scientific Spirit of American Humanism* (Baltimore: Johns Hopkins University Press, 2020).

Charles Devellennes, *Positive Atheism: Bayle, Meslier, d'Holbach, Diderot* (Edinburgh: Edinburgh University Press, 2021).

Introduction

The return of religion, de-secularization, the post-secular turn, or the new visibility of religion – there were many concepts seeking to grapple with one of the most dynamic phenomena in scholarship and in society at large at the end of the 20th century and the first decades of the 21st. This concerns the notion that religion – after a modernist phase of being relatively marginalized – was returning to the very center of both international and domestic politics, as well as in cultural and intellectual debates inside and outside of academia. This triggered a heated debate on the validity of secularization theory/narratives, a rethinking of intellectual-historical scholarship, and not least a discussion and critique of secularism initiated by authors from various academic fields, such as Talal Asad, José Casanova, Joan Scott, and Charles Taylor, to name a few.[1]

This essay considers one element of the wider recent and renewed intellectual interest in understanding religion and its boundaries: namely the growing body of historical research considering individuals and institutions having consciously and explicitly turned away from a belief in God or gods and organized religion, thereby trying to formulate the possibilities of living in and organizing societies without a belief in God. This research is sometimes linked to the scholarship on secularism and secularization mentioned above – sometimes drawing inspiration from it, sometimes criticizing it – but is nevertheless broad enough to make out a corner of its own, a specific research field in which scholars of different national and his-

---

Acknowledgments: My work on this essay was financed with a grant from the Swedish Research Council (Vetenskapsrådet 2019–02873). I am grateful to the editors who have read and commented on earlier drafts of the text.

[1] Talal Asad, *Formations of the Secular: Christianity, Islam, Modernity* (Stanford: Stanford University Press, 2003); José Casanova, *Public Religions in the Modern World* (Chicago: University of Chicago Press, 1994); Charles Taylor, *A Secular Age* (Cambridge: Belknap Press of Harvard University Press, 2007); Joan Wallach Scott, *Sex and Secularism* (Princeton: Princeton University Press, 2018). For discussions on secularization and de-secularization, see, for instance, Rodney Stark, "Secularization, R.I.P.," *Sociology of Religion* 60, no. 3 (1999); Peter L. Berger, ed., *The Desecularization of the World: Resurgent Religion and World Politics* (Grand Rapids: Eerdmans, 1999); Steve Bruce, *Secularization: In Defence of an Unfashionable Theory* (Oxford: Oxford University Press, 2011). For a discussion on the return of religion and scholarship in intellectual history, see, for instance, Alister Chapman, John Coffey, and Brad S. Gregory, ed., *Seeing Things Their Way: Intellectual History and the Return of Religion* (Notre Dame: University of Notre Dame Press, 2009).

torical contexts communicate with one another.[2] The phenomenon studied – the turning away from, or absence of, a belief in God or gods – is often labeled atheism. While this is the most common umbrella term, a certain conceptual complexity exists, which I return to below.

Moreover, there are interesting points of contact in relation to the burgeoning field of history of knowledge, which is promoted in this yearbook. For many historical atheists, "knowledge" represented an important concept opposite to religious belief. More specifically, modern science and scientific knowledge have played an important role for many of the individuals and communities that consciously turned away from organized religion, both during the freethought movement of the 19th century and our more contemporary atheism of the 21st century. While the history of knowledge has addressed many issues and topics, religion and detractors of religion have not been prominent topics in the field, meaning that there are possibilities for further work where the link of these two fields could create synergies.[3]

Intellectual historian Nathan Alexander points out in a recent text on the historiography of atheism that the "topic has frequently attracted partisans on either side."[4] That is, much of historical interpretations of unbelief have adopted either an atheist or secularist perspective or a decidedly Christian one. The fact that the history of various subjects attracts scholars who also have a stake in them personally is obviously common and is not necessarily a problem. At times, however, such historiography risks tipping over to become more of identity politics than high-quality scholarship. Secularist *Heilsgeschichten* on how at least the Western world has shaken off the religious burden of less developed eras have been common, as have, conversely, narratives regarding the destructive decline of Christianity or the perils of a world without God. These were more common in the 19th century, but as shown by Alexander, there are echoes of them also later, even in our own era.

---

[2] An institutional manifestation of this is the International Society for Historians of Atheism, Secularism, and Humanism (ISHASH), which hosts webinars and conferences, among other things. See https://atheismsecularismhumanism.wordpress.com/ , accessed May 31, 2023.
[3] On religion and the history of knowledge, see the discussion by Kajsa Brilkman and Anna Nilsson Hammar, "Religion as Knowledge," https://newhistoryofknowledge.com/2019/04/24/religion-as-knowledge/, accessed May 31, 2023. For a discussion on the importance of religion in the field of history of knowledge with a focus on interdisciplinarity, see Simon Goldhill, "How Interdisciplinary Is God?" *KNOW: A Journal on the Formation of Knowledge* 1, no. 1 (2017).
[4] Nathan G. Alexander, "Histories of Atheism: Key Questions and Disputes," in *The Cambridge History of Atheism*, ed. Michael Ruse and Stephen Bullivant (Cambridge: Cambridge University Press, 2021), 14.

Two books that came out in 2014 may bear witness to this. Mitchell Stephens, a historian and professor of journalism published a history of atheism titled *Imagine There's no Heaven: How Atheism Helped Create the Modern World*. The title gives away its somewhat simplified narrative: from ancient times up until today, there has been a more or less dichotomous struggle between brave disbelievers, who have stood for good and modern things – science, reason, individualism, tolerance, etc. – and narrow-minded and reactionary religious people. Atheists and doubters were the ones who "helped lead the way to the modern world."[5] Another overview of the history of atheism, with a similarly ingenious title, is Nick Spencer's *Atheists: The Origin of the Species*. Spencer works at the Christian think tank Theos and may thus be considered a representative of the camp opposite from that of Stephens. Indeed, what Spencer takes issue with in his introduction is what he refers to as the "creation myth" of atheism – simplistic accounts of how reason and science triumphed over superstitious religion. Spencer's way of countering this is to offer a more complex story, in which modern atheism rather had to do with the "(ab)use of theologically legitimized political authority than with developments in science and philosophy."[6] While *Atheists* is quite nuanced, it clearly represents a historiography in the service of contemporary religious debates. In fact, Spencer ends it by levelling critique at the so-called New Atheists, who were influential at the beginning of the 21st century.[7]

Whatever you think about New Atheism, it seems as if it has contributed to the growth of the field of the history of atheism, secularism, and humanism. Works like the ones just mentioned relate to this movement quite explicitly, but it is plausible to assume that the wave of New Atheism, together with the above-mentioned discussions on the "return of religion" and the "postsecular," was instrumental in also bringing forth a more profound historical scholarship on the topics of atheism and related issues. One example is another book from 2014, intellectual historian Todd Weir's *Secularism and Religion in Nineteenth-Century Germany: The Rise of the Fourth Confession*, which departs from contemporary discussions regarding secularism, such as the work of Talal Asad. However, in contrast to the more sweeping narratives of Stephens and Spencer, this work marked a high standard

---

[5] Mitchell Stephens, *Imagine There's No Heaven: How Atheism Helped Create the Modern World* (New York: Palgrave Macmillan, 2014), 2.
[6] Nick Spencer, *Atheists: The Origin of the Species* (London: Bloomsbury, 2014), xv.
[7] Spencer, *Atheists*, 247–257. New Atheism was coined as a term to describe a new wave of writers, scientists, and philosophers propagating atheism. The most famous exponents were Richard Dawkins, Sam Harris, Christopher Hitchens, and Daniel Dennett.

in the writing of a more contextualist case study of a specific society, influenced by both intellectual and social history.⁸

Weir has not been alone in carrying out new studies of great quality. Overall, the 2010s and the 2020s have so far been a highly productive period for the historiography of atheism, secularism, humanism, and freethought, a period crowned by the magisterial new *Cambridge History of Atheism* published in late 2021. This new standard work, edited by philosopher of science Michael Ruse and theologian and sociologist Stephen Bullivant, contains 60 chapters over some 1,200 pages in two volumes (including texts by Weir and four of the authors whose works I discuss here). While having a historical perspective, stretching from antiquity to our own time, it includes scholars from various disciplines and offers both thematic and geographical overviews, as well as tackling contemporary issues and topics such as transhumanism and the internet. This two-volume work, impressive in terms of its breadth and up-to-date character, however, is for various reasons left outside this essay.⁹ Instead, I present a selection of recent monographs to paint a picture of how the history of atheism and related phenomena is written at the moment.

In selecting these works, a few criteria were taken into consideration. They had to be recent and are all published in the last five years. Although I wanted them to be representative of the trends in English-language research on this topic, I also wanted to include topics not addressing the dominant cases of the US and the UK. This means that a few books on these national contexts were left out.¹⁰ However, the ones included offer a good picture of how research is car-

---

8 Todd H. Weir, *Secularism and Religion in Nineteenth-Century Germany: The Rise of the Fourth Confession* (New York: Cambridge University Press, 2014). He was not alone in the first half of the 2010s, see also Laura Schwartz, *Infidel Feminism: Secularism, Religion and Women's Emancipation, England 1830–1914* (Manchester: Manchester University Press, 2013).

9 One reason is its sheer size, another is that I focus on monographs, while a third is that I have co-authored a chapter. Apart from Todd Weir, Nathan Alexander, Christopher Cameron, Alec Ryrie, and Victoria Smolkin also contribute with chapters related to their respective field of expertise. Michael Ruse and Stephen Bullivant, ed., *The Cambridge History of Atheism* (Cambridge: Cambridge University Press, 2021). For an introductory review, see Clare Stainthorp, "Book Review: The Cambridge History of Atheism," *Global Intellectual History*, published online, 2022.

10 A few more recent works that did not make it here, either because of the predominance of Anglo-American works or because they were published a bit too late in the writing process include James Bryant Reeves, *Godless Fictions in the Eighteenth Century: A Literary History of Atheism* (Cambridge: Cambridge University Press, 2020); Matthew Wilson, *Richard Congreve, Positivist Politics, the Victorian Press, and the British Empire* (Cham: Palgrave MacMillan, 2021); Leigh Eric Schmidt, *The Church of Saint Thomas Paine: A Religious History of American Secularism* (Princeton: Princeton University Press, 2021); Patrick J. Corbeil, *Empire and Progress in the Victorian Secularist Movement: Imagining a Secular World* (Cham: Palgrave MacMillan, 2022); Suzanne Hobson, *Unbe-

ried out at the moment, while also featuring a selection of specific angles, topics, and time periods, thereby highlighting a breadth of approaches. While a few highly interesting edited volumes have been published recently, I have here prioritized monographs since these represent more coherent projects.[11]

I have already used many terms for the object of this research field. This might constitute a drawback but is almost unavoidable. Concepts such as atheism, secularism, humanism, freethought, unbelief, nonbelief, disbelief, doubt, and irreligion are not all synonymous but are nevertheless sufficiently related to make out a historical phenomenon to be studied. Sociologists may decide on "non-religion" as an analytical concept and be content with that, while historians make different choices depending on their tradition and the specific case they study. Quite frequently, they use these terms more or less synonymously.[12] Still, one might ask

---

lief in Interwar Literary Culture: Doubting Moderns (Oxford: Oxford University Press, 2022); Renny Thomas, Science and Religion in India: Beyond Disenchantment (London: Routledge, 2022); Callum G. Brown, David Nash and Charlie Lynch, The Humanist Movement in Modern Britain: A History of Ethicists, Rationalists and Humanists (London: Bloomsbury, 2023). Schmidt's previous book also needs mentioning as an important study from the last decade: Leigh Eric Schmidt, Village Atheists: How America's Unbelievers Made Their Way in a Godly Nation (Princeton: Princeton University Press, 2016). Looking beyond works in English, there are a few solid German monographs from the last ten years: Lisa Dittrich, Antiklerikalismus in Europa: Öffentlichkeit und Säkularisierung in Frankreich, Spanien und Deutschland (1848–1914) (Göttingen: Vandenhoeck & Ruprecht, 2014); Christoffer Leber, Arbeit am Welträtsel: Religion und Säkularität in der Monismusbewegung um 1900 (Göttingen: Vandenhoeck & Ruprecht, 2020); Claus Spenninger, Stoff für Konflikt: Fortschrittsdenken und Religionskritik im naturwissenschaftlichen Materialismus des 19. Jahrhunderts, 1847–1881 (Göttingen: Vandenhoeck & Ruprecht, 2021).

11 Niels De Nutte and Bert Gasenbeek, ed., Looking Back to Look Forward: Organised Humanism in the World: Belgium, Great Britain, the Netherlands and the United States of America, 1945–2005 (Brussels: VUB Press, 2019); Carolin Kosuch, ed., Freethinkers in Europe: National and Transnational Secularities, 1789–1920s (Berlin & Boston: De Gruyter, 2020); Tomáš Bubík, Atko Remmel, and David Václavík, ed., Freethought and Atheism in Central and Eastern Europe: The Development of Secularity and Non-religion (London: Routledge, 2020); Jenny Vorpahl and Dirk Schuster, ed., Communicating Religion and Atheism in Central and Eastern Europe (Berlin & Boston: De Gruyter, 2020). In other languages, see, for instance, Patrice Dartevelle and Christophe de Spiegeleer, ed., Histoire de l'athéisme en Belgique (Brussels: Aba éditions, 2021); Ellen van Impe and Rik Röttger, 50 jaar debat & verbinding: De Unie Vrijzinnige Verenigingen en haar leden 1971–2021 (Brussels: ASP, 2023), both of which focus on Belgium.

12 For instance, Nathan Alexander in his book discussed below states that "I use the terms 'atheism,' 'freethought,' 'nonbelief,' and 'irreligion' interchangeably." Nathan G. Alexander, Race in a Godless World: Atheism, Race, and Civilization, 1850–1914 (Manchester: Manchester University Press, 2019), 13. For a discussion on the term non-religion from a sociological perspective, see Lois Lee, Recognizing the Non-religious: Reimagining the Secular (Oxford: Oxford University Press, 2017), especially Chapter 1.

whether all the phenomena included here could be said to be related or whether it is not too much of a stretch to include, say, 16th-century blasphemy, 19th-century freethought worldviews and popular movements, and 20th-century communist state atheism in the same discussion. One of the points I make toward the end of this text is that they are sufficiently related and that scholars of a particular time and place may learn much from research on other contexts.

A further point I make is what I hinted at already at the outset: that scholars should be careful not to write partisan histories and that atheism is not an eternally homogenous phenomenon, but that social and political contexts play a key role in which form it takes. This leads me to another point, which is that attentiveness to religious contexts is key also for historians of atheism. A noticeable and positive trend is that quite a few of the monographs discussed here move into the 20th century. I want to point out the importance of continuing this trend as earlier centuries have been dominant in the field. Further, the field is dominated by research on the US and the UK. While the scholarship on these contexts is great and possible to learn from, I would like to stress that understanding atheism as a global phenomenon would be richer with more perspectives both from other parts of the Christian West and from other parts of the world, Christian and non-Christian. More comparative, entangled, and global histories are thus called for. Finally, I would like to encourage historians of atheism, secularism, and humanism to ask what their research can bring to other fields and topics and to reflect upon what we can bring to historiography in general. Specifically, I also try to point out how this research does and could further relate to the field of the history of knowledge.

All these points and suggestions for future directions are discussed further in the concluding part. Before we get to this part, I discuss seven recent books, somewhat grouped geographically, starting with three works dealing with the United States, followed by moving across the Atlantic to a number of transnational and European studies. Apart from discussing the contents of these books, I also want to highlight methodology, materials, what they bring to the field, and how they relate to each other.

US History in Focus

Increasingly looking upon history through the lens of racial relations has been a noticeable development in recent years, especially in the United States, undoubtedly related to current events. In the field of the history of atheism and secularism, two books written by intellectual historians do this in different ways. Nathan Alexander, mentioned at the outset, has written a book about the history of race and racism, which I come back to in the next section, while Christopher Cameron focuses on secularism in the history of African American political and intellectual life.

Cameron presents a clear and straightforward argument in his exciting *Black Freethinkers: A History of African American Secularism*. Contrary to common depictions of African American communities and traditions as being especially religious, yes, even "naturally religious," freethought and atheism have played a key role in black political and intellectual life since the 19th century.[13] Another prejudice that does not hold is that atheism has often been – in the words of a 19th-century slaveholder referred to by Cameron – the preserve of "educated and cultivated minds" – that is, white people.[14] In a sense, Cameron also argues against the narrative on how reason and science represented the primary source of non-belief in modern society by claiming that in the long run, the brutal experience and legacy of slavery resulted in a loss of faith for many African Americans.

The argument directly relating to slavery is naturally more prominent in the first of four chapters in this chronologically structured book: a chapter discussing slavery and the immediate aftermath of the Civil War, when slavery was still a very prevalent argument. The following chapters focus on the Harlem renaissance, radical left-wing politics of the interwar era, and the civil rights movement, respectively. In a concluding afterword, Cameron touches upon a few contemporary black freethought organizations and individuals. The structure of Cameron's narrative is in this sense tied to the general development of modern African American history. While it outlines this broad narrative, Cameron's method in many ways concerns focusing on specific individuals. From Frederick Douglass to Alice Walker, we get short narratives on a diverse set of characters with different backgrounds, ideals, and expressions, who nevertheless had one thing in common in that they were "black freethinkers." Here, Cameron analyzes different sorts of material: speeches and various theoretical and political writings, but also novels and autobiographies.

One interesting theme throughout the book is that Cameron spends a fair amount of time on retelling why these people left a religion they typically grew up very close to. As mentioned above, slavery was one reason for abandoning religion. Frederick Douglass experienced violence from a white Christian farmer he worked for, which led him to a feeling of "cosmic abandonment and self-reliance."[15] Later black freethinkers did not have this direct experience of slavery, and there were also other reasons for leaving one's religion. Sometimes, it could be quite simple, such as having been included and received education in free-

---

[13] Christopher Cameron, *Black Freethinkers: A History of African American Secularism* (Evanston: Northwestern University Press, 2019), x.
[14] Cameron, *Black Freethinkers*, ix. See also p. xii.
[15] Cameron, *Black Freethinkers*, 27.

thought circles, which was the case when Alain Locke encountered Felix Adler's Ethical Culture Society.[16] The gravitation toward atheism could also be the result of studying existentialist philosophers (Huey Newton) or communist theoreticians (Stokely Carmichael).[17] Many black freethinkers told stories about how they at a formative age lost their faith after they had experienced hypocrisy and immorality in Christianity, either in relation to racial hierarchies in a Christian United States (James Baldwin) or within the African American community (Richard Wright).[18]

Such personal stories – or "freethought conversion narratives" as Cameron terms them – in themselves represent a form of secularist speech act, in that they were often publicly expressed in a stylized fashion.[19] Cameron points out that what childhood story novelist Richard Wright related in his autobiography *Black Boy* – about a greedy preacher who took the best parts of the chicken in front of hungry children – is almost a literary trope, a part of African American lore.[20] Apart from autobiographies, Cameron also analyzes other literary works. In his words, Nella Larsen's novel *Quicksand* is "probably the most extensive exploration of religious skepticism in African American literature before 1930."[21] While fiction is a different form of source material from argumentative or theoretical texts, as a genre, it is no less important in terms of conveying secularist messages. At a time when women were more seldom than men elevated to the highest positions as leaders and ideologues, they instead found other channels to communicate their ideas, such as writing fiction. Novels may thus serve as a genre in which to find voices other than those of the most famous male theoreticians. Thus, while it sometimes feels as if many individuals and various materials are included in Cameron's compact book, there are good reasons for doing so. *Black Freethinkers* is a rich work that adds something important to the study of the history of atheism.

In terms of the focus on individuals, there are affinities to the latest book by historian Kimberly A. Hamlin, a biography of Helen Hamilton Gardener (1853–1925, born Alice Chenoweth). Gardener was a champion of women's rights throughout her life. She was a writer, a novelist, but primarily an activist for various causes having to do with sex, science, and politics; for instance, campaigning for raising the legal age of consent for women (girls). In the 20th century, she was involved in

---

16 Cameron, *Black Freethinkers*, 47–48.
17 Cameron, *Black Freethinkers*, 129–136.
18 Cameron, *Black Freethinkers*, 56–57, 154–155.
19 Cameron, *Black Freethinkers*, 46.
20 Cameron, *Black Freethinkers*, 56–57.
21 Cameron, *Black Freethinkers*, 75.

the suffrage movement and a key player in the adoption of the Nineteenth Amendment. The political establishment recognized Gardener's work, and she received a seat on the Civil Service Commission in 1920, making her the highest-ranking and highest-paid woman in the federal government.

Gardener was a "free thinker," as stated in the title of the book, but she was also a freethinker in the narrower sense more relevant to this essay. The freethought movement in the latter half of the 19th century was her passageway into public life. In her late twenties, Gardener had read John Stuart Mill, Herbert Spencer, Thomas Paine, and freethought periodicals, starting to formulate her own texts, often related to sex and gender roles. She shared these with the "Great Agnostic" Robert Ingersoll, a famous freethought orator and later the leader of the American Secular Union.[22] Ingersoll encouraged Gardener to continue writing and in 1884 invited her to speak at a public meeting in New York. Her lecture "Men, Women and Gods," in which she lambasted the creation story in Genesis, was not only a success that night but quickly earned her a reputation and gave her a prominent role in the freethought speaking circuit. She was touring eastern United States in 1884, started publishing in the freethought paper *Truth Seeker*, and worked as an editor in *Freethinkers' Magazine/Free Thought Magazine*. This was not without frictions: some questioned the quick rise of "Ingersoll's favorite," and Gardener argued with another freethought leader, Samuel Putnam, regarding his view on women. For a short while, however, Gardener had an important position in the freethought movement, hailed as "Ingersoll in soprano."[23]

Hamlin's biography of Gardener is not only an impressive empirical achievement but also a great read. While it is not only a work primarily focusing on the history of atheism and freethought, it also demonstrates the viability of biography as a method in this field. Gardener was a life-long agnostic and critic of Christianity, but in a sense, this was not what brought her to the freethought movement. Hamlin points out that in the late 1870s, freethinkers were more or less "the only people openly talking and writing about marriage and sex," and "rationally discussing the restrictions of patriarchal marriage and the sexual double standard."[24] Gardener's primary loyalty was to the women's cause and not to critique Christianity for its own sake, something that her public polemics with Putnam made clear.[25] This also meant that she later moved on, focusing her work on the *National American Woman Suffrage Association*.

---

[22] Kimberly A. Hamlin, *Free Thinker: Sex, Suffrage, and the Extraordinary Life of Helen Hamilton Gardener* (New York: W.W. Norton & Company, 2020), 52–54, 61–62.
[23] Hamlin, *Free Thinker*, 67–82, 144.
[24] Hamlin, *Free Thinker*, 54.
[25] Hamlin, *Free Thinker*, 75–76.

Focusing on a single individual may thus tell us something about the broader conjunctures of the freethought movement: the other political and social causes it related to, what made it attractive to certain segments of the population, and how this changed over time. Biographies of long-time leaders who spent their entire life in the movement are important, but biographies of other individuals who may have come and gone, such as Gardener, also offer an interesting diachronic perspective placing freethought into the broader workings of the history of politics, society, and knowledge. As it were, Gardener entered freethought as it experienced its "golden age," when the movement served as an important vehicle for various sorts of radical opinion formation. For her, this intellectually and politically radical milieu became a springboard into other engagements.

In a sense, Hamlin's work can be read together with – as a complement to – another recent monograph on US history of freethought in a broad sense. While devoting a couple of chapters to the 19th century, Stephen Weldon's *The Scientific Spirit of American Humanism* mainly focuses on the 20th century and another stream of the breaking loose from the Christian tradition. Weldon's story is a history of (secular) humanism, to some extent focusing on the American Humanist Association (AHA), but by no means exclusively on this organization. It is interesting to note that neither Gardener, Ingersoll, nor Putnam figure in Weldon's work, and it is clear that the roots of the tradition he portrays were different. There were ties to the Ethical Culture Society, but in many ways, humanism rather grew out of Unitarianism and liberal and unorthodox interpretations of Christianity and not out of the 19th-century freethought movement, as represented by figures such as Ingersoll et al.

In his history, Weldon not only writes a commendable history of secular humanism in the United States, which will be useful for a long time to come, but also addresses a few issues that might be of wider interest. First, as the title makes clear, science plays a structuring role in the book. Science and religion are still seen by many as eternal opponents. Historians of science and ideas have debunked this simplified dichotomy – the "conflict thesis" – for a long time now, but while there might not be an eternal battle, it is clear that science and scientific knowledge have been invoked as a tool or weapon in debates on the validity and position of Christianity in society, not least during the last 150 years.[26] Therefore, nuanced empirical studies on this changing and multi-faceted relation, such as Weldon's, are valuable.

---

26 John Hedley Brooke, *Science and Religion: Some Historical Perspectives* (Cambridge: Cambridge University Press, 1991); Peter Harrison, *The Territories of Science and Religion* (Chicago: The Univer-

As expected, there is plenty of evolution and creationism in *The Scientific Spirit*, as the struggle over primarily the teaching of evolution has been a "persistent aspect" of modern US culture and an issue having engaged famous humanists.[27] But the most important takeaway from this work is that while science has been an ideal throughout the history of 20th-century humanism, its appearances and ideals have varied. In a kind of ideal type distinction, Weldon outlines two poles: one where science is more holistic, even spiritual, linked to values such as democracy, equality, and faith in the goodness, freedom, and dignity of man. On the other side, there has been a more reductionist, mechanistic, and deterministic view of science, in this version perceived as a value-neutral endeavor. If the first was linked to pragmatist philosophy dominating the humanist movement in the first half of the 20th century, the second was rather related to positivism and an Anglo-American analytic tradition of philosophy. These different ideals could come into conflict, which became clear in, for instance, humanist debates regarding eugenics and behavioristic psychology.[28]

This dichotomy is in many ways related to another question having occupied the humanists themselves as well as observers: is humanism "religious" or not? It certainly was for most people at the beginning of the movement. They viewed humanism as a religion of a new, higher sort, freed from superstition and transcendence and placed within a naturalistic worldview. This position was close to that of the large number of Unitarian ministers who developed the movement early on but also to a pragmatist philosopher such as John Dewey. In his *A Common Faith* from 1934, he wrote about how religious intensity and experience were deeply human but did not have anything to do with God.[29] Positions like these became less dominant throughout the years. As Weldon concludes, the humanist movement "began as a radical religion and gradually secularized. It started with a largely pragmatist worldview and became more positivist in outlook later."[30] Whether or not humanism was a religion was not only a theoretical question but could also involve highly practical concerns: the categorization as a religious organization is linked to highly tangible things such as taxation and conscientious objection.[31]

---

sity of Chicago Press, 2015); Thomas Dixon and Adam. R. Shapiro, *Science and Religion: A Very Short Introduction* (Oxford: Oxford University Press, 2022).
27 Stephen P. Weldon, *The Scientific Spirit of American Humanism* (Baltimore: Johns Hopkins University Press, 2020), 191–208.
28 Weldon, *The Scientific Spirit*, 3–4, 117–129, 148–149.
29 Weldon, *The Scientific Spirit*, 6, 71.
30 Weldon, *The Scientific Spirit*, 214.
31 Weldon, *The Scientific Spirit*, 176.

Weldon succeeds in his aim to connect humanism to the wider religious and intellectual history of the United States. He tells the story in episodes or thematic chapters, which are well-connected to one another. One theme he discusses, and which is interesting to relate to Cameron's work, is the question of race. Weldon shows how humanism was very much a preserve of the white, well-to-do middle class. While most of the time being progressive with regard to race, the humanist movement with its strong emphasis on science was not particularly attractive to African American nonbelievers and freethinkers, who came to their convictions based on different concerns. The challenges of a racist society "made many of the debates about science and religion almost superfluous to them," as Weldon puts it.[32]

The three books discussed so far present three different angles on the turning away from Christianity in the modern United States and together present a rich history of this process. An additional piece of the puzzle in this development is the book we now move on to discuss.

Traveling across the Atlantic

Stephen Weldon touches upon the question of race in his work on science and humanism. The relationship between science and race also plays an important role in the already mentioned monograph by Nathan Alexander. Alexander's work relates to the ones we have discussed thus far, but he adopts a broader geographical perspective. Rightly pointing out that the freethought movement in the 19th century was transatlantic, he includes both the United States and Britain in his *Race in a Godless World: Atheism, Race, and Civilization, 1850–1914*. The point of departure of this book is a debate at the intersection between religious identity, morality, and history: what is the link between secularization and racism? Did the formation of more secular societies starting in the late 19th century help open the way for racism or did it provide new ways of challenging it? The first position is often based on the idea that God created humankind as one, in the image of God, and when this diminished as a governing social idea, new ways opened up in terms of creating racial hierarchies and even dehumanizing certain people, frequently with support from supposedly value-free science. The second position points to how Christians have often used their faith to defend racial hierarchies and oppression, such

---

[32] Weldon, *The Scientific Spirit*, 223, see also 127–129.

as slavery, that there is a strong tradition of Christian anti-Semitism, and that secularization, as a result, rather was a boon in the fight against racism.[33]

Alexander claims that while versions of these positions are often found in debates on modern atheism and the secular, this has never been systematically researched in relation to actual freethinkers, who were pushing for society to secularize. He here chooses to focus on the late 19th century up until the beginning of the 20th century based on two reasons. First, this was a period when racial attitudes were very prominent on both sides of the Atlantic. This was not only an age of British imperialism – as well as abolitionism, civil war, and the introduction of the Jim Crow laws in the US – Alexander focuses also on how racial science grew strong during this period. Second, as mentioned above with regard to Hamlin's work, this was the golden age of freethought, when organizations, journals, and individual activists emerged in large numbers.

These freethinkers make up the source material for Alexander's study. Periodicals in focus here include the American *Boston Investigator* and *Truth Seeker* and the British *Reasoner*, *National Reformer*, and *Freethinker*, in addition to numerous other works by freethinkers and atheists such as Robert Ingersoll, W. E. B. Du Bois, George Holyoake, Annie Besant, and Charles Bradlaugh. Using this material, Alexander carries out a number of thematic case studies: on evolution, on the anthropological debate on polygenesis and monogenesis, on ideas of civilization and savagery, on the view of the Far East, and more. Alexander then uses these cases to discuss the broader question concerning secularization, secularism, and racism.

Alexander shows that there is no easy either-or answer to this question. Or, as he concludes toward the end, "The central theme of this book has been ambivalence."[34] As discussed above, many white freethinkers had radical political ideas, including abolitionism and anti-racism. Here, Robert Ingersoll again deserves mention, as he argued against prejudice and for equal civil rights for African Americans, while also protesting against slavery and lynching.[35] And the freethinkers' position as outsiders with regard to the Christian establishment could mean that they took on more sympathetic views than others toward "other races," both "savages" in Africa and the "wise men of the East," who were sometimes presented as having more advanced religious views than the superstitious Christians of the West. This, however, does not mean that there were no negative stereotypes of non-white people among freethinkers. There were also quite clear cases of promot-

---

[33] This argument reverberates throughout the book but is neatly summed up at the outset: Alexander, *Race in a Godless World*, 1–2.
[34] Alexander, *Race in a Godless World*, 205.
[35] Alexander, *Race in a Godless World*, 157–166, 173.

ing racial hierarchies and outright and vile racism, such as when the *Truth Seeker* editor Eugene MacDonald in 1903 compared black men to animals and described people of African descent as an "inferior race."[36]

The question posited about racism and the secular society is strongly dichotomous, and it is thus no surprise that the answer is that things are more complicated than that. Furthermore, studying freethinkers in the long 19th century only represents one piece of the larger puzzle. This does not mean that Alexander's work is not worthwhile. *Race in a Godless World* offers a great deal of empirical historical flesh to a potentially controversial question, which otherwise risks being simplified. He also offers a very rich material and in many ways presents not only a fascinating glimpse into complex racial discussions in the late 19th century but also a wonderful, updated overview of the movement and the intellectual history of freethought in general. In a concluding chapter, Alexander also moves the question further into the 20th century and into our own age. There are parallels but also massive differences. Above all, he notes how nonbelievers in the 19th century and today differ a great deal in their relations to established society, as they have now moved into the mainstream, even in the United States. This consideration of social position is something any scholar of this topic needs to take seriously.

Going back further in history, but still traversing national boundaries, is Alec Ryrie's *Unbelievers: An Emotional History of Doubt.* Ryrie is a British professor of the history of Christianity as well as a professor of divinity. As he "in the interest of full disclosure" states in his introduction, he is also a religious believer and a lay minister in the Church of England.[37] If there are two camps, as discussed in the introduction, Ryrie clearly falls into the Christian one. This, however, is no work of Christian lament regarding the decay and decadence of a godless world. If Ryrie's Christian background shows up here, it is mostly in his focus and expertise. *Unbelievers* is in a sense a church history of atheism, focusing on doubt in the early-modern Christian community (primarily but not exclusively in England). Doubt has always been part of Christianity, and in the period covered by Ryrie, it always bordered on, and sometimes fell into, sheer unbelief.

Ryrie states that "anxious doubters were not bold pioneers of freethought. If they were atheists, they were reluctant, even horrified ones."[38] This captures a few of Ryrie's points. According to this perspective, unbelief is not a *Heilsgeschichte* in which bold men and women in a clearly defined camp throughout history fight

---

36 Alexander, *Race in a Godless World*, 171. Regarding hierarchies, see, for instance, 66–82.
37 Alec Ryrie, *Unbelievers: An Emotional History of Doubt* (London: William Collins, 2019), 11.
38 Ryrie, *Unbelievers*, 127.

against another clearly defined team. It is rather something emerging slowly in complex, sometimes unexpected ways. In this sense, his book is related to Nick Spencer's *Atheists*. Further, "anxious" is a key word here, as Ryrie promises "an emotional history of doubt." His opening chapter takes a stand against writing the history of doubt, atheism, and by extension, secularization, as a purely intellectual history. Before there were clear and well-formulated systems of atheism, which emerged toward the later parts of the 17th century, there was blasphemy, doubt, and unbelief – the latter being entangled with, or fueled by, strong emotions. In the early modern period he focuses on, he discerns two specific types of emotional unbelief: the unbelief of anger, which concerned grudges against the church and clerics, against a Christian society, or even against God. The unbelief of anxiety was one in which pious women and men found themselves beset by fears and uncertainties that they could not reason away.[39]

All in all, Ryrie's take on doubt, unbelief, and, by extension, atheism is one of a dialectic departing from within Christianity. It seems, he argues, that it was frequently the ones who initially took Christianity the most seriously who ended up being disappointed with it, or even abandoning it. People noticed moral inconsistencies or intellectual uncertainties regarding the truth of Christianity and their own salvation. And, if Christianity did not live up to high standards of ethical and ontological certainty – perhaps it was not anything to count on at all?

Ryrie's book is more toward the broader, essayistic end of the spectrum, covering a lot of time and space rather than representing archive-based research on a single case, like most other works discussed here. It is, however, an erudite, interesting, and commendable read. His model of the emotional history of doubt is not always clearly and consistently put to work; above all, "anger" disappears somewhat in the early part supposed to focus on this very theme. Here, the book ironically reads rather like a classical history of ideas, discussing the intellectual influences of Renaissance humanism and the Protestant Reformation as well as the religious thoughts and doubts of household names in the intellectual history canon such as Machiavelli and Montaigne (Spinoza and Hobbes turn up toward the end of the book).[40] However, his general points are interesting, and I certainly see how his categories are valuable for understanding unbelief and that they may be transposed to other times and locations. Much of the conversion narratives described by black freethinkers in the 19th and 20th centuries that we encounter in Christopher Cameron's work, for instance, are certainly bound up in emotions, not least feelings of disappointment and anger toward a hypocritical Christianity.

---

39 Ryrie, *Unbelievers*, 5–6, 181–182.
40 Ryrie, *Unbelievers*, 35–39, 61–65, 71–72, 175–180.

A key argument of *Unbelievers* is that doubt and unbelief existed before there were elaborated philosophical arguments and systematic ideas concerning atheism. Ryrie's story ends in the late 17th century as this was the time when unbelief "came out into the open and claimed philosophical respectability for itself" – the intellectual history of atheism followed from then on.[41] The early phase of that intellectual history is covered in another recent book on atheism, Charles Devellennes' *Positive Atheism: Bayle, Meslier, D'Holbach, Diderot*. Devellennes pinpoints the birth of more systematic positive framings of atheism at about the same time as the previous author, the late 17th century, and states that this represents the natural starting point for writing the history of this topic. While Devellennes does not deny that atheism has a prehistory of unorthodox religious speculation and doubt, or that the concept of atheism existed as an accusation for a long time, he claims that it makes more sense to write a history of atheism focusing on its explicit positive versions, "if one is concerned with taking atheism seriously."[42] In a sense, this position does not correspond with that of Ryrie, but Ryrie is not the writer he argues with here, rather taking issue with previous historiographers of atheism, such as Michael Buckley and Charles Kors.

Devellennes focuses on what he refers to as the move from negative to positive atheism. Negative atheism could mean both an accusation, a label imposed on others, but also the mere denial of the gods or religious system it questions. Devellennes, however, directs his interest to the moment when atheism becomes positive; that is, in two different formulations: "seeks to set philosophical bases for a life without god" or "bringing together a coherent worldview without gods."[43] Based on this, Devellennes moves into an exegesis of the thoughts of four more or less well-known Enlightenment figures: Pierre Bayle (1647–1706), Jean Meslier (1664–1729), Baron d'Holbach (1723–1789), and Denis Diderot (1713–1784).

The point of Devellennes is not that all these thinkers were necessarily atheists in that we can be sure they did not believe in God or that they clearly identified themselves as such. No, he rather claims that neither Bayle nor Diderot were atheists in a simple sense, contrary to what some scholars have argued.[44] When it comes to Baron d'Holbach and Jean Meslier, a Catholic priest who denied God and is sometimes called the first self-avowed atheist in history, things are different – they were more clearly atheists. However, what matters here is not exactly how they explicitly identified themselves, nor what they personally believed in terms of

---

41 Ryrie, *Unbelievers*, 181.
42 Charles Devellennes, *Positive Atheism: Bayle, Meslier, d'Holbach, Diderot* (Edinburgh: Edinburgh University Press, 2021), 3.
43 Devellennes, *Positive Atheism*, 12, 189.
44 Devellennes, *Positive Atheism*, 34–39, 56–62.

the existence of God, but that they all framed atheism as a positive system of thought. While Devellennes argues that Bayle himself was a religious believer, he points out the importance of how Bayle still made the case for the existence of virtuous atheism – yes, how an atheist society could be just as virtuous as any other.[45]

Devellennes shows that he possesses detailed knowledge of the lives and works of these four thinkers, and his presentation of the religious, social, and political thoughts of these *philosophes* is highly instructive and makes this an important study. This applies to the single chapters (Meslier, above all, has not been covered to a great extent in English-language scholarship) as well as to the comparison between them, which highlights the lively philosophical and political era of Enlightenment France. This is obviously an era that continually needs to be discussed and (re)interpreted in the intellectual history of atheism.

A discussion partner for Devellennes throughout *Positive Atheism* is intellectual historian Jonathan Israel, who is one of the leading and most productive scholars of the Age of Enlightenment in our century. Devellennes to some extent draws on Israel, but also points out that 18th-century France was more complex compared to Israel's division into moderates and radicals.[46] Still, Devellennes keeps the idea of radicalism but tries to complicate Israel's points. This is not entirely to the book's advantage, since when pointing out that radicalism can be seen in at least four different ways, and then using this term throughout the book to point out how the four thinkers were "radical" in different ways, it loses some of its power as an analytical concept. Radicalism thus ends up meaning many different things, and I am not entirely convinced that this wide concept of radicalism then serves as an important framework for historically understanding these authors in their context, certainly not as a group. The reason, as Devellennes himself points out, is that there are clear differences in their thinking.

Devellennes, who is not solely an intellectual historian but also a political theorist, toward the end of the book looks up from the 18th century and discusses possible lessons from the philosophy he has presented. In Diderot, he finds an inclination that he terms metatheism, something he claims also goes beyond positive atheism. This is a position that transcends a sharp division of belief and non-belief,

---

45 Devellennes, *Positive Atheism*, 39–42.
46 It is not possible here to further analyze Jonathan Israel's discussion on these thinkers or the Enlightenment and belief. However, for an interesting recent publication by Israel on Pierre Bayle's fideism and skepticism, see Jonathan Israel, "Pierre Bayle's Correspondence and Its Significance for the History of Ideas," *Journal of the History of Ideas* 80, no. 3 (2019). For a critical view of Israel's work, above all his dichotomous view of a radical and moderate Enlightenment, see Samuel Moyn, "Mind the Enlightenment," *The Nation*, May 12, 2010.

is skeptical with regard to its own positions and assertions, and is not afraid to discuss a spiritual understanding of the world.[47] If Ryrie wrote from a humble, Christian perspective, Devellennes' work is then one of humble, atheist thinking.

While all the books covered here have strong merits and in different ways bring something lasting to the field of the history of atheism, secularism, and humanism, the last work I comment on stands out as arguably being the strongest and most important work in this field in recent years. While there have been prior studies on Soviet atheism, also in English, Victoria Smolkin's *A Sacred Space Is Never Empty: A History of Soviet Atheism* promises to be a new standard work.[48] The state atheism of the Soviet Union, a very different 20th-century path for atheism than it took in Western Europe or the US, represents a key case in the history of atheism. And in a nuanced but exciting monograph, based on extensive archival work, Smolkin succeeds in retelling this long and very complex story.

The state communism in the Soviet Union is often perceived as a political or *Ersatz* religion. This is not least the case for thinkers wanting to disassociate the communist experience in the USSR from rational secularism. Hence, Mitchell Stephens, discussed in the introduction, writes that "Stalin, Mao and Pol Pot *were* in a sense religious" (thus enabling him to handily exempt these communist dictators from his story of good atheism).[49] In another recent book on atheism, British philosopher John Gray claims that Bolshevism was religious in that it served as a channel for the "millenarian myths of apocalyptic Christianity."[50] Applying the categories of traditional religion to (totalitarian) politics may certainly be a valid analysis, but it also risks remaining a rather crude portrayal of certain political experiences and historical developments. In the case of the USSR and atheism, it is much more interesting to see what actually went on in the godless superpower, how the leaders of party and state sought to disband, replace, or refocus traditional religion, and what this meant for the development of Soviet society. This is what Smolkin has done in her work.

The goal was clear: an atheist society where traditional religion – perceived as an enemy to communism – was to disappear. However, the intensity and methods of this project varied greatly throughout the some 80 years that the Soviet Union existed. Without discussing this in any detail here, we may note a couple of shifts.

---

47 Devellennes, *Positive Atheism*, 201–209.
48 See, for instance, Daniel Peris, *Storming the Heavens: The Soviet League of the Militant Godless* (Ithaca: Cornell University Press, 1998).
49 Stephens, *Imagine There's No Heaven*, 221.
50 John Gray, *Seven Types of Atheism* (London: Allen Lane, 2018), 72. Gray here bases his account on thinkers such as Eric Voegelin and Norman Cohn.

With a nod toward Devellennes' work discussed above, we may say that one development was the shift from negative to positive atheism. Earlier persecutions of Christians, destruction of churches, and rational debunking of superstitious beliefs in the name of science proved insufficient. The people still believed not only in Lenin and Khrushchev, it turned out, but also in God, and in the homes of ordinary people, the party program was placed next to prayer books.[51] Therefore, during the post-war era, there were conscious efforts from the state to replace religion by trying to fulfill spiritual needs, thus taking control over the Soviet soul. Communicating a communist worldview and ethics represented one tool in this project; another was the expansion of socialist rituals connected to important events in human life, such as weddings and funerals.[52]

Smolkin's book will become important in Soviet historiography. In this context, however, it is more interesting to note its relationship to the historiography of atheism and secularism. Atheism in the Soviet Union played an important part in 20th-century atheism in general, also in Western countries – an inspiration for some, but a threat to or a big Other for most.[53] Shifts in Soviet atheism may thus mean shifts in religious and atheist identity in other societies. This is certainly true in the case of the US, and Smolkin relates to the "cultural war" of the Cold War. This warfare, for instance, led cosmonauts and astronauts to discuss theological matters (German Titov did not see God in space, he proudly declared, while John Glenn claimed that his God was not of the kind you could see from a spaceship).[54]

It is also interesting to note some similarities to the Western hemisphere during the Cold War. First, the belief in, and connection of atheism to, science represented a backbone also in Soviet atheism. Here, the non-believing cosmonauts were heroes, promoting the proud scientific and technological advances of the atheist state.[55] Second, the "return of religion" to public life in the late 20th century was also noted in the Soviet Union. However, the background for this phenomenon was different. If Western Europe first experienced a "religious crisis" in the 1960s and 1970s, when especially the youth lost faith in traditional religion, an inverted

---

[51] Victoria Smolkin, *A Sacred Space is Never Empty: A History of Soviet Atheism* (New Jersey: Princeton University Press, 2018), 83.
[52] Smolkin, *A Sacred Space*, 165–193.
[53] The impact and legacy of Soviet atheism are still noticeable in Finland and the Baltic states, see Teemu Taira, Atko Remmel, and Anton Jansson, "The Nordic and Baltic Countries," in *The Cambridge History of Atheism*, ed. Michael Ruse and Stephen Bullivant (Cambridge: Cambridge University Press, 2021).
[54] Smolkin, *A Sacred Space*, 84–85.
[55] See especially Chapter 3 in Smolkin, *A Sacred Space*.

development took place in the USSR. Youth and intelligentsia about this time seemed to turn to religion. This could thus be seen as opposite to the development in the West but also a parallel: if the religious crisis in the West signaled dissatisfaction with the establishment of the older generations, similarly the turn *to* religiosity in the Soviet Union was a turn away from the establishment, an "opposition to the socialist way of life" or even "inner migration."[56] This serves as an additional example of how national and political contexts matter in the development of belief and non-belief.

So, atheism was an integral part of the social and political history of the globally vastly important Soviet state. Another example of this is how Smolkin reads the demise of the Soviet Union through atheism. In the 1980s, the state under Gorbachev increasingly came to accept the Russian Orthodox Church and its representatives. This was, in a sense, a break from atheism, which signaled the end of the ideological coherence between official party ideology and state practice. Such inconsistencies meant that the monopoly of truth was put into question, thus resulting in the moral authority and political legitimacy of the Soviet rulers crumbling.[57] This is an interesting example of how atheism may play a role also in social and political issues going beyond the mere question of the existence of God and the role of religious institutions.

Conclusion: Trends and Future Directions

It may be hard to discern *one* common trend in the historiography of atheism, freethought, etc. based on the seven books discussed here. Nevertheless, some things can be noted. Many of these works in a very fruitful way move in the borderlands between intellectual, social, and political history. Ideas are circulating in social movements, as we see in the works of Alexander and Weldon, are promoted in state policy, as in Smolkin's work, move in broader historical shifts, as in Ryrie's work, or take shape in relation to gender politics, as made clear in Hamlin's work. The importance of canonized thinkers – Spinoza, Diderot, Paine, Marx, Nietzsche, Darwin, and others – is duly noted as significant, but their texts are not necessarily analyzed in depth.[58] The materials used also mirror this: the au-

---

56 Smolkin, *A Sacred Space*, 225–226; Hugh McLeod, *The Religious Crisis of the 1960s* (Oxford: Oxford University Press, 2007).
57 Smolkin, *A Sacred Space*, 228–246
58 There may be exceptions. One recent work that could have been included even though the author does not directly relate it to this field is Frederick C. Beiser, *David Friedrich Strauss, Father of Unbelief: An Intellectual Biography* (Oxford: Oxford University Press, 2020).

thors here have not shied away from using a wide assortment of sources. Philosophical and scientific works, yes, but also periodicals, newspapers, archival material of various kinds, correspondence, novels, autobiographies, and, in Smolkin's case, interviews. This mirrors the broader history of atheist ideas in movements, in contexts, and in circulation. This represents a constructive way of writing this history. As we have seen, social and political contexts matter a great deal for the various ways in which atheism and secularism take shape.

As mentioned at the outset, research on the history of atheism has often lent itself to partisan narratives exhibiting hagiographic or speculative tendencies. While there are surely also current researchers who are motivated by their personal belief or non-belief and engagements in corresponding organizations, the historiography considered here is nuanced and well-grounded, rather than serving as identity formation dressed up in academic garb. To produce a tenable historical understanding, the historiography of atheism cannot be too one-sided. This also means that those who research non-believers and the turning away from religion need to be knowledgeable regarding religious contexts and consider them in their analysis. First, this is because doubt and humanism may grow out of religious traditions, as made clear in the works of Ryrie and Weldon. Second, and more importantly, due to the fact that religion is a clear opponent to most atheists and freethinkers, religion is productive in the history of the latter. All religious traditions are to some extent malleable, and an understanding of the particular position and ideals of the dominant religion or religions in a given context helps explain the motivations and specific engagements of atheists. What did they specifically dissent from or criticize? Was this the same as in other national contexts?

US history is an outlier when it comes to religious identity in the 20th century, and its specific Christian experience needs to be taken into account if we are to understand how and why unbelief in the US differs from, say, Scandinavian unbelief.[59] Weldon, for instance, to some extent contextualizes his story about humanism with the broader religious history of the US and how shifts in Christianity are related to developments in humanism. Generally, however, theological and church-historical aspects could be strengthened in works in this field. In various ways, modern secularism and modern Christianity are mutually constitutive. One example of this is highlighted by Todd Weir, mentioned in the introduction. He has re-

---

[59] The United States has always been an anomaly for those advocating the correlation between modernity and secularization, being a society much more infused and dominated by religious beliefs – primarily Christianity –than otherwise similar richer, "modern" Western European countries. For a discussion on this and how this nevertheless seems to be changing, see David E. Campbell, Geoffrey C. Layman, and John C. Green, *Secular Surge: A New Fault Line in American Politics* (Cambridge: Cambridge University Press, 2020).

cently written about how Christians and secularists in interwar Germany were involved in a cultural war, where they in their "apologetics" shared the stage and therefore learned a lot from one another.[60]

There are recurring themes in these books. Science is hard to avoid when studying the history of atheism, but its centrality here is certainly related to developments in the 21st century. New Atheism was science-based, and this in a way perceived by many as crude and ahistorical. In this historiography, we can thus discern a wish to better understand science and atheism in context. Race is key for Alexander and Cameron and also occurs in the works by Weldon and Hamlin. Here, it is easy to see the echoes of contemporary US politics where this is a defining issue, not least in the 21st century. In this sense, while these works are not part of some partisan debate, they do reflect contemporary concerns.[61] This is obviously not something that should surprise us. As Jacob Burckhardt put it, history is "the record of what one age finds worthy of note in another."[62] Apart from this, we may note how one of the most dynamic "turns" in historical research in recent times, the history of emotions, has also found its way into the field, in Ryrie's work.

There is also a potential in the research in this field to join forces with another growing research field, namely history of knowledge, where this yearbook serves as a central arena and important exponent. The characterization of how the intellectual and social history of non-belief is currently written rhymes well with the dynamic, contextual, and cultural understanding of knowledge proposed by historians of knowledge.[63] There are more specific aspects where synergies could be found. As discussed above, the dichotomies of science vs religion and belief vs knowledge have been crucial in the history of freethought and atheism, as have knowledge-related concepts such as doubt, which is the focus of Ryrie's work. And while historians of science and knowledge have done much to debunk

---

60 Todd H. Weir, "The Apologetics of Modern Culture Wars: The Case of Weimar Germany," in *Defending the Faith: Global Histories of Apologetics and Politics in the Twentieth Century*, ed. Todd H. Weir and Hugh McLeod (Oxford: Oxford University Press, 2021).
61 Science is notable also outside these particular books. Apart from it being central to Weldon and important for Smolkin, Alexander, and to some degree Hamlin, it is the focus of attention also in Thomas, *Science and Religion in India*; Spenninger, *Stoff für Konflikt*. Race is central to Corbeil, *Empire and Progress*.
62 Jacob Burckhardt, *Judgments on History and Historians* (Indianapolis: Liberty Fund, 1999), 168. The German original reads: "Sie ist der jedesmalige Bericht dessen, was Ein Zeitalter am andern Zeitalter merkwürdig findet." Jacob Burckhardt, *Historische Fragmente: aus dem Nachlass gesammelt von Emil Dürr mit einem Vorwort von Werner Kaegi* (Stuttgart: K. F. Koehler Verlag, 1957), 198.
63 For a presentation with further references, see the introductory text of this journal from 2022: Charlotte A. Lerg, Johan Östling, and Jana Weiß, "Introducing the Yearbook History of Intellectual Culture," *History of Intellectual Culture* 1 (2022).

these as eternal categories of conflict, it is clear that in certain instances, religious belief and certain types of knowledge claims have come into conflict and that these have been important for the identity and practice of various non-believing communities. This could then illustrate the historically shifting roles and contentions of knowledge as well as how knowledge intersects with identity and belief. Within these communities, there are also plenty of actors and arenas of knowledge that have been instrumental in the circulation of certain types of knowledge, not least shown in Stephen Weldon's work. Connecting with this field could thus be of interest to historians of knowledge interested in circulating practices, while historians of atheism, secularism, and humanism could benefit from theoretical tools such as knowledge actors, public arenas of knowledge, and circulation.[64] More at a meta level, furthermore, the relatively sudden turn from social sciences dominated by secularization theory to the post-secular where religion quickly returned to scholarship around the turn of the 21st century could in itself be of interest for historians of knowledge, specializing in modern academic knowledge production.[65] These are just a couple of suggestions for how these fields could benefit from interactions and collaborations.

A positive development is that quite a few of these works have moved into the 20th century. It is safe to say that the historiography of atheism and freethought has focused on the 19th century, which is not surprising given the golden age of freethought and how many new strands of materialist and naturalist thinking came into existence at that time.[66] However, to historicize the 20th century and

---

[64] See, for instance, Johan Östling, "Circulation, Arenas, and the Quest for Public Knowledge: Historiographical Currents and Analytical Frameworks," *History and Theory* 59, no. 4 (2020); Johan Östling, "Circulating Knowledge in Public Arenas: Toward a New History of the Postwar Humanities," *History of Humanities* 6, no. 2 (2021).

[65] A point of departure in José Casanova's classic *Public Religions in the Modern World* was that he had noticed a dramatic paradigm shift: his colleagues were in the process of abandoning a previous paradigm dominated by the secularization theory "with the same uncritical haste with which they previously embraced it." Casanova, *Public Religions*, 11. Secularization theory and what many have seen as a secularist domination of mid-19th-century scholarship could thus also be an object for empirical studies by historians of knowledge. For an attempt focused on Sweden, see Anton Jansson, "The City, the Church, and the 1960s: On Secularization Theory and the Swedish Translation of Harvey Cox's *The Secular City*," in *Histories of Knowledge in Postwar Scandinavia: Actors, Arenas, and Aspirations*, ed. Johan Östling, Niklas Olsen, and David Larsson Heidenblad (Abingdon: Routledge, 2020).

[66] A typical 19th-century work not mentioned thus far is Michael Rectenwald, *Nineteenth-Century British Secularism: Science, Religion, and Literature* (London: Palgrave MacMillan, 2016). Of course, even though they are clearly fewer, there have been some works focusing on the 20th century. Apart from the above-mentioned volume edited by De Nutte and Gasenbeek, see, for instance,

try to note breaks and continuities with the preceding and following centuries is an important task and one where I think we will see more dynamic work in the future. The research of Smolkin, Weldon, and Cameron may here inspire and assist.

Further, these works bear witness to a curious situation facing current scholarship: the fact that English is both the dominant common language of the international research community and the native and particular research language for some scholars. The specific interests of the latter then naturally take up more space in what is also an international field. All scholars discussed here are based in the US and the UK, and while there are works on France and the USSR, the majority cover Anglo-American history. The selection of books here is obviously my own, but it reflects a strong tendency that English-language monographs on the history of atheism primarily tend to focus on North America and the UK. As noted in the beginning, the case here is rather that there are more books on these areas that could have been included.

In one sense, this is natural, but the international research community could also gain from more in-depth stories concerning other countries and language areas, not least since the United States is no default case in the history of religion and secularism. We non-English-language scholars should work toward this, but it is also something that academic publishers and editors should consider. In the meantime, we could also revel in the fact that there are great edited volumes in which fascinating national and sometimes even entangled cases flower, such as *Freethinkers in Europe* (edited by Carolin Kosuch), *Freethought and Atheism in Central and Eastern Europe* (Bubík, Remmel, and Václavík), or *Looking Back to Look Forward* (De Nutte and Gasenbeek).[67] In these works, other European, and mostly Christian, countries come to the fore, but more works relating to non-Christian and non-European traditions are also needed.[68] All in all, works on other national cases as well as comparative, entangled, and global histories are something to hope for in the future.

Tina Block, *The Secular Northwest: Religion and Irreligion in Everyday Postwar Life* (Vancouver: UBC Press, 2016).
67 Kosuch, *Freethinkers*; Bubík, Remmel, and Václavík, *Freethought and Atheism*; De Nutte and Gasenbeek, *Looking Back*.
68 *The Cambridge History of Atheism* contains good chapters on atheism in non-Christian and non-Western settings, but there are fewer recent monographs with a clear historical perspective. One work touching on the history of atheism that is worth mentioning is Thomas, *Science and Religion in India*. For a work that is a few years older and with partly but not solely a historical angle, see Johannes Quack, *Disenchanting India: Organized Rationalism and Criticism of Religion in India* (New York: Oxford University Press, 2012).

Initially, I raised the question of whether all works on the history of atheism and freethought necessarily belong to the same research field. We have here seen that these works focus on quite different parts of history. However, there are also many parallels, both expected and unexpected. The peripheral 18th-century atheist priest Jean Meslier, one of Devellennes' main characters, was erected as a statue in the Soviet Union, while German philosopher Ludwig Feuerbach not only inspired Karl Marx's critique of religion but was also read by black freethinkers, such as Frederick Douglass and Zora Neale Hurston, as pointed out by Christopher Cameron.[69] Emotions were tied into belief and unbelief not only in the 16th century but also in the 20th century. So, historians working on atheism in one century and on one continent may still learn from reading and communicating with researchers working on completely different eras and locations. The existence of differences is obviously a necessary component for constructive comparisons, which help getting a better understanding of one's own case and context.

However, we have also seen how these works speak to other research fields and other historical phenomena than the ones discussed here. And it is my conviction that histories of freethought, atheism, secularism, and humanism could benefit research on other topics. As discussions on the "return of religion" in recent decades have made clear, questions of belief and non-belief represent a permanent and active part also in modern societies. The works mentioned here may bring something to the historical study of race, philosophy, knowledge, and science as well as to the wider history of religion and politics. Seeking out ways to contribute to this also represents one of the most interesting challenges to experts in this lively and interesting field.

About the contributor

Anton Jansson is an associate professor of the History of Ideas and Science at the University of Gothenburg, Sweden. Jansson has carried out research on both German and Swedish history in the 19th and 20th centuries, mostly with a focus on religion and secularization. He is currently working on a research project funded by the Swedish Research Council: "Visions of a Society without God: The History of Atheism in Sweden 1879–1968."

---

69 Cameron, *Black Freethinkers*, 33, 55.

HIC Conversation with Marnie Hughes-Warrington, Chiel van den Akker, and Moira Pérez, edited and introduced by João Ohara

Pasts and Futures for the Theory and Philosophy of History

Abstract: In this conversation, we explore some of the current questions approached in the theory and philosophy of history. Three participants in the field reflect on their professional trajectories, the intellectual traditions from which these stem, and the theoretical questions surrounding historical knowledge and our historical condition.

Keywords: philosophy of history, theory of history, historicity, historical knowledge

It is often said that historians are "theory-averse," whatever meaning we attribute to the term "theory." There is some truth to this claim: at least some historians have had a complicated relationship with the (social and cultural) theory they need to borrow from sociologists and anthropologists. Some were even more reticent regarding literary theory, and perhaps most historians either ignored or bemoaned what little philosophers had to say about the epistemology of historiography. Nevertheless, at least in some countries, such as Brazil or the Netherlands, history departments have for quite some time now had in-house specialists in the "theory of history," and journals and events dedicated to this specialty have been organized with plenty of submissions.[1] So, it is perhaps safe to say that just as *some* historians are averse to talking about theory, *others* have shown a great deal of interest in the theoretical aspects of their discipline (again, whatever meaning they attribute to the term "theory").

We could tell many different stories about such a specialty. For some, it is the story that goes from the "speculative philosophy of history" through the "analytical philosophy of history" to "narrativism." Others prefer to frame it in the spirit of the German genre of *Historik* and its developments. Others still start from neo-Kantianism and go all the way to "French theory," "postmodernism," and the

---

[1] For instance, the International Network for Theory of History (INTH) has organized conferences in Belgium, Brazil, and, most recently, Mexico. Meanwhile, journals such as *History and Theory* (USA), *Rethinking History* (UK), *Historein* (Greece), *Historia y Grafía* (Mexico), or *História da Historiografia* (Brazil) have been published for many years, sometimes decades, without interruptions.

like. Sometimes, these strands even intertwine, even though the labels used only rarely assume the same meanings across different traditions.[2]

All these different genealogies have an impact on our present practices. Some have made a distinction between the philosophy of historiography, in which philosophers address more traditional philosophical questions, and the theory of history or historical theory, where historians deal with an eclectic mix of problems in an equally eclectic multitude of ways. Others see no such distinction, looking upon "philosophy of history" and "theory of history" as interchangeable terms. For some, the legitimate questions of the field are somewhat related to the questions addressed in the philosophy of science regarding the sciences. Others see no reason to privilege one specific flavor of the philosophy of science (the analytic one) over the others. Furthermore, there are those who see no reason to privilege philosophy at all, thus also bringing to bear insights and questions from social theory or the history and sociology of knowledge.

We can readily see how quickly we get to a kaleidoscope of sorts. We also face the task of either figuring out what these historians and philosophers do or proposing ways forward. In this conversation, I have asked three practitioners about their own trajectories and perceptions regarding the field. The resulting discussion gives us some intricate details on three different backgrounds and intellectual contexts that, in the end, are part of the diverse set of questions and approaches that make up what we could refer to as "the theory and philosophy of history."

1) Our professional labels

"Theory of history," "historical theory," or "philosophy of history" are some of the labels we often use to classify our work. However, it is not always clear whether we understand each of these labels as having the same meaning or if there are meaningful differences between them. In fact, the works we classify using each of these labels are so diverse that finding a common denominator has proven difficult. Nevertheless, we still use these terms, and we use them in ways suggesting that we at

---

2 See, for example, Jouni-Matti Kuukkanen, "A Conceptual Map for Twenty-First-Century Philosophy of History," in *Philosophy of History: Twenty-First-Century Perspectives*, ed. Jouni-Matti Kuukkanen (London: Bloomsbury, 2021), Christophe Bouton, "The Critical Theory of History: Rethinking the Philosophy of History in the Light of Koselleck's Work," *History and Theory* 55, no. 2 (2016): 163–184, or Jörn Rüsen, "A Turning Point in Theory of History: The Place of Hayden White in the History of Metahistory," *History and Theory* 59, no. 1 (2020): 92–102.

least see some family resemblance tying our work together. How did you end up working in this field and which kinds of questions have you engaged in lately?

Marnie Hughes-Warrington: Historiography has a broad meaning. I have always understood it to accommodate a range of approaches to understanding the past, including historical methods, sociology, psychology, and philosophy. For this reason, it makes sense to at first glance describe my work using the label "philosophy of history." This is what you will see in profiles of my work, as it is a good way for people to understand how I approach my research.

As a student, though, I majored in history and philosophy. I have always viewed them as equal subjects. They are like the left and right hands of my work, and my aim is not just to be ambidextrous, but to join those hands together. History brings insights to philosophy; philosophy brings insights to history. I first saw the potential of joining them together when I read R. G. Collingwood's inaugural professorial lecture on the topic of historical imagination. It was by sheer coincidence that I read this in history class when I was simultaneously studying imagination in philosophy class. As an undergraduate, I was intrigued that the two subjects crossed over on this topic, and my DPhil (PhD) topic was formed in that moment.[3]

Collingwood's approach has influenced my work deeply. He was committed to joining philosophy and history together and to being a public intellectual. I hope that people see in my work a celebration of both history and philosophy, while they in my work as an administrator and for community groups see a commitment to public thought. By deepest training and inclination, I am most interested in metaphysics and in world and global history, but I have always sought to advance our understanding of the nature and purpose of history in broad spaces such as schools, film, museums, and universities. For this reason, I also use the words "history theory" to describe my work. I do so to invite other people in.

I do this as I do not think that the discipline of history "disciplines" tightly. The boundaries and nature of our work are fuzzy and shift over time, including the labels we use to describe it. In *Big and Little Histories*,[4] I argued that this is the case due to ethical reasons: history making is in part an invitation to an *ethos* or the effort of ethics, as Aristotle saw it.

---

[3] Marnie Hughes-Warrington, *"How Good an Historian Shall I Be?": R. G. Collingwood, the Historical Imagination and Education* (Thorveton: Imprint, 2003).

[4] Marnie Hughes-Warrington and Anne Martin, *Big and Little Histories: Sizing Up Ethics in Historiography* (London: Routledge, 2022).

We have to do the work of understanding the nature and purpose of history for ourselves.

People know that I talk about "history makers," for example, to capture the histories made outside of universities. I have pursued the logical implications of this by looking at as wide a range of history-making activities globally as I can. I hope that, like others, I have encouraged students and scholars to see themselves in history theory or philosophy of history. I do not mind which label they use; my role is to encourage them.

This interest in the breadth of history making has brought me to my current work, on whether artificial agents can make histories. Even if we do not think that they can, and even if tools such as ChatGPT make us feel uncomfortable, I hope to further amplify people's interest in the logic of history and encourage those interested in history to contribute to decisions and debates regarding artificial intelligence. We are not just another voice in those decisions and debates. I see artificial intelligence as a fundamentally historical activity, as this concerns the ways in which machines process and reprocess information and past data. Collingwood wrote a critical essay on the gramophone, and I am sure he would have had many critical ideas about machine intelligence. Just like him, I hope that people will not be sure which label to use to describe my work and that they will forge their own path in history. That is my aim.

Chiel van den Akker: Perhaps we may view the distinction between historical theory and philosophy of history as analogues to the distinction between political theory and political philosophy.[5] There are no generally accepted distinctions regarding any of these, although there are differences in terms of emphasis. Philosophy of history is less eclectic and often more ambitious (for better or worse) than theory of history. We may also think of this distinction in institutional terms. Historical theory is taught and studied at history departments just as political theory is taught and studied at political science departments, whereas philosophy of history, just like political philosophy, is taught and studied at philosophy departments. Anyway, I am fine with each label. But how did I end up here? After graduating in historical theory, I wrote a PhD thesis in philosophy on the nature of historical representation, which I finished in 2009.[6] I sent my PhD thesis to an indi-

---

[5] Cf. Andrew Reeve, "Political Theory," Oxford Reference, https://www.oxfordreference.com/view/10.1093/oi/authority.20110803100334775

[6] The PhD thesis has been published as *Beweren en Tonen. Waarheid, Taal en het Verleden* (Rozenberg Publishers: Amsterdam, 2009).

vidual, Chris Lorenz at the Vrije Universiteit Amsterdam, who then asked me if I would be interested in pursuing an academic career. A colleague of his at the VU, Susan Legêne, was advertising for a post-doctoral position in which historical theory was one of the requirements. I applied for the position, got it, and quit my job as a history teacher in secondary education. After Chris went to Germany, I took over his undergraduate and graduate courses in historical theory, after which I was eventually offered a tenured position as lecturer at the VU. In the Netherlands, all undergraduate students in history take a course in historical theory, which explains why there is a small job market for historical theorists in the Netherlands.

I am currently working on two projects. The first is a short book on how narratives make the past intelligible to us. It is intended for a wide range of scholars and students interested in history writing. The other project is still in *status nascendi*. It concerns the relationship between history and justice. It takes me to the Athenians in the second half of the fifth century B.C., such as the sophist historian Thucydides, whose work is part of the greater debate on the relationship between human nature and written and unwritten laws and customs, and to his contemporaries, the playwriters who in their tragedies addressed the relationship between free action, fate, and justice. This project also takes me to the German idealists for whom the relationship between history and justice plays a key role in their philosophies of history (idealists such as Hegel were also very interested in these ancient Athenians for that very reason). What I am mainly interested in at the moment is the recent interest in Hegel in analytical philosophy and the sporadic interest in his philosophy of history in that tradition. Curiously, most people working on Hegel's philosophy of history are rather ignorant of developments in contemporary philosophy of history. As stated above, however, the whole project is still in its very early stages, and perhaps it leads nowhere (this is also the sort of project for which it is hard to find funding). Anyway, I have given some lectures on parts of the project on different occasions, and one publication is forthcoming early next year.

Moira Pérez: The matter of defining the field is an old question in philosophy, and we somehow just got used to not really knowing what our discipline is about. I say I do philosophy of history as I studied philosophy and as I feel that I have a philosophical way of thinking, but I would not be able to say exactly what that means. Still, the question of disciplinary boundaries is interesting because, on the one hand, you use these to communicate to others an idea of what you do (and, of course, to apply for jobs and grants), but at the same time when we engage in work that goes beyond what is usually perceived as part of our discipline, we are in a way expanding its boundaries: we say that "this can also be a part of philosophy of history" and open up that possibility for people following in our footsteps.

I became interested in this field as an undergraduate student, when I took philosophy of history as part of the mandatory program for the orientation in practical philosophy at the University of Buenos Aires, Argentina. I had always been interested in political issues, questions of marginalization, oppression, resistance, and social movements. When I took this course offered by Verónica Tozzi Thompson, the professor who subsequently became my supervisor and mentor, I was immediately fascinated by the opportunity to understand the role of historical narratives and representations in these phenomena and in the turbulent political history of my country and region. The first topic I studied was the relationship between historical presence (being included in historical narratives) and political presence (having a say in the public sphere and in decisions affecting our lives). I also specialized in queer theory, which was not at all that common in Argentina prior to the 2010s, and I started to bring both approaches together as I noticed, with some surprise, that this had not been done before. I dedicated my PhD thesis to exploring what a queer philosophy of history would look like.[7] Along the way, I realized that other factors such as ableism, coloniality, and cissexism also had to be included if I really wanted to grasp how historical representations reproduce or resist marginalization. This resulted in my thesis being somewhat more intersectional, which was unusual both for mainstream philosophy of history and for queer theory. With time, questions of coloniality became more central to my work, but I still feel that queer theory informs my perspectives, particularly in relation to temporality, normativity, utopia, and my understanding of identities.

My research still revolves around the exclusion of certain collectives from historical narratives and, through these, from the public sphere. On the one hand, I am interested in epistemic injustice and epistemic violence as pervasive phenomena in historiography, with grave epistemic and political consequences. On the other hand, I study the uses of public space and temporality to exclude certain collectives as part of broader structural

---

7 Moira Pérez, "Resumen de tesis de Doctorado: Aportes queer para la representación del pasado: aspectos políticos, epistemológicos y estético-formales," *Cuadernos de Filosofía* 63 (2014): 106–108, https://doi.org/10.34096/cf.n63.3138. See also Moira Pérez, "Queer Politics of History: On Progress Narratives and Its Outcasts," *Lambda Nordica* 21, no. 3–4 (2018): 15–34, http://www.lambdanordica.org/index.php/lambdanordica/article/view/525

oppression. I am currently a fellow at the Forschungsinstitut für Philosophie in Hannover, Germany, where I am working on the global movement to bring down colonial monuments, which may serve as a way of resisting these exclusions, but also a way of whitewashing them. I hope to contribute to discussions on what to do with historical objects, such as monuments or artworks, that constitute blatant expressions of colonialism or white supremacy. I get the feeling that in the next few years, I will turn more to questions related to temporality, futurity, and utopia, perhaps because the world looks so grim right now...

2) Thinking across traditions

In all the different types of work we nowadays do in the theory and philosophy of history, we can discern at least a handful of different intellectual traditions engaged in understanding our historical condition and the ways in which we produce knowledge of the past(s). This scenario is very different from the times of "analytic philosophy of history," where a small number of philosophers could more or less agree on a core conceptual framework. But while diversity is and should be embraced for our field to thrive in the contemporary academic landscape, it also presents challenges in terms of collective efforts if we lack some minimal common ground where exchanges and collaborations may occur. How can we foster such a community? What does such a community look like in our case? Can someone studying the epistemology of historiography work together with someone studying indigenous conceptions of time in Latin America, Africa, or Asia? In sum, how can we work together across multiple boundaries?

MHW: My training was in analytic philosophy of history. I am still grateful to this day for the rigorous nature of the training I received. It is very helpful for reading all kinds of texts, and I enjoy reading analytic work. Collingwood's work did not, however, fit that approach. To explore his arguments, I read Kant, Hegel, Croce, Sartre, Plato, Aristotle, as well as Wittgenstein and the professors of my time, such as W. H. Dray, Morton White, Hayden White, Alan White. For a short time, I thought you had to have the family name White to be a philosopher! Once I got the philosophy bug, I started reading Derrida, Heidegger, Dworkin, Rorty. I am still an avid reader today, always interested in new approaches and reflections. I do not believe that I understand these philosophies as well as those who are fluent in their first languages, but the effort of seeking to understand is what philosophy is all about. More recently in my life, I have looked to the fusion of approaches in Asian philosophies. And perhaps most significantly, I have sought to learn about Australian Aboriginal philosophies. Aboriginal people have a tradition of welcoming you to their country. They see everything as connected in their country. I have tried to reciprocate their welcome and generosity by learning. I learned about some Ngunnawal ideas in Canberra, and a senior elder is teaching me Kaurna philosophy in Adelaide. He teaches me two ideas at a time. This slow journey together is one of trust and generosity. It is like the profound act of trust and generosity in Aunty Anne Martin's gift of telling and knowledge in *Big and Little Histories*. We often assume that our world is falling into conversations in which we talk past one another. That is not my experience. Trust, listening, learning, respect, and caring for other people still matter and still have currency. That requires letting go of knowing the answers, speaking, and disciplinary labels. It is for these reasons that I only now see myself as really learning philosophy.

CvdA: These are difficult questions, and I doubt whether I have anything substantial to offer in response. I agree that the celebrated polyphony marking the field of historical theory all too easily turns into a cacophony. Here, however, journals, conferences, networks, study groups, and companions have a role to play. They all allow for exchanges in which a common ground and community may be established. There are several interesting journals in the field,[8] each with their specific mission and identity, as well as several important networks organizing conferences and online presentations.[9] Perhaps the field needs to be more self-conscious about who we see as predecessors and contemporaries working on similar or related issues and how a conversation with these may be initiated and continued.

MP: My background is also in analytic philosophy and, just like Marnie, I am extremely grateful for that, as it has provided me with a set of skills to do my work regardless of which topic I study. However, it is also true that the prevalence of Anglo-Saxon philosophy in our work and background is part of the international division of intellectual labor, which is rooted in deeper structures of domination, most notably colonialism. My hope

---

8 For instance, *History and Theory, Journal of the Philosophy of History, Rethinking History,* and *Storia Della Storiografia*.

9 Especially the Centre for Philosophical Studies of History in Oulu (Finland), the UK-based IHR The Philosophy of History Seminar, and the International Network for Theory of History (INTH) based in Gent (Belgium).

is that our intellectual community will look more and more like a diversity of traditions and backgrounds that we can draw from, which may open up dialogues and enable us to learn from each other when an opportunity arises.

There are currently countless lines of inquiry in philosophy and theory of history, and we are not necessarily always going to work together, which is fine. The connections and feedback between various subfields, methods, and traditions are dynamic. They depend on the context and topics attracting the interest of scholars. I feel that when this happens, scholars in our field are open to exploring these connections, which, in my opinion, makes it one of the most exciting subfields in philosophy.

I feel that the discipline gains enormously from expanding its boundaries and diversifying its perspectives, topics, and methodologies. For contexts historically seen as being at the center, this can be revealing but also challenging, as scholars in these contexts have to learn about what is being done elsewhere and learn to converse with people from very different backgrounds. For those of us working in Latin America, this is in some way easier as we are already aware of what is happening in the North and as we share a language and, to a certain extent, also a history (including an intellectual history of sorts). But this does not mean that there is no resistance: our foundation is Eurocentric, and we too must learn to read and respect what is being done at home. Of course, there is also financial and editorial pressure to work on topics that are trending in the North, which pushes us to be more creative in order to find ways of working with what interests us and is relevant to our contexts, while still securing access to global academic networks.

3) Our relationships to the past(s)

Historical knowledge and our cognitive relationships to the past(s) have been privileged objects in theoretical and philosophical reflections on history. And although they still retain much of their significance, authors from vastly different backgrounds have started to turn their attention to other kinds of relationships we establish with the past(s) – for instance, pragmatic ones where the past(s) becomes either an arena or a tool (or both) in present struggles. Anthropologists, literary theorists, historians, and philosophers have come to realize that these other relationships to the past were not relics of a bygone era having been superseded by a strictly intellectual interest in the past. These relationships seem to be the very foundation, the very reason some of us look for reliable answers about the past in the first place. Do you see this shift as something that may circle back and enrich our understanding of historical knowledge? Could it open up unexplored pathways that are worth exploring even if they take us farther away from cognitive problems?

MHW: These shifts delight me, because I see them in no small part as the return of metaphysics after a strong period of analytic approaches. I also see in them a wide variety of historical methodologies as informing theoretical and philosophical reflections on history. I always wondered why our approaches to theory were narrower than approaches to history making, and I am pleased that approaches to epistemology have broadened. This will help us better understand even the most basic things that we take for granted, such as conditionals like "if, then."

CvdA: I am not sure how to conceive of the shift you refer to and whether there is such a shift in the first place. History should serve life, as Nietzsche argued already a century and a half ago, and his distinctions between the antiquarian, critical, and monumental senses of history include different kinds of relationships to the past, each of which is a mixture of dispositions, desires, and beliefs. His essay still serves as a basis for any understanding of the use and abuse of history, and I do not see which new relationships are discovered compared to the ones he distinguished. (I do think he missed the importance of historically articulating the beliefs we hold dear.) The different uses of the past in present struggles certainly fit within Nietzsche's conceptions.

Perhaps there is, and has been, a strictly intellectual interest in the past in some academic circles at some points in time. Such a strictly intellectual interest has, I guess, to do with increasing our knowledge of the past without there being any use for it. But who is interested in knowledge of the past as an end in itself, except for the antiquarian and, as Hayden White once put it, the cultural necrophile?

MP: As I stated above, in my experience, the interest was always in the politics of history. Even when exploring epistemic practices in historiography, or in representations of the past more broadly, this represented a means for understanding how certain subjects, collectives, and ways of life are excluded from the past, how others are affirmed in the present, and so forth. Maybe it is this inclination that leads me to think that the political cannot be understood without the epistemic, and vice versa. Feminist and anti-colonial epistemologies, and what I have more broadly referred to as "epistemologies from the margins,"[10] have proven that there is a great epistemic loss in the belief that we can explain a cognitive phenomenon, such as the study of the past, through "purely epistemic" factors. Social epistemology has also shown how our epistemic practices are rooted in epistemic dependence, meaning that knowledge does not occur in a vacuum but rather in our interactions with others and from a specific social location. So, I do not think that exploring these paths will necessarily lead us away from cognitive problems (unless, obviously, we want them to). Rather, they will allow us to better understand the epistemic facets of our relationships to the past.

4) Questions unanswered or not yet posed

Narrativism has allowed us to pose new kinds of questions regarding how historical texts could possibly represent past phenomena in an intelligible way. We were able to pose additional questions by turning to memory, to testimony, and then to non-Western experiences of time. However, just as there are probably many kinds of questions yet to be posed, many of those we did pose remain partially or entirely unanswered. Which questions still unanswered grab your attention? And which questions yet to be posed do you think might be on the horizon?

MHW: There are plenty of wonderful philosophers of history working on narrative, so I doubt that I am able to add to that topic. I am most interested in the question of whether you have to be a human to make a history. I have indicated that I am working on whether artificial agents can make histories, but I have also noted in *Big and Little Histories* that algorithms derived from insect movements are being used to sort information. Do we see insects as helping us create histories? I think this is one of the most important questions of our time. I also wonder whether history is, well, not historical enough. If information is constantly being updated and modified on digital platforms, what does this mean for print media, journal papers, and even forums like this? Do we get the chance to revisit our answers to your questions over and over again? I hope so.

---

10 Moira Pérez, "Epistemologias das margens e disputas sobre o passado," in *Epistemologias feministas, ativismos e descolonização do conhecimento*, ed. Mariana Prandini, Breno Cypriano, and Eduardo Mattio (Porto Alegre: Zouk, 2023). See also Verónica Tozzi Thompson and Moira Pérez, "Epistemology," *Bloomsbury History: Theory and Method* (online) (London: Bloomsbury, 2021), http://dx.doi.org/10.5040/9781350970809.005

CvdA: The question of how history and justice are related, which I mentioned above, has obviously been answered in the past. But given the nature of our field, we constantly reexamine past answers in relation to new contexts. This is how the reflections on our existence in time and history as a discipline "works." Think, for example, of how postcolonial theory offered a reexamination of old questions in relation to the new post-colonial context. Scholars such as David Scott do important and inspiring work in this regard, not by raising new questions, but by reexamining old questions and their answers in relation to new contexts. It is only by reexamining old questions that we continue the conversation of humankind, as Richard Rorty called it. And this is something we should do, rather than starting a new and parochial conversation. This is thus a question that also grabs my attention: how best to continue the conversation of humankind and reeducate our forebears, if needed, as Rorty[11] urged us to do?

MP: I believe that the theory and philosophy of history hold great potential in terms of contributing to questions that are at the forefront of current debates in the public sphere. For instance, neo-conservative movements around the world are feeding on fake news, misinformation, and active ignorance to promote their agendas and expand their power. How may historiography and uses of history more broadly help us resist these movements? How should we do and disseminate history to effectively counter contemporary forms of genocide denial, neo-fascism, and conservative backlash?

On the other hand, our discipline itself must be reexamined. The challenges posed by collectives that are historically marginalized from scholarly work (except as objects of study) lead to us facing urgent questions regarding the methods, practices, and ethics of intellectual work. Philosophy, in particular, has been extremely reluctant to engage with this incitation, and it might ironically be the most resistant to self-critique regarding its racist, sexist, ableist history and habits. So, there is a lot to be done in this respect, not only in our subfield but also in philosophy and the academy more broadly. For example, how can we work with historically marginalized forms of knowledge (you mentioned non-Western experiences of time, indigenous conceptual frameworks, and so forth) without this resulting in extractivism? How can we build truly horizontal conversations? This

---

11 Richard Rorty, "The historiography of philosophy: Four genres," in: *Philosophy in History: Essays on the historiography of philosophy*, ed. Richard Rorty, J. B. Schneewind, and Quentin Skinner (Cambridge: Cambridge UP, 1984), 49–75, at 54 and 71.

brings me to a question that is at the root of it all and that might not have an answer: Is Western Europe really ready for the difficult task of provincializing itself?

About the contributors

Chiel van den Akker is a lecturer in philosophy of history at the Vrije Universiteit Amsterdam, the Netherlands. His research focuses on narrative and the relationship between justice and history. He is editor-in-chief of the *Journal of the Philosophy of History*.

Marnie Hughes-Warrington, AO PFHEA, is a Rhodes Scholar and graduate of University of Tasmania and Oxford. Marnie is a metaphysician who studies how the past shapes our present and future. A scholar having received over AU$18 million in grants, her work has been applied to many contexts. Her most recent book is *History from Loss* (together with Daniel Woolf, 2023), and she is currently researching historical logic in AI. Marnie is Deputy Vice-Chancellor: Research and Enterprise at University of South Australia and an honorary professor of history at the Australian National University. In 2022, she was made an Officer in the Order of Australia for distinguished service to higher education governance, leadership, and mentoring.

João Ohara is an assistant professor (with tenure) of theory of history at the Federal University of Rio de Janeiro, Brazil. His current research focuses on the social epistemology of historiography. His most recent publication is the book *The Theory and Philosophy of History: Global Variations* (2022).

Moira Pérez is an assistant researcher at the Argentine National Council for Scientific and Technical Research and professor at the University of Buenos Aires, Argentina (Department of Philosophy). She directs the Research Group on Applied Philosophy and Queer Politics (PolQueer) and works from a queer, anti-colonial perspective on the interactions between violence and identity. Her recent publications include "The practical past as an instrument of epistemic resistance: The case of the Massacre in the Seventh Ward" (*Estudios de Filosofía* 66, 2022) and "Contracting imaginations: On the political and hermeneutical monopoly of identity politics" (*Dialectical Anthropology* 47, 2023).

Contributors

Chiel van den Akker is a lecturer in philosophy of history at the Vrije Universiteit Amsterdam, the Netherlands. His research focuses on narrative and the relationship between justice and history. He is editor-in-chief of the *Journal of the Philosophy of History*.

Carlos Alves is a researcher at the Center for the History of Society and Culture, University of Coimbra, as well as a visiting assistant professor at the Faculty of Arts and Humanities, University of Coimbra, and the Faculty of Religious Studies and Philosophy, University of Saint Joseph, Macau. His main interest is the history of science, knowledge, and universities. His recent publications include the co-authored "The Study of Natural Law in Coimbra, Seville, and Santiago de Chile (Eighteenth and Nineteenth Centuries)" in *Comparative Legal History* (2022) and "The Teaching of Anatomy at the University in the South of Europe" in *The Spaces of Renaissance Anatomy Theatre* (2022).

Elena Falco is a doctoral candidate in science and technology studies based at University College London. Her work is interdisciplinary and rooted in the philosophy of technology and STS. Her doctoral project analyses how epistemic values are embedded in Wikipedia's website. In parallel, she works on ageism in technology, having co-authored a chapter on "Digital Ageism, Algorithmic Bias and Feminist Critical Theory" that is forthcoming in *Feminist AI – Critical Perspectives on Algorithms, Data, and Intelligent Machines* (2023).

Jean-Pierre V. M. Hérubel is Professor of Information Studies in the Libraries and School of Information Studies, Purdue University. His interests include historiography and theory, history of scholarly publishing, history of academic disciplines, and mapping historical scholarship. He has published studies on disciplinary cultures, bibliometric analysis, and scholarly communication.

Marnie Hughes-Warrington, AO PFHEA, is a Rhodes Scholar and graduate of University of Tasmania and Oxford. Marnie is a metaphysician who studies how the past shapes our present and future. A scholar having received over AU$18 million in grants, her work has been applied to many contexts. Her most recent book is *History from Loss* (together with Daniel Woolf, 2023), and she is currently researching historical logic in AI. Marnie is Deputy Vice-Chancellor: Research and Enterprise at University of South Australia and an honorary professor of history at the Australian National University. In 2022, she was made an Officer in the Order of Australia for distinguished service to higher education governance, leadership, and mentoring.

Anton Jansson is an associate professor of the History of Ideas and Science at the University of Gothenburg, Sweden. Jansson has carried out research on both German and Swedish history in the 19th and 20th centuries, mostly with a focus on religion and secularization. He is currently working on a research project funded by the Swedish Research Council: "Visions of a Society without God: The History of Atheism in Sweden 1879–1968."

Charlotte A. Lerg is assistant professor of North-American History at Ludwig-Maximilian University Munich and managing director of the Lasky Center for Transatlantic Studies. She also serves on the board of the Bavarian American Academy. Her research focuses on the cultural history of knowledge, visual media, and historical theory. Publications include *Universitätsdiplomatie: Prestige und Wis-*

senschaft in den transatlantischen Beziehungen 1890–1920 (2019). She also edited The Diary of Lt. Melvin J. Lasky (2022).

João Ohara is an assistant professor (with tenure) of theory of history at the Federal University of Rio de Janeiro, Brazil. His current research focuses on the social epistemology of historiography. His most recent publication is the book The Theory and Philosophy of History: Global Variations (2022).

Johan Östling is Professor of History, Director of the Lund Centre for the History of Knowledge (LUCK), and Wallenberg Academy Fellow. His research is mainly devoted to the history of knowledge, but he has a more general interest in the intellectual, political, and cultural history of modern Europe. His recent publications comprise Circulation of Knowledge (2018), Forms of Knowledge (2020), Histories of Knowledge in Postwar Scandinavia (2020) and Knowledge Actors (2023).

Elisavet Papalexopoulou is a PhD researcher at the European University Institute in Florence. Her research focuses on intellectual history with an emphasis on female thinkers and gender in the Age of Revolutions. Her publications include the artle "Tracing the Political in Women's Work" (2021) and a forthcoming chapter on Maria Petrettini in the edited volume Gender and Cultural Mediation in the Long Eighteenth Century: Women Across Borders.

Moira Pérez is an assistant researcher at the Argentine National Council for Scientific and Technical Research and professor at the University of Buenos Aires, Argentina (Department of Philosophy). She directs the Research Group on Applied Philosophy and Queer Politics (PolQueer) and works from a queer, anti-colonial perspective on the interactions between violence and identity. Her recent publications include "The practical past as an instrument of epistemic resistance: The case of the Massacre in the Seventh Ward" (Estudios de Filosofía 66, 2022) and "Contracting imaginations: On the political and hermeneutical monopoly of identity politics" (Dialectical Anthropology 47, 2023).

Chelsea A. Rodriguez is a PhD candidate in the history of education at the University of Groningen (Netherlands). She is interested in educational debates and the mediated communication of educational ideas in the public sphere. Her dissertation investigates the history of education news in the United States, specifically how the institution of The New York Times circulated particular forms of knowledge about U.S.-American education to readers during the post-war era.

Bennet Rosswag is a research assistant at the chair of early modern history at the University of Giessen. He is interested in trans-epochal media history, the construction, legitimization, and function of early modern power, bureaucracy and states, as well as the application of sociological theories in historiography. His PhD project focusses on the role of media in the administrative reform in territories of the Holy Roman Empire around 1800.

Anastassiya Schacht works at the Department of History at the University of Vienna, where her project received a grant from the Vienna Doctoral School of Historical and Cultural Studies. Her PhD research explored how the conflict concerning the political abuse of psychiatry in the 1970s and 1980s evolved, intertwined with tensions of the Cold War, and shaped governmental strategies and professional agendas. This project analyzed the strategies of self-construction and legitimation in international psychiatric networks, action spaces for scholarly autonomy and responsibility, as well as state involvement in the field of science in authoritarian regimes.

Christoph Schmitt is an academic assistant in the History Department at the University of Education Schwäbisch Gmünd. His research interests include theory and methodology of history, social history, and social mobility. His doctoral thesis deals with the epistemic construction and formation of social history in the FRG (1960–1990) in exchange with different systems, using the example of social rise and social mobility.

Carl-Filip Smedberg is a researcher at the Department of the History of Science and Ideas, Uppsala University. His research focuses on social taxonomies, social identities, and the history of the social sciences. His present project studies the history of the knowledge society and debates concerning educational differences in post-war Sweden.

Jana Weiß is DAAD Associate Professor at the University of Texas at Austin. With a focus on U.S. and transatlantic history, her research interests include 19th and 20th century immigration, knowledge, and religious history as well as the history of racism. Her most recent publications include *The Continuity of Change? New Perspectives on U.S. Reform Movements* (co-edited with Charlotte A. Lerg, 2021), and (with Nicole Hirschfelder) "Overcoming Barriers: An Interdisciplinary Collaboration in a Transatlantic Research Network on the Black Freedom Struggle", in *Entgrenzungen: Festschrift zum 60. Geburtstag von Andrea Strübind*, ed. Sabine Hübner and Kim Strübind (Berlin: Duncker & Humboldt, 2023).

www.ingramcontent.com/pod-product-compliance
Lightning Source LLC
Chambersburg PA
CBHW061714300426
44115CB00014B/2680